Pushpesh Pant is an academic, food critic and historian. Born in 1946 and homeschooled in Mukteshwar, a small town in district Nainital, he subsequently studied History, International Relations, and Law in Nainital and Delhi. He retired from Jawaharlal Nehru University (JNU) after a long teaching career spanning four decades. He has written over fifty books on cuisine, culture, religion, and foreign policy in English and Hindi. Pant is a regular contributor to English and Hindi newspapers and periodicals. He also anchors TV programmes and produces documentaries from time to time.

ALSO BY PUSHPESH PANT

Buddhist Peace Recipes (2004)
Classic Cooking of Punjab (2004)
Food Path: Cuisine Along the Grand Trunk Road (2005)
Hindu Soul Recipes (2007)
India: The Cookbook (2010)
The Indian Vegetarian Cookbook (2018)

From the KING'S TABLE *to* STREET FOOD

A Food History of Delhi

PUSHPESH PANT

SPEAKING TIGER

SPEAKING TIGER BOOKS LLP
125A, Ground Floor, Shahpur Jat, near Asiad Village,
New Delhi 110049

First published by Speaking Tiger Books in 2024

The excerpts on Pgs 133, 134 and 168 are from *Smoke Without Fire: Portraits of Pre-Partition Delhi* by Abdul Rahman Siddiqi, published by Aakar Books, 2011; and on Pgs 45, 46 from *The Last Spring Part 1: The Saga of the Great Mughals* by Abraham Eraly, published by Penguin India, 2014, and are reproduced here with the kind permission of the publishers.

ISBN: 978-93-5447-808-6
eISBN: 978-93-5447-972-4

10 9 8 7 6 5 4 3 2 1

Typeset in Adobe Garamond Pro by SÜRYA, New Delhi
Printed at PRINTWORKS, New Delhi, India

This book is for my beloved son Indrajit and my equally beloved granddaughters Sehar and Sara for whom Delhi is, and will forever remain home wherever they are.

Contents

Preface

This book has no pretensions of scholarship. There are others who have contributed substantial volumes on the subject, among them Narayani Gupta's *Delhi Between Two Empires*[1] is breathtaking in its scope and amazing in a rigorous marshalling of details. I have reread it many times and always put the book aside deeply humbled.

William Dalrymple has over the past four decades revised the way we look at Delhi very significantly. From the impressionistic *City of Djinns*[2] to *White Mughals*,[3] he has dealt with the subject of British and post-British Delhi with great warmth, objectivity and compassion.

Rana Safvi's trilogy, *Where Stones Speak*,[4] makes even forgotten and neglected monuments come alive. Her primary interest is not food but she has many an interesting nugget when she mentions the snack she enjoys during her backbreaking fieldwork. The way she describes the city makes it very easy for those who follow in her footsteps to overlay a food map on the cityscape.

Nor does this book purport to be a food guide for residents and tourists, far less does it aspire to explore the multiple cuisines in the city with encyclopaedic curiosity. My intention when I embarked on this venture was not to write a history of Delhi with food as a garnish, or the story of the city's food spiced up with anecdotes from its history.

Essentially, this is a personal memoir of someone who came to Delhi as a young student and made it his home, metamorphosing from a refugee from the hills to a Dilliwala who identifies equally with the shehar, the various avatars of New Delhi and the bursting at the seams NCR.

One has been an eyewitness to the transformation of Delhi and the foodscape for over six decades. But, as I summon up forgotten flavours and lost aromas, memory tends to play strange tricks as you grow old and revisit old haunts, remembering them very differently. Not all the old beauties have aged gracefully, and at the same time, new temptations and seductions are encountered at each step. This is as true of food as of the costume and language, traditional crafts and performing arts of a city.

The seeds of this book were sown some years back when Premola Ghosh, the brilliant graphic artist and multifaceted program officer at the India International Centre, asked me to curate a special banquet inspired by the royal meals described in the epic, the Mahabharata. This was to be the curtain-raiser for a series of menus curated from 'the kitchens of Undivided India'. Tetei Towchhwang was extremely supportive in getting the project to take off. Babso Konwar, a passionate foodie from Mumbai, and I joined hands and we spent many happy hours going through the various translations of different editions of the great book.

Finally, the menu included not only the delicacies mentioned at the banquets at the palace but also the food eaten by the Pandava princes in the forest and in distant kingdoms during their exile. The challenge was considerable, as the recipes had to to be recreated imaginatively through meagre information provided by their names. To cut a long story short, this was about the foods and flavours in the very first imperial capital that existed, Indraprastha, where many cities followed with different names in the next few millennia. The prince among foodies, Rocky Mohan, extended a helping hand to source ingredients hard to get in Delhi.

This event led me to think about the many layers of foods and cuisines in Delhi. Ravi Shankar, who wears many hats as cartoonist, novelist, satirist, graphic designer and editor, asked me to contribute a piece based on the Mahabharata banquet, for the *Sunday Standard* which provided another opportunity to revisit the subject.

The 'kitchens of Undivided India' project motivated me to embark on a more substantial work that would go beyond menus and unveil the gastronomic heritage of Delhi.

Perhaps it would be best to make it clear at the outset that when we talk of history, a distinction must be made between what is corroborated by verifiable facts, and legend lore and myths. This is not to dismiss legend lore and anecdotes as useful sources of historical knowledge, but the need to cross-check evidence from several sources—archaeological, literary, and accounts of foreign travellers—remains the touchstone. When we apply this definition strictly, the reliable records for food in Delhi are available only for the last two centuries or so.

Another difficulty is that legendary food shops have created their own backstories and there are plenty of rival claims about inventing signature dishes that are difficult to verify.

What this volume strives to do is to sketch the foodscape in broad strokes using a diversity of sources from the prehistoric period depicted in the Mahabharata to the foundation of historical capitals in succession.

We have relied mostly on accounts of court chroniclers and foreign travellers to glean information about delicacies prepared in palace kitchens as well as the staple diet of common people. The difficulty here is that little is available besides the names of dishes or ingredients in most cases. As far as European travellers are concerned, the atmospherics seem to overpower the observer and often the descriptions suffer from exoticism and exaggeration. Most of the writers have focused on what the Mughals ate, tending to overlook that very few ruled from Delhi and this was the food consumed in capitals like Agra and Lahore. This is not to deny that the Mughaliya influence on the food of the city is significant, but perhaps no more than other culinary streams like the Turko-Afghan, Punjabi (the pre-Partition original settlers when the city was founded) and Awadhi.

Some of the later Mughals employed cooks from Lucknow in their kitchen and at least one of them had spent many years in exile in Awadh. It is only from the latter half of the eighteenth century that we have more comprehensive descriptions of food in the city by the visitors. It was not until the advent of the British that systematic documentation of the food consumed by Indians and foreigners began. Some of the British officers got Persian cook books translated and these have rich nuggets of relevant information.

Though Delhi claims a millennia-old lineage but in fact, the city we live in today has had its unique identity shaped by tumultuous events in the past two and a half centuries. What needs to be underlined is that the history of the food consumed by the residents of Delhi can only be credibly narrated in the context of the past 175 years or so, more specifically in the post-Mutiny period when the life of the nation changed drastically due to the impact of the World Wars, pandemics, the freedom struggle and the carnage of Partition. The food in the city has actually evolved in the last seventy-five years, as Delhi was rebuilt, suffered other hardships but continued to enjoy traditional as well as innovative recipes with the indomitable spirit of the survivor.

One

Becoming a Dilliwala

United Coffee House, Connaught Place, Delhi
Source: @UCH_Delhi on X (formerly Twitter)

I had tasted the treats of Delhi long before I visited it. My parents were food lovers and asked relatives or family friends coming to the hills in the summer as our house guests, to bring some *sohan halwa* from Ghantewala, Delhi's oldest halwai, and a tin or two of the *Sindhi halwa* from Chaina Ram, both iconic sweet shops in Chandni Chowk. *Sohan halwa* came in large, thick hard-to-break discs and had a sticky texture like stickjaw toffee. One could feel the ghee oozing out as the flakes splintered and melted slowly in the month. The *Sindhi halwa* aka *Bombay halwa* or *Karachi halwa* was packed in attractive small tins, each rectangle in a different hue, wrapped in translucent butter paper, and studded with melon seeds and nuts. As children, we were intrigued as neither confection resembled even vaguely the *suji ka halwa* that we were familiar with. Common to these two halwas, apart from their chewiness and enrichment with extravagant amounts of ghee, was their long shelf life. Doled out to us in small portions, the exotic sweets lasted months. What made them exotic was that neither was prepared with *khoya* or *chhena*. When the refugees from Punjab reached the small hill town where I was growing up, another delight was added to the list—this was Paljee's eggless fruit cake.

The taste of Delhi I encountered in childhood was not confined to sweets. When the Balis came as long-stay guests, they brought with them a large canister of thin crisp *mathhis* with a black peppercorn adorning each *mathhi*, like a precious gem. At tea time, they were handed out generously and paired with pickles spiced very differently from *achars* made at home. Father was very fond of the *amla murabba* made with the large, almost fibreless *kalami* variety of the fruit, by Harnarain Gopinath. We used to be well stocked with a large *martban* of this *murabba*.

The maximum temperature in Mukteshwar in district Nainital

in Kumaon Hills where my childhood was spent never rose beyond 25–26 degrees, so *sherbets* were not required to keep cool. However, mother specially procured a bottle of Rooh Afza as she abhorred the taste of lemonade, ginger ale and Vimto that could be ordered from the club.

Mr Bindra was posted for a short while as the administrative officer at the Indian Veterinary Research Institute. His wife introduced us to chicken *tangri*. Not done in a clay oven but pan grilled, and exceptionally succulent due to expert marination. Chicken was seldom cooked in our house. Rarely did mother prepare a *murgh musallam*, stuffed with biryani and boiled egg, for it entailed a day-long effort. Jassi, Bindra's son, was a few years older than I. He informed us that his mother's *tangri masala* was as good, if not better, than a leg carved from Moti Mahal's *tandoori murgh*.

I have no recollection of *mah-di kali dal*, *chole-bhature* or *rajma* from my childhood days. Before the pressure cooker came to be used, it was very tedious to cook these beans and lentils in the hills. The Punjabi families also managed without these dishes familiar to them.

Father used to visit Delhi every year in the winters, to spend a few weeks with his sister, my buaji. She had been married very young, when he was in the first year of medical college in Lucknow. Her husband, a hardworking man from a village near Almora, worked in the Defence Headquarters and had slowly worked his way up from a lower-division clerk to a gazetted officer. The couple lived in government accommodation near Connaught Place and Gole Market, with a large brood of children and members of the extended joint family. The place was cramped and buaji was an ultra-orthodox housewife. Father doted on his sister and spent at least a few days with her before shifting to other friends' homes for a longer and more comfortable stay.

Our excitement would build up as the train approached the Delhi

Junction (Old Delhi), via the double-decker steel bridge spanning the Yamuna. My parents would prod us to appreciate this technological marvel where the motor vehicles and the trains moved at different levels. We were received here, or later, at the New Delhi Railway Station, by our cousins and transported in tongas with the unwieldy luggage—trunks, hold-alls, bags, large and small—to Jaffery Square or Peshwa Road. We passed through Connaught Place and chattered excitedly about the visits planned to spots in this fairytale place.

After a day's rest, our parents fulfilled their promises. The walk began at Hanuman Mandir. The fair-like atmosphere there cast its magical spell. There were sellers of cheap toys, tinsel bow-and-arrow sets, cardboard swords covered with foil, kaleidoscopes and 'dark glasses' made with thick paper and tinted film. Candy floss vendors along with balloon sellers tried to solicit the children. The crowd of devotees, waiting to enter the temple for darshan, made father uneasy. He was paranoid about kids getting lost in the melee. Father was greatly relieved when the clockwise circumambulation of the inner circle started after the darshan ritual was over.

Father never forgot to buy a couple of chameli gajras. One for Mother, to adorn her juda with, and the other to wrap, rakishly, around his wrist. We gaped at life-like mannequins displayed in large show windows of stores and pedal-driven motorcars displayed in toy shops. Our midway stop used to be at Wenger's where we were treated to patties and pastries. Our cousins weren't quite sure if they should succumb to the temptation of preparations containing meat, which were prohibited at home. They took hesitating bites of the forbidden delights when assured by 'Mamu' that their parents wouldn't scold them for the transgression. More often than not, this was followed by flavoured milk sold in bottles at the Keventers counter at the corner.

For us, the forbidden stuff, that made us drool, was *tikki* and *chaat* sold by *khomcha walas* in the verandahs or on the peripheral pavements of Connaught Place. Father could spot disease-bearing, deadly germs without a microscope. Whenever the cousins recommended a particular vendor, he would mutter words like cholera and typhoid, to push us not very gently onwards to safer edibles. Mother was made of sterner stuff. She ate what she wished and treated the cousins to what they were more used to. After splurging on *tikkis* and *golgappas*, she would buy some *lakkad hajam patthar hajam chooran* as a digestive and never forget to take back some sweet and sour *aam papad* with her. Just before we returned to the hills, pickles and preserves were stocked up from Harnarain Gopinath 'by appointment to Their Majesties the King Emperor and the Queen,' including *kalami amla* and *baans ka murabba*; the *sohan halwa* and *Sindhi halwa* stocks were replenished.

Birla Mandir was a half-day excursion, where it was customary to get oneself photographed against the backdrop of a curtain painted with Hindu gods and goddesses. Jantar Mantar was a pleasant enough walk in the winter sun, where Mother would regale us with stories of the ancient Indians' achievements in astronomy. The observatory was built in the reign of Aurangzeb but was enough for her to 'take off' to explore the stratosphere.

Phuphaji shifted to a small bungalow on Atul Grove Road, just off Telegraph Lane, before his retirement. Our sightseeing destinations also changed. The Mughal Gardens in Rashtrapati Bhawan, with flowers in full bloom, and the India Gate lawns, abutting shallow canals with boats, were easily reachable via a radial road from Connaught Place. Bhistis sprinkling water over the grass and flowerbeds were a novel sight.

Those were the days when an expedition was mounted to visit Qutub Minar in Mehrauli. If memory serves me right, a friend's car was borrowed for the picnic. How far it seemed from the heart of the city! Climbing to the top, to get a panoramic view of the city, was an attraction. Going up the narrow winding staircase, however, one suffered claustrophobia.

I finally arrived in Delhi in 1965, not yet out of my teens, a slightly precocious youngster from a small hill town in Uttar Pradesh. (Later, in 2000, Uttar Pradesh was split into two, with my hometown being allocated to the newly formed state of Uttarakhand.) I was wide-eyed, curious and excited about living on my own in the capital of India.

The country was facing an acute shortage of food grains then and many were living literally from 'ship to mouth' on the PL-480 (Public Law-480) food aid from the United States. The mess manager in the hostel asked me to bring a properly authenticated copy of the ration card, which showed my name scratched out, before he could add it in the mess register! A cereal-less day was observed every week and the Guest Control Order (1965) was strictly enforced. Not more than five dishes—most prepared with good old potato—were permitted, and a sharp eye counted the number of guests invited. Newspapers carried disturbing reports and pictures of famine in some drought-stricken districts in Bihar. Shortages and scarcity were more painful in the big city than back home in Mukteshwar or Nainital.

Yet, the joys of exploring the food scene were many. Shankar Market, close to Connaught Place, was within walking distance from where I was staying, the Gomti Hostel, annexed to Sapru House on Barakhamba Road. I vividly remember the meal I had one day at Azad Dhaba—four *tandoori rotis* with free dal for 70 paise! One could supplement this with half-plate of sabzi for 25 paise more. The pangs of hunger could be quelled for even less at another nameless dhaba in Refugee Market, sprawled behind the Modern School campus, next door to Bengali Market.

At first, I stayed with my aunt, Manjula Pandey, in Vinay Nagar. I often walked back from Sapru House, past the Safdarjung railway crossing (there was no flyover then), and stopped for a cup of coffee or tea at a khomcha in the Vinay Nagar (now Sarojini Nagar) market. What struck me was that apart from a sweet shop that also sold *chaat*, there was no proper restaurant here.

Sharad Dutt, media personality, entered my life almost as soon as I arrived in Delhi. We shared many interests: books, Hindi films, music and food. He had a wide circle of friends, many of whom belonged to old families in Shahjahanabad. The accomplished sitarist, Mahmud

Mirza Sahib was one. Sharad also introduced me to the Sajjadanashin Khwaza Sahib at the Nizamuddin Dargah where we partook of the exquisite langar more than once. Through Sharad, over the years, I met interesting writers, poets and painters, actors and singers; what brought them together was potluck in Sharad's flat in Bengali Market. Rashmi Dar cooked some of the most memorable Kashmiri meals. (Her family is one of an old Kashmiri clan settled in Delhi.) Her rendering of Kashmiri recipes is akin to Pravasi Bengali recipes, slightly modified traditional recipes, partly due to non-availability of Kashmiri ingredients, as well as changes in tastes from imbibing local influences over time. Rashmiji loves food and was particularly helpful in evaluating Kashmiri eateries in Delhi and NCR. Some of them have been around for more than half a century.

My friends in Sapru House introduced me to the foods of their city, which was not then my own. Shahid, whose father was then the Deputy Mayor of Delhi and who stayed in the heart of Old Delhi, a short distance away from Jama Masjid, often invited us home and let us taste delicious *pasande*, *qorma* along with *shami* kebabs that his mother cooked. He also took us to Flora Restaurant, near Jama Masjid, that was preferred by discerning diners in the mid-1960s.

The restaurants Karim's and Al-Jawahar were considered good enough only for the tourists. Shahid packed his lunch box with enough goodies from home to supplement the hostel lunch we subsisted on. Mohammed Siddique, the prankster, chipped in with *saag gosht* and *keema* in different forms. Both these friends taught us to distinguish between home cooking and what is available in commercial eateries. It is important to keep this distinction in mind when discussing food and flavours.

Alok Rai, from Allahabad, had become a close friend in the summer of 1965. He introduced me to Atul Rai, his younger cousin, who stayed in Hauz Khas. After Alok left for Oxford, Atul was a constant companion. We explored many eateries together, big and small, in Connaught Place and elsewhere. He had a car all to himself and this made it easy to go around the city, even to places at a distance.

His father, Sripat Rai, whom we called 'chacha', was a reclusive person, a painter of substantial talent and a gifted editor and publisher. On a good day, Atul treated us to coffee or a meal at a restaurant we couldn't afford. His mother hailed from Banaras. When in Delhi, she cooked *qormas* and *salans* in the Banarasi style. This helped me understand that although dishes may share a name, the recipes vary from place to place and there is a vast gulf in their tastes. The *aloo gosht* served at Karim's or Al-Jawahar's was remarkably different from the *aloo wala salan* that Ammi cooked at R-7 Hauz Khas.

The fare at the Triveni Tea Terrace, on the premises of Triveni Kala Sangam, near Bengali Market, was always there to break the monotony of hostel food. Puran Devi Acharya, who ran the Triveni Tea Terrace, was a gracious hostess, with exceptional charm. Parantha with *keema matar*, phulka with *shami* kebab, cheese toast—the menu was limited but the place was spotlessly clean, great value for money, and the small dining area was packed with poets, painters and actors from the National School of Drama.

Mrs Acharya ensured that the boys working for her were well groomed and smartly dressed. Smiling adolescents from Uttarakhand like Makhan Singh, bubbling with enthusiasm, worked in the kitchen and doubled as waiters. One saw them grow up as young men, upgrading their skills.

Makhan Singh later found employment at Vinod Dua's house in Civil Lines and stayed with the family in Vinod's lifetime. Vinod, then a part of Shri Ram Centre Repertory Company, was a regular at the Triveni Tea Terrace like many (then) budding actors from the National School of Drama and other theatre groups, like M.K. Raina, Balraj Pandit, Dinesh Thakur and Shobhana Bhutani.

Overlooking the Tea Terrace was the small amphitheatre that provided hours of free entertainment. There would be Manipuri dancers—protegés of Guru Rajkumar Singhajit Singh—rehearsing and describing incredible leaps, with pung drums hanging round their necks. Walking in and out of the Triveni building, one could view the paintings on display in the two art galleries. Artists like Gieve Patel, Bhupen Khakkar, and Rameshwar Broota exhibited there.

There were a few 'messes', like the Nair Mess, tucked away and operating out of servant quarters in the bungalows on Feroze Shah Road or Curzon Road. They provided meals to regulars—lower middle-class and upwardly-mobile Malayali and Tamilian patrons—who were staying alone and didn't have access to a kitchen. At times, when my hostel mates Suryanarayan or Ramchandran, both Tamilians, were pining for a taste of home, they headed to Nair's Mess, crossing Barakhamba Road and walking through Harishchandra Mathur Lane. On chilly winter evenings, the steaming *rasam*—peppery and tamarind tinged—beat the fancier French onion soup at Triveni Tea Terrace.

Lining the roads that converged at the Mandi House roundabout—Feroze Shah Road, Sikandara Road, Tolstoy Marg, Bhagwan Das Road, Barakhamba Road—were the bungalows of the rich and the powerful. On Barakhamba Road, the Royal Nepalese Embassy, the J.K. House and the Modern School took up most space. On Sikandara Road, there was a cluster of hutments for upper-middle-level officers that merged into the compound of Lady Irwin College that stretched up to Hardinge Bridge. Across the road, was Bhawalpur House, home to the offices of the United States Information Service (USIS) till it shifted to Kasturba Gandhi Marg. In brief, it was the canteens, messes and shops in Bengali Market and Refugee Market that provided succour to the hungry. Peons and menials brought tiffin boxes from home and had lunch during the break either in the canteens or on the grassy roundabout.

Connaught Place remained so close yet so far, out of reach for youngsters like me, subsisting on small scholarships and/or a dole from home. But still, there were places to where one could go at times and splurge.

Indian Coffee House, better known as PRRM (short for 'Price Rise Resistance Movement Coffee House'), had a menu offering *dosa-masala* and small deep-fried vegetable hamburgers for 27 paise each; and a cup of coffee added another 27 paise to the bill. The odd pricing was due to addition of 2 paise as tax. A single-egg omelette with a slice of bread was a wee bit more expensive. The eatery was run as a cooperative by workers, who had an easy relationship with the regulars. This was the preferred rendezvous of writers, painters, unemployed loungers and argumentative Indians of different generations.

The Coffee House occupied the 'roof space' where the underground Palika Bazaar now operates. It was very close to the Theatre Communications Building that housed the editorial offices of *Young India*, edited by the then Congressman, Chandra Shekhar, the original 'Young Turk' in politics, later to be prime minister, and of *Secular India*, that spearheaded the battle against communalism, under the leadership of D.R. Goyal.

I first caught a glimpse of legendary painter M.F. Husain, with his trademark foot-long brush in hand, at this coffee house, and spotted Dr Ram Manohar Lohia, surrounded by his admirers and followers. This is where I met Prayag Shukla, poet and art critic, who became a lifelong friend. Indeed, much can happen over a cup of (affordable) coffee. This was much more than an eatery, it was a genuinely democratic public space to express dissent and disagree stridently. Not surprisingly, it became an eyesore to Sanjay Gandhi who ordered its demolition during the Emergency. No bulldozers were sent, but pliant authorities got the space vacated and allotted it to a glitzier and far more expensive restaurant, Rambles.

This was the time when I began to understand the close relationship between affordable food, freedom of expression and democracy. The Coffee House rose like a Phoenix after the dark days of Emergency but that is another story. Like many others of my generation, I kept up an affectionate relationship with the PRRM Coffee House.

When I started teaching at Ramjas College, in Delhi University, in 1969, most of my lunches were at the Law Faculty coffee house, across the road. There were waiters who welcomed you with a warm smile and didn't wait for the order. They knew what one liked—fluffy *vada*, soaked in *sambar*, or an omelette with steaming strong coffee. Some were familiar faces from the PRRM at Connaught Place. Joseph from Kerala and Durga Singh from Uttarakhand remain deeply etched in my mind. Durga later moved to Kake da Dhabha and continued to progress; the last I encountered him was in the air-conditioned Chinar restaurant, in the middle circle of Connaught Place. I never saw Joseph after I left Delhi University and joined the Jawaharlal Nehru University.

When the money order arrived from home (yes, those were pre-bank transfer days) or scholarships were disbursed, one splurged at the Kwality restaurant in Regal Building, Connaught Place. Soup, hamburger, steak, plus a scoop of ice-cream burnt a hole in the pocket—but not bigger than ten rupees, and this included the tip! When good friend, Alok Rai, won the Rhodes scholarship, this is how we celebrated the special occasion.

Gay Time Grill in the Regal Building sold deep-fried mutton hamburgers closer in size and resembling the ones at PRRM—the patties and buns were smaller, though the softy ice-cream dispensed by the machine made the combo attractive. The eatery was cramped but that added to its charm. Standard restaurant was located on the first floor of the Regal Building. Gentle ladies took their kids there for milkshakes and pastries. Coffee came with a complimentary brownie in a translucent paper envelope. There was a juke box for entertainment. As years passed, it lost favour with patrons and no one noticed when the restaurant closed down.

The Children's Film Society had its office in the Sapru House basement. Other floors were occupied by the Indian Council of World Affairs (ICWA) and Indian School of International Studies. The ICWA library, on the ground floor, was open to all and had rich resources. The spacious lawn, well shaded, was no less attractive. Its central location and the functions organized here—speeches, seminars and conferences, musical recitals and dramatic performances—made Sapru House a unique cultural hub. The Sapru House canteen, which served samosa, leaf tea, buttered toast and cold drinks, was popular with the arty crowd. *Pista barfi* and salted roasted cashew nuts were brought from Nathu's Sweets, in Bengali Market, on order.

The stream of visitors and audiences ensured the canteen on the mezzanine/first floor had a steady respectable income. The canteen was the gateway to the auditorium where I experienced the enchantment of Indrani Rahman and fell under the mesmerizing spell of Ustad Vilayat Hussain Khan Sahib. Gandharva Mahavidyalaya celebrated the annual Vishnu Digambar Jayanti Sangeet Samaroh here and legendary and emerging performers mingled with research scholars and journalists in the canteen. The menu was limited but the quality of the snacks was exceptional. Journalists conducted interviews here; and the coin-operated STD booth provided the lifeline to temporarily separated love-birds.

Gulzar Sahib, dressed in his trademark spotless white kurta and pyjama, often came to 'our' canteen with Pandit Narendra Sharma, who was then teaching at the Modern School next door. Jagmohan, then serving as Deputy Commissioner, Slums, at the Delhi Development Authority, came straight from his office to enjoy his regular cuppa of Green Label before immersing himself in the pile of books stacked on his desk in the library. Mohan Thakur (Mohan Da to the hostellers), the Kumaoni proprietor/manager of this canteen, took great pride in his job. He often reminisced with a smile about the time when Pandit Nehru had walked in during the recess in a conference to have a cup of tea. He knew well the artistes, visiting scholars and impresarios. The helpers, Bhuwan Upadhyaya and Kundan Singh, like their peers at Triveni Terrace, forged bonds of friendship with us, though without a hint of over-familiarity. Many of them later found permanent employment in hostels at the Jawaharlal Nehru University.

By the mid-1960s, Rabindra Bhavan and the National School of Drama had shifted the centre of cultural gravity from the AIFACS (All India Fine Arts and Crafts Society) on Rafi Marg to Mandi House roundabout. Kamani Auditorium, Kathak Kendra, originally established as the Kathak wing of the Shriram Bharatiya Kala Kendra, and Little Theatre Group offered their stages which were swankier than the one at the old dowager, Sapru House.

Evening snacks at Nathu's and Bengali Sweets in the Bengali Market were within easy reach. Nathu's Sweets was established in 1939, the year the Second World War broke out. The shop was proximate to Connaught Place and some busy rail tracks separated it from the ten uninhabited tracts of land that stretched from Turkman Gate to Khooni Darwaza in Daryaganj. The *chaat*, *dosa*, *chole-bhature*, with Coke or Fanta, at Nathu's fell somewhere in the middle between PRRM and Kwality. The eateries in Bengali Market primarily catered to middle-class Indians, who preferred desi snacks and sweets, and had not yet acquired a taste for what the more expensive eateries in Connaught Place offered. Bengali Market had half a dozen grocers, and a couple of vegetable and fruit shops, a dry cleaner and the Post Office. There were three paan shops that also sold cigarettes and cold drinks.

No dinner in the Gomti Hostel was complete without a trip to Bengali Market. The pangs of hunger quelled, one would have a craving for something more. Some of us drank a digestive-soda with masala—others ordered a celebratory Coke in the company of a boy/girlfriend. A few were addicted to paan. There were two shops at the corner—Jawahar, with a lush white moustache that would do a Rajput warrior proud, was always dressed in spotless white and donned a starched cap. Madan owned the shop next door. Younger, darker in complexion, with a much smaller moustache and oiled hair, he was assisted by his adolescent son, whose face bore pockmarks. He prepared paan with less of a flourish but it tasted better. Limca had just been launched and was enticing with its lime-n-lemony taste. Home-grown Gold Spot was giving a tough fight to Fanta, marketed by a multinational. It was an inexpensive treat that almost anyone could afford once in a while. Boys working in the hostel mess, when they came to splurge on a cigarette or two out of a whole pack, to taste some luxury beyond the foul-smelling *bidis* they shared by the dozen during the day, often rubbed shoulders with research scholars there.

New Delhi, at least this part, where government servants lived, went to bed early. The sweet shops had done most of their business by 9.30 p.m. Besides the Sapru House regulars, the other customers at the paan shops were a few theatre artistes, musicians and dancers living on campus in Bharatiya Kala Kendra, or residents of staff quarters in Modern School.

There were times when fellow hostellers pooled resources to splurge on a Chinese meal at Ginza in the outer circle of Connaught Place. Mr Wang, the chef in-charge, was a Calcutta Chinese who dished out Sweet and Sour Chicken, Fish and Pork, pan-fried noodles and some Manchurian concoctions for the vegetarians. Till then I had only tasted 'Chinese' Fried Rice and stir-fried vegetables at Ranjana in Lucknow. Suvarna Bhatt, my classmate, was a vegetarian but loved the Chinese soups. Vasanti Damle, from Baroda, joined the School of International Studies in 1968, and became a core member of our group. She was fond of Chinese food and with her constant encouragement and generous contribution, our visits to Ginza became more frequent. Soups were ordered split one into two—Chicken, Sweet Corn, Hot and Sour, Wonton or Manchow. Most of the time, dessert was a fruit gateau—not part of any Chinese repertoire. The more expensive Nirula's China Room remained out of reach.

The same year, in 1968, I went for fieldwork to Singapore and Malaysia where I stayed with Chinese families. They initiated me into the different streams of Chinese regional cuisines. I also mastered the art of eating with chopsticks and was invited by friends to help order a 'proper' Chinese meal. The Sechzuan style endeared itself to the Delhi palate, though many Chinese chefs hailed from Calcutta where the Chinatown was inhabited predominantly by Cantonese.

Gufa, opened as part of the Nirula's Hotel in the 1960s, was reinvented as La Boheme. It was a chic exotic place, dimly-lit, where a couple could switch off the lamp that illuminated their table and remain unseen by other guests. Their presence was only betrayed by suggestive whispers and barely-suppressed sounds of lip-locking kisses. Discreet waiters kept filling up flasks of Cona Coffee as one nibbled on dainty chicken patties. I was introduced to La Boheme by Sunil Gupta, a friend of Alok Rai from Allahabad, who had come to Delhi for an interview as management trainee at Hindustan Levers. He later joined the IAS (Indian Administrative Service). At some point, the management had to remove the light switches from the lamps, much to the disappointment of passionately romantic pairs, who could no longer remain unseen. A few years later, Nirula's Cafetaria opened and offered many interesting menus for small meals. Grilled, not fried, hamburgers with sesame studded buns, coleslaw and relish, omelettes with potato hash, freshly squeezed (by machines, not hands) orange juice and pastries. This remained the real McCoy for decades till the arrival of McDonalds. Another major attraction was Nirula's Ice Cream Parlour round the corner, with twenty-one flavours to tempt one with: Rum Raisin, Kulfi, Kesar-Pista, and Coconut, besides Strawberry, Chocolate, Coffee, Mango, Flavour of the month, Cassata and more.

Bankura, a stylish restaurant, where artistes visiting the Chemould gallery, the brainchild of Roshan Alkazi, could meet, nestled in the premises of the Cottage Industries Emporium, at that time housed in barracks built for 'Tommies'. Coffee there was aspirational and finger food and bite-sized nibbles were elegantly presented. I don't recall anything substantial. Only the culture vultures hung around there. It wasn't affordable, except for the well-heeled. I was taken there once or twice by 'Chacha', Sripat Rai.

Briefly, there was Shuddha Shakahar, in Regal Building, that attracted diners who were strict vegetarians, with stuffed tomatoes and capsicums. Paneer hadn't annihilated other vegetables dishes till then. Suryanarayan, a fellow student at the Indian School of International Studies, introduced me to the place when he celebrated in style his award of a fellowship.

Tea House stood at the corner where Regal Building met Parliament Street. It was the favourite haunt of the better-off writers and intellectuals. Namvar Singh, the Hindi literary critic, held court here and one could spot other literary stars like Mohan Rakesh and Kamleshwar. The hall was spacious and it had a few innovative items on its menu like *keema dosa*. Later, The Cellar, the city's first disco, was opened in 1968, in its basement. The submarine sandwiches served there were a novelty. The place has been donning different garbs since those days.

The restaurant Volga was, for the old timers, the new kid on the block. It had opened only in 1956. The interiors were ornate, with lots of mirrors on the ceiling, recalling a Bombay film set. This was more expensive than Kwality and ranked a notch lower than Gaylord. Its menu was a mélange of Continental fare, Italian dishes (spaghetti with meatballs), along with some Indian curries. This is where I first met the publisher of my Hindi stories, Kanta Pittie, the owner-editor of the prestigious Hindi magazine *Kalpana*. On another occasion, I was treated to high tea by the eminent writer Krishna Sobti. Krishna ji was a larger than life, most colourful, character. She was always dressed in a gharara and covered her head with an odhani. Her eyes remained hidden behind thick dark glasses. She had in her youth served as a guardian to a brood of royal children in Patiala and moved with an effortless grace. She could change colours like a chameleon. She could in a blink be transformed into a naughty teenager, bent on pulling the leg of the person overawed by her public persona. Very encouraging to youngsters, she was a marvellous raconteur and full of stories about the pre-Partition years. Later, I had the good fortune to collaborate with her on the television serial *Buniyaad*, scripted by Manohar Shyam Joshi.

The decor at Volga was kitsch but the food was consistently good. It afforded more privacy for intimate conversation than other restaurants in the inner circle of Connaught Place.

Around sixty years back, the late Madan Lamba, a first-generation Punjabi restaurateur, had bought a bar in Lahore from a Russian and named it after the Russian river. The Lambas shifted to Delhi in the aftermath of the Partition and Volga was resettled in Connaught Place's B Block. The once trendy restaurant, however, suffered a steady decline over time—from a classy eatery to a cheap beer bar—culminating in its slow, unlamented death, as it refused to read the writing on the wall.

Wenger's, started by a Swiss couple in 1926, was another of Krishnaji's favourite haunts. She has recounted an amusing incident on her literary life, when poet Agyeya had accepted one of her stories, 'Sikka badal gaya' for publication in *Prateek*. She was excited to meet over coffee the legendary novelist-poet-editor, who had been jailed in his youth as a revolutionary and had later served in the British-Indian Army during the Second World War. The live band was playing and Krishnaji couldn't resist flirting mildly with the band master, as an aside. She sent him a chit with a request to play her favourite number. The man acknowledged with a nod and went on to play the song next.

Wenger's was a familiar place from my childhood days. It was a grand eatery, sprawling over two floors, with an expansive verandah enhancing the sense of space. The café Rendezvous was the place for the city's elite to be seen. Till Independence, its clientele was largely British and aristocratic Indians. It enjoyed a matchless reputation for its Swiss bakery items. For us, the pastries didn't quite match up to those offered by Sackley's, the Swiss confectionary in Nainital. By the 1960s, Wenger's exuded a quaint charm that had already started fading. The live band was a muted memory. Though richly carpeted, the place felt stuffy—past its prime. The restaurant finally shut shop in 1979.

The bakery counter at the ground floor bravely tries to keep the flag flying. Their cakes and pastries, patties, sandwiches, and deep-fried, spicy *shami* kebab added later on, continue to enjoy a loyal patronage. The place with its jostling crowd queuing up at different counters to place orders, collect tokens, pay the bills, and for delivery, feels no different from popular desi mishthan bhandars. The ambience and elegance matching the exquisite offerings are a thing of the distant past.

Keventers had a small counter, as one turned into the middle circle of Connaught Place, where flavoured cold milk was dispensed. The Keventers dairy used to operate from a corner plot in what is now posh Chankyapuri. Keventers Lane survives to mark the location. Many years later, poet Agyeya built his tree house here and spent the last years of his life with his companion and muse Ila Dalmia, whose family owned the property. A young man from Shilling village, near Kanda, was employed as a salesman in Connaught Place during the 1980s and was delighted to learn that I had many kinfolk related to him. He wouldn't let us pay and to avoid embarrassment I used to give the shop a miss.

United Coffee House, in the inner circle of E-Block, one of the oldest restaurants in Connaught Place, was far less intimidating. As we walked up to Connaught Place along Barakhamba Road, this was the first restaurant that greeted us. And when we circumambulated the inner circle clockwise, we ended our journey at this point, turning back to Sapru House. It served both Continental and Indian dishes. A jukebox was its special attraction and, in 1965, for 25 paise, you could play the music of your choice—Bollywood numbers from the years when Melody was Queen or Top of the Pop charts. They had a butter chicken on the menu, milder and more aromatic than its cousin in the dhabas in the Municipal Market, on the periphery. No one rushed you if you lingered over a cup of espresso coffee, waiting for a friend to join you. Till the 1980s, it was one of my son's favourite places for eating out. He always ordered the same—a dish of butter chicken with naan. Rajinder Puri, the brilliant cartoonist, and C.P. Ramachandran of *Hindustan Times*, Ram Singh of *Thought*, then considered a forum of anti-communist ideas and literary features, were regulars.

In the mornings and evenings, the place wasn't very crowded and one could find the favourite corner table or the comfortable red sofas on the mezzanine floor.

Much later, I learnt that the United Coffee House was started by Lala Hardayal Kalra, who had a flourishing liquor business in Sialkot. He had migrated to Delhi not as a penniless refugee but as a man of means, who was looking forward to diversifying his business interests, much before the Partition, and had settled down before the tumult that preceded Independence. Most of those who patronized the United Coffee House were not anglicized brown sahibs but affluent Indians, many of them vegetarians, residing in Civil Lines—Kayasthas, Baniyas, and Khatris. Vir Sanghvi has perceptively observed that like many other eateries, 'the Punjabi owners cooked for largely Punjabi guests.'

The refugees struck new roots, slowly but steadily, with the more resourceful securing tenancy rights in shops in Municipal Market that developed on the periphery of Connaught Place. This was a half-circle, stretching from State Entry Road, leading to the VIP platform on the New Delhi Railway station, to Shankar Market, shy of the Fire Brigade station.

Kake da Dhaba bore testimony to the indomitable spirit of the refugees, determined to succeed against all odds. It was established by Lala Amolak Ram, a freedom fighter from village Kanda, near Lahore. He used to run a small hotel in that city. According to family lore, Lalaji had once shared a prison cell with I.K. Gujral, who after Partition assumed charge as Vice Chairman, New Delhi Municipal Corporation (NDMC). When the Municipal Market was planned for resettling refugees operating from the verandahs of Connaught Place, on its outermost circle, Lalaji succeeded in renting out a plot in a prime location and Kake da made its Delhi debut in 1948.

The subsequent story of Kake da is a tale of gentrification of the quintessential dhaba. The shack-like kiosk rose from the ground level to a stand-up counter. Spotless degh were arranged symmetrically on it, to dole out 'classic' dhaba fare—*mutton masala*, *chicken curry*, *tandoori chicken*, *saag gosht*, *keema-kaleji* and *mah-di-dal*. This 'hole in the wall' eatery served only Punjabi dishes, cocking a snook at the Old Delhi 'hotels' claiming to be inheritors of the Mughal culinary legacy. Dishes in the menu weren't labelled *qorma* or *salan*. Perhaps the Hindu-Sikh refugee was pushing back against the Mughal/Muslim hegemony in the culinary realm.

The atmosphere was rustic and no one bothered about how the guests were dressed or behaved. The conversation was loud—orders had to be shouted—the sound of gargling emanating from the direction of the washbasin wasn't exactly music to genteel ears. The tables were cramped and the appreciative belches of diners there assured those awaiting their turn that the food was indeed lip-smacking. There was no pretense at sophistication—patrons weren't inhibited about displaying their approval of a satisfying meal by making assorted noises, cracking the bones to extract the marrow while talking at the same time. Waiters topped up the gravy without being asked for it. Those who'd finished eating contributed to these sounds, rinsing their mouths in the washbasin placed outside and often gargling.

Kake da was essentially a curry place and remained one. Crowds thronged, lured by its gravies with desi ghee floating on top. Sliced onion rings and halved lemons to go with the curry, were always plentiful.

National dhaba, next door, was the preferred place for all those who liked their meats roasted or grilled. It had strongly spiced *seekh*, *barra* and *tikka*. Neel Batra, ex-Royal Air Force, news reader and columnist, gently guided me through its menu one late night. *Tandoori roti* and naans were the only breads here.

Glory, another eatery adjacent to it, catered to the vegetarians with *bharta*, *paneer*, and *saag*.

Years later, reading Malavika Singh's extremely engaging short biography of Delhi, *Perpetual City*,[5] it dawned on me that Connaught Place has always meant different things to different people. What has shaped perceptions and different images of this heart of New Delhi is social class. The rich and the beautiful, those born to privilege, did not have to rub shoulders with the masses who thronged the PRRM coffee house and carefully counted even the fraction of a rupee burning a hole in their pocket. For adolescent children, progeny of the elite, The Cellar, Gaylord were not exotic places but almost a normal progression from home via Gymkhana Club to Connaught Place. Life was not a struggle but sheer excitement and being trendy.

She recollects late morning parties at Gaylord, over tall etched glasses of cold coffee and hot cups of Cona coffee, with chicken patties, laced with green chillies in vinegar—good girls from good families were checked out for good boys from good families. 'Those were the days!' Neither did the old and new overlap nor did the rich and the poor.

The author doesn't mention that both places had notices prominently displayed at the entrance proclaiming 'Right of Admission Reserved'. Neither was inexpensive or affordable, even for the middle-class youngsters or the elderly, for occasional visits. When she uses 'we', it is just a little less than regal. People like her were a minuscule minority who 'watched noon shows in boxes (in Regal Cinema) where lunch from The Cellar would be served to them.'

In the same breath, she adds: 'As teenagers, we would spend hours at the club (The Gymkhana)—play tennis, use the library and swim. Sitting out on the lawns, we would devour chicken sandwiches, dipping them in ketchup, drinking ghastly aerated cola called Vimto...'

The Cellar, according to Malavika Singh, was the brainchild of her brother-in-law. She says in *Perpetual City*: 'Our young generation came together regardless of cultural differences, language, caste or colour on the back of the music of the moment and international dress code of blue jeans...A liberation of the spirit was happening and we were part of that psychedelic change.'

In the mid-1960s, the foreign exchange situation was tight and stringent import restrictions were in place. This didn't cramp the style of the epicurean elite. Malavika Singh has described how an enterprising Sikh, 'K.D. Singh, an old Delhi boy from Baird Road,' and his partner, Kuldip Shankar, set up Steak House in Jor Bagh, importing and stocking 'cheeses of many types, cold cuts, cans of Mexican chillies, Tabasco and HP sauce, not to forget rolls of soft toilet paper.' She recalls sitting in the rear room, eating her favourite ham sandwiches with dollops of mustard there and adds, 'The clients ranged from prime ministers to common mortals like us.' Including herself among the latter, without a touch of self-consciousness or irony.

She notes in passing, remarking with a touch of condescension that the Chinese restaurant Ginza was more 'authentic'. It was popular with upper-crust journalists like Sham Lal and Girilal Jain, and her parents, Romesh and Raj Thapar. A comfortable place to debate socio-political issues over talu-mein soup and pork spare ribs!

Consumption of ham sandwiches, imported cheeses, chillies and sauces were palate ticklers for the minuscule upper crust of society, the rulers—foreigners or Indians and the courtiers.

Two

Echoes from the Past

Purana Qila by Thomas Daniell (1790s)
Courtesy: The History Collective Visual Archive

My deep dive explorations into the food culture of Delhi made me curious about what this was like in Indraprastha, the first city of Delhi, celebrated in the epic, the Mahabharata.

Serendipitously, Premola Ghose, the then program officer at the India International Centre, suggested one day that I should consider curating a series of special thematic dinners based on Delhi's colourful past. It was decided that the curtain-raiser would be a flashback inspired by the tales in the Mahabharata set in the 'first city' of Indraprastha.

The tales of blood and gore, lust, sexual deviations and moral pontifications in the Mahabharata—literally, the Great Land of Bharat, have gripped the imagination of Indians over centuries. The epic, however, contains much more than the engrossing tale of warring cousins, deceits and treachery, cowardice and valour; it is a mine of priceless nuggets of information about how our civilization has evolved.

It chronicles the celebration of marriages and housewarmings, crowning ceremonies and *yajnas* (rituals to ensure people's welfare) and fabulous feasts.

Royal banquets were held where vassal kings feasted, and Brahmins were honoured in spectacular ceremonies. The delicacies served on these occasions are described in mouth-watering detail. These include roasted venison, char-grilled or pan-fried fish, rice cooked with condiments, sweets like laddoo and *apoop* (the original Sanskrit term for *pua*, an eggless banana pancake found in Bihar and West Bengal). Ingredients were brought as tribute to the Imperial city from faraway places—saffron from Kashmir, bamboo shoots from Pragjyotisha, present-day Assam.

The period of peace and prosperity was short-lived. Indraprastha, founded on the ashes of a living forest, it appears, was under a curse. The new city caused great heartburn among the Kauravas as Hastinapur, their capital, paled in its shadow. Duryodhana, the crown prince of the Kauravas, was persuaded by his advisers to take Indraprastha from the Pandavas. A game of dice was organized and Yudhisthira, the eldest of the Pandava brothers, who was addicted to gambling, staked all on one throw. The dice was loaded and he lost all—his kingdom, his wife and his reputation. Draupadi was molested in open court and the Pandavas forced into exile for twelve years.

During their wanderings, the banished princes explored different regions of the subcontinent, some falling in love and marrying aboriginal princesses and siring children of mixed blood. They also acquired exotic, alien tastes and learnt new cooking techniques.

The return of the Pandavas after twelve years and the Kauravas' betrayal in keeping their word to them, led to the genocidal fratricide at the battle of Kurukshetra. The Pandavas' victory was phyrric. The city was reduced to a sea of decaying corpses, internal dissensions tore the allies apart, and Yudhishtira renounced the throne, became an ascetic and seeking salvation, left for the Himalayas.

The devastated city of the dead and the dying struck by plagues and pestilence was swallowed by wilderness. Not a trace of it remained.

The Age of Darkness had descended.

The city remained forgotten for over three thousand years, indeed, until the twentieth century, recalled only when mythic memories were stirred, blurring lines between fact and fantasy.

Growing up in Mukteshwar, I remember accompanying my parents once to Bhimtal, and nearby, the Nal Damyanti Tal. These two small but beautiful water bodies are associated with figures in the Mahabharata. Local lore maintained that Bhimtal was created when Bhim, seeking water to quench Draupadi's thirst, struck the hard earth with his powerful fist. The flat colourful fish swimming in the Nal Damyanti Tal, according to the villagers, were descended from ancestors who had jumped back from the frying pan into this pool—depriving Nal, struck by adversity, from a hard-earned meal. From our house, we could see the five snow-capped peaks, Panchachuli, shining in the sunlight. Legend had it that these were remnants of chulhas (stoves) set up by Draupadi on the family's final heavenward journey.

About the Mahabharata, it is said that whatever one may encounter elsewhere is present here, and if it isn't, it cannot be found anywhere else. What has intrigued me no end is that, despite its enduring enchantment, food has not received due attention in the epic. Feasts are part of the narrative and delicacies are mentioned, at times with some of the ingredients used but details like recipes are missing.

The most exhaustive treatment about the Indian philosophy of food is available in the seventeenth chapter of Srimad Bhagvad Gita that dwells in detail about the correspondence between three types of persons and three types of foods—Satvik, Rajasik and Tamsik. It provides most interesting, thought-provoking insights into body types, psychological predispositions and nutritional requirements. Combined with the concept of gunas–doshas (inherent properties of various ingredients and imbalance caused by changing cycle of seasons) this is what provides the firm philosophical foundation for Indian gastronomy.

There are countless references to food in the Mahabharata. According to legend, King Nala, ruler of Nishadha (present-day Chhattisgarh) was not only an amazing mathematical genius with phenomenal computational skills, who could accurately 'count' the number of leaves on a tree as his chariot raced past, but also a fabulous cook. The magic in his hand controlled wild horses and temperature in large cauldrons with equal skill. Bhima must have acquired enough culinary skills to wear successfully the disguise of a professional cook when the Pandavas spent a year in anonymous exile in the court of King Virat, ruler of Matsya. He may have been exceptionally fond of laddoos but he was surely capable of rustling up many a dainty dish 'fit enough to be placed before the king.'

Dronacharya was alienated from his childhood friend Drupad,

when made acutely aware that even a learned Brahmin could not expect to feed his children like his companion princes did (Dhronacharya's wife constantly complained of having to prepare 'mock milk' by grinding rice grains and mixing it with water to feed their son, unlike his affluent friends). Another poor Brahmin, Sudama, was nagged by his wife to seek favours from his powerful schoolmate Krishna and packed off to Dwarka with a small parcel of parched pounded *rice-choora* that sustains the abjectly poor in what is derisively described as the Cow Belt. Krishna took great delight in being able to savour the 'riches of poverty', snatching the parcel from Sudama who was reluctant to bring it out—afraid that his royal friend would take offence. How can one forget Krishna's boon to Draupadi, that even when rendered a refugee, her pot will remain full to feed family and guests? Or, the ravenous undiscriminating appetite of Bhima, who could not be laid low by overeating poisonous laddoos?

When Yudhishthira performed the Rajasuya *yajna*, kings, who had been subdued, came from the four corners bringing with them precious tributes, including hampers of exotic food ingredients like saffron, honey and aromatic substances.

Indraprastha then, like Delhi and NCR today, was a confluence of food and flavours. The ruler of Indraprastha could command the choicest produce from different regions of his empire, from saffron in Kashmir to bamboo shoots from Pragjyotish in Assam, lentils from Madra (present-day Madhya Pradesh), rice from Patna, and pepper, cardamom and cloves from Southern India. For special royal banquets, expert cooks could also be invited to cater to princes and priests. Today, one might have access to all these ingredients, but we have no knowledge of the recipes for the dishes cooked in Indraprastha. One can, however, speculate with some justification, that the Pandava princes, during their years spent in exile in the forest, travelling all over the land, acquired a taste for foraged foods and mastered cooking techniques from different regions. This must have enriched their culinary repertoire.

Three

Enter the Sultans

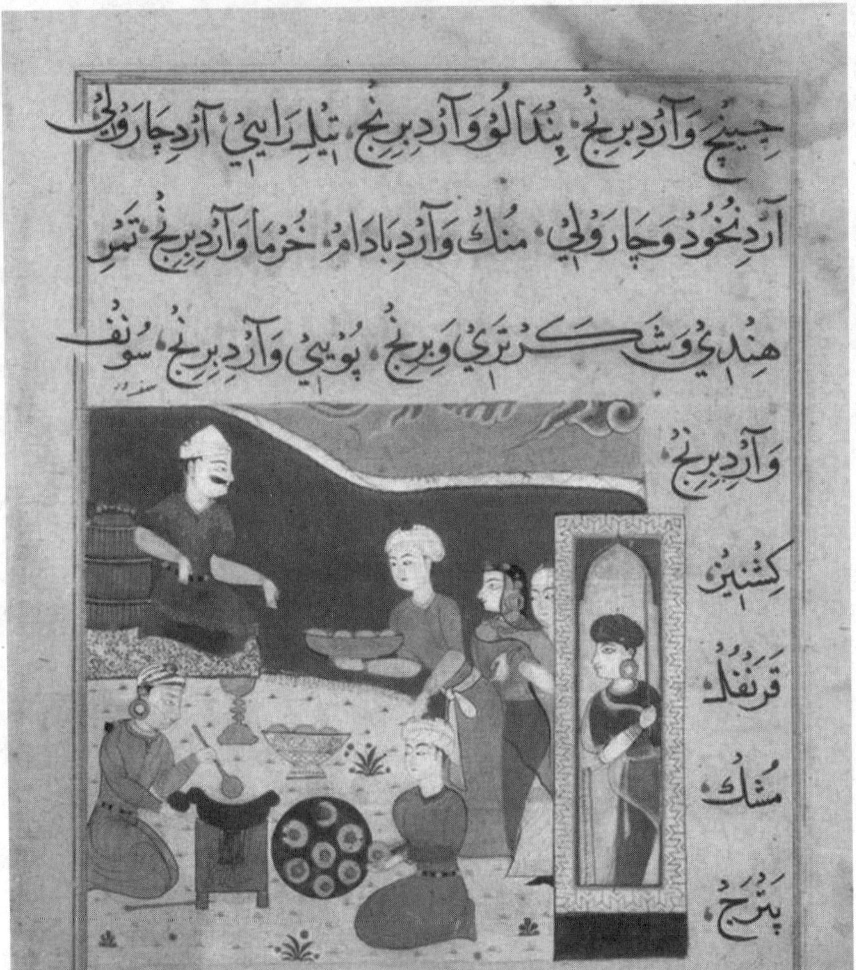

A cook frying sambusak (Samosa) for the Sultan

Source: Wikimedia Commons

Historians agree that the documented history of Delhi begins in the eleventh century, when King Iltutmish shifted his capital to the city from Lahore. Between 'The Age of Darkness' and the eleventh century, we hear of a king called Dillu who founded the capital of his kingdom here. Folklore has it that the word 'Delhi' commemorates this local chieftain. Another tradition maintains that the word is related to 'dehali', which means a threshold. Delhi was, indeed, at the threshold of the Gangetic Plain. Lal Kot, the city built in the eleventh century by King Anangapal II, popularly known as Anangapal Tomar, was known as Dillika before his reign. In any case, not much is known of what was eaten by the people who inhabited these now forgotten cities.

The newly-conquered territory was governed by successive rulers of the Slave Dynasty (1206–1290). Qutb-ud-din Aibak demolished the buildings existing in Lal Kot/Rai Pithora and used the rubble to erect impressive mosques and minarets. The foundations of a new city, Siri, were laid.

Information about crops grown and food eaten by the rich and the poor begins as a trickle but substantially increases with the establishment of the Turko-Afghan Sultanate in India at the end of the twelfth century. Hagiographers, courtiers and travellers have left chronicles of what the Emperor ate, how some of them tried to bring about market reforms to control prices and improve the lot of common people by ensuring subsistence.

Many of the contemporary eyewitnesses were awestruck by the massive fortifications erected by Sultan Ghiyas-ud-din Balban. As Shams Siraj Afif recorded in *Tarikh e Firoze Shahi*, written a hundred years after the Sultan's death, 'Walls of Delhi, width 11 arms, length 17 feet tall, small rooms to house guards, to keep vigil on city gates, stores for grains, catapults, arms slots on city side to let light in, lower part of stone, upper of brick, numerous watch towers.'

The rule of Mamluks, also known as the Slave Dynasty, the first of the Turko-Afghan rulers, ended effectively with Balban. When Razia, Iltutmish's daughter, assumed the reins, she was met with resistance by powerful nobles who refused to bow down before a woman. What complicated matters was her affair with Yakut, who was not considered a noble. Razia tried valiantly to assert herself but was unsuccessful; eventually, she was killed along with husband, Altunia, who was once her opponent. After the reigns of a couple of weak and debauched successors, power passed to the Khiljis.

The Khiljis were Indian Muslims who had served as vassals of Mamluk Sultans, who were Turkish. Among the Khilji sultans, Alauddin Khilji is arguably the most remarkable ruler of Delhi in the medieval period—but also the most vilified. Well known is the story of his being enamoured by the beauty of Queen Padmavati, his siege and sacking of Chittor Fort to take her, and Padmavati's performing sati to avoid capture by him. Folklore has mythologized history, making it difficult to sift the grain from the chaff. Alauddin had in all probability attacked Chittor to subdue and subordinate the pre-eminent Rajput kingdom for strategic reasons.

Another of Alauddin's famous military campaigns was his invasion of Devagiri (later renamed Daulatabad). He commanded the imperial troops on behalf of his uncle who was then the Sultan. In this case also legend and lore have muddied history and demonized Alauddin. He is portrayed as a cruel villain and a plunderer. It is true that the booty the young commander brought back from the Deccan was fabulous—dozens of elephants laden with gold and silver, precious gems and a handsome slave, who became his favourite. Historians agree that these riches helped Alauddin in buying his way to power back in Delhi. It is also believed that losing patience with his aged uncle, he engineered his demise. Once enthroned he proved himself to be an able administrator and a just ruler.

One of his major ambitions was to curb the black market in food grains and to impose price controls. The Emperor issued orders that wheat was to be sold at the fixed price of 7 ½ Jitals per maund (equal to 50 kilos). Barley, a millet used by the poor, was even cheaper, at 4 Jitals for a maund. Rice was only a little more expensive, at 5 Jitals per maund. This was the price at about which most lentils (maash—black *moong* unhusked, gram, *moth*) were to be sold. Sugar remained expensive, the poor could hardly get to taste it; their preferred sweetener was jaggery. The price for *misri* (candied sugar) was fixed at the rate of 2.5 Jitals per seer. Salt, that everyone used, was sold at 5.5 Jitals for 40 kilos.

The Sultan tried to ensure that the essential provisions were made available at fixed prices to public kitchens run by caravan sarais like Ramzan Qalandar, Malik Yaar Praan and Syed Mohammad Gesu Daraz. It appears that before Alauddin Khilji's price control measures, there was a large number of people who found it difficult to make both ends meet and that is why public kitchens sprouted across the city.

After Alauddin's passing, the Tughlaks captured the throne of Delhi. Sultan Ghiyas-ud-din Tughlak, founder of the dynasty, was irked by the popularity of the Sufi saint, Nizamuddin Aulia. It is said that he once summoned him to his court but the Pir refused to respond. An uneasy truce existed for years, but the Sultan was unrelenting. He vowed that once he returned from a military expedition, he would punish the recalcitrant Pir. According to legend, when his worried devotees carried this news to the saint, he laughed it off, saying 'that Delhi is yet far' (*Hanuz Dilli dur ast*), implying that the Sultan might never make it back to his capital. Uncannily, the Sultan died in a freak accident, when a stage constructed to welcome him collapsed and he was buried under it. It was suspected that this 'accident' was engineered by his nephew, who was in a hurry to ascend the throne.

The Sultan, before this 'accident', had built a new capital city for himself, which was not surprisingly named Tughlakabad. There is an interesting story about Tughlakabad. When Mohammed bin Tughlak, the nephew and heir-apparent, remarked that this was perhaps not the best place to build a magnificent capital, his uncle, irritated, had retorted, 'You can build the capital wherever you desire, when you become the Sultan.' It is believed that the city never flourished because it was cursed by the saint Nizamuddin Aulia, who had famously pronounced '*Ya rahe ujad, ya base Gujar*,' which may be literally translated as, 'This place will remain barren, occupied only by nomadic Gujjar tribals, grazing their goats amidst ruins.'

Muhammed bin Tughlak, who succeeded his uncle, was an exceptionally talented and obsessively ambitious individual. He envisioned 'Jahanpanah' as his capital, a sprawling city that would encapsulate the existing or abandoned cities within its periphery, from Tughlakabad to Siri, including the area near Hauz Khas. This mega-project could never be completed because the Sultan was repeatedly distracted by his whims and fancies.

One such fanciful idea was to shift the capital from Delhi to Daulatabad in the Deccan (Devagiri), a more central location for the sprawling empire. As is well known, the forced migration of Delhi's inhabitants and their return to the city proved to be a huge misadventure that depleted the exchequer greatly. There were not enough funds to complete the Jahanpanah project. (All that remains of the Jahanpanah are the remnants of a wall on its eastern side and the sluice gate between this site and Tughlakabad.) There were other hair-brained schemes implemented by the Sultan, described by some as a man ahead of his times. He initiated copper coinage, creating panic among the populace, who feared that the gold and silver coins being taken out of circulation would suddenly impoverish them. The Sultan also mounted an expedition to conquer Tibet, but his armies had to retreat after depredations in the mountainous territories. The Deccan revolted in 1347, and the Sultan died fighting in Gujarat in 1351.

The turbulence that marked the Sultans' reigns in general was hardly congenial for pursuits of finer culture, especially of food. Sultan Muhammad bin Tughlak's reign was an exception. Regardless of his travails, the Sultan maintained a glittering court and enjoyed a lavish lifestyle.

Food cooked and served for the Tughlak Sultans is described in some detail by Ibn Battuta who visited Delhi during the reign of Muhammed bin Tughlak. He has listed a number of dishes, including the samosa, which appear to have travelled along the Silk Road, which passed through India.

> The spread comprising thin round bread cakes; large slabs of sheep mutton, round dough cakes made with ghee and stuffed with almond paste and honey; meat cooked with onions and ginger; sambusak made of minced meat enriched with almonds, walnuts, pistachios, onions, and spices placed inside a piece of thin pastry; rice with chicken topping, assorted cakes and sweetmeats after meals, ended with paan. The main dishes were accompanied by a variety of pickles prepared with mangoes, ginger and peppers; jackfruit and barki, a yellow gourd with sweet pods and kernels; sweet oranges; wheat, chickpeas, lentils and rice.

Though the foreign traveller mingled with nobles and emirs and shared their rich repast, Ibn Battuta wasn't blind to the plight of poor subjects. He has observed that common Indians subsisted 'largely on a diet of millets that were pounded to prepare a thick porridge. Only the relatively rich could afford to add milk and sugar to make this gruel palatable.' They had a breakfast of peas and *moong dal* cooked with rice and ghee.

Amir Khusrau mentions that Sultan Muhammad bin Tughlak's royal kitchen cooked for about 20,000 people daily and that the Imperial dastarkhan had a spread of hundreds of delicacies. More details are available in his famous epic poem *Mathnavi dar Sifat-e-Dehli*. The royal feast included '*sharbet, labgir, naan-e-tanuri, sambusak*, pulao and halwa.' Wine accompanied the meal that concluded with *tambul*.

Other varieties of bread, *naan-e-tunuk*, a lighter bread, and *naan-e-tanuri*, bread baked in a tandoor, are mentioned. In addition, Khusrau mentions as delicacies, exotic dishes prepared with sparrow and quail, along with a variety of *sherbets* made from roses, pomegranates, oranges, mangoes and lemons.

Ibn Battuta was greatly impressed by the city he saw:

> On the next day we arrived at the city of Dihli (Delhi), the metropolis of India, a vast and magnificent city, uniting beauty with strength. It is surrounded by a wall that has no equal in the world, and is the largest city in the entire Muslim Orient...Everywhere domes rose white to the sky, water sparkled in the sun and the streets were gay with the bustle and colour of metropolitan life. In spite of its tribulations Delhi had never before been so large and magnificent.

Delhi at this time stretched from Mehrauli and Lal Kot to Siri, near the village of Shahpur Jat. On the western extremity, lay the great tank built by Alauddin Khilji that was called Hauz Shamsi at the time of its construction. Plain, barren land stretched till Tughlakabad towards the east. There once existed a water body between Jahanpanah and Tughlakabad.

Public kitchens continued to flourish during the reign of successive sultans at the langar khaana maintained by Sufi khaneqahs associated with different orders of mystic-saints. Among the most prominent Sufi orders were the Suhrawardi, the Ishaqia, who dressed in yellow robes, the Haideri, who wore heavy chains round their neck, and the Firdausi, the Qadri and the Naqshbandi. The Chishtia silsila was the dominant one. Many of the khaneqahs served as serais, where travellers could stay for three nights without paying anything. Hazrat Nizamuddin Aulia, when he first came to the city with his mother from Badaun, stayed at Namak ki Serai before shifting to a more modest Rakabdar Serai. Not all serais were attached to khaneqahs or madrasas, some operated as inns on a commercial basis.

Stability returned to the affairs of state when Firoz Shah, Mohammed Tughlak's nephew, succeeded him. Firoz was ambitious and commissioned the city of Firozabad that is known at present as Feroz Shah Kotla. He is also credited with building the first canal on the Yamuna River. To beautify the new city, he transported two Ashokan pillars and constructed a hunting lodge on the Ridge.

Firozabad remained closely connected with the earlier settlements at Tughlakabad and Siri. Peace prevailed during Firoz Shah's reign and because of this, perhaps, it was not considered necessary to build thick protective walls. The Yamuna River served as a natural moat on Firozabad's eastern flank.

Firozabad was the 'New Delhi' of the fourteenth century. When the palace had been completed, suburbs grew up around and outside the walls. Two cities coexisted: one at the Qutub/Mehrauli and the other at Firozabad, separated by a few miles. Firozabad wasn't girdled by thick protective walls as no traces of fortifications have been discovered. The palatial apartments and mansions have been reduced to rubble.

Firoz Shah also built a madrasa, with a small beautiful mosque, at Hauz Khas. He liked the site very much and selected a suitable spot for his own mausoleum. Firoz Shah died in 1388, and with him departed the glory of the Tughlaks.

The 'Old Delhi' at Mehrauli in the vicinity of the Qutub continued to flourish. This was the city which Timur occupied in 1398. His march left a huge trail of devastation, as if locusts had passed that way. The city never quite recovered from this blow.

Sultan Mahmud Shah, the last Sultan of the Tughlaks, returned enfeebled and dispirited. Rebellious governors challenged his authority and sought to set themselves up as rival centres of power. Mahmud died in 1414, and this marked the end of the Tughlak dynasty. Though Firozabad remained the capital in name for another four decades, it had lost all its glitter. Soon the Lodis from Afghanistan claimed the throne of Delhi. Firozabad continued to be a substantial settlement until the middle of the eighteenth century.

Though Delhi is littered with Lodi tombs, none of these Sultans had the time or resources to build a new city, commemorating the dynasty. The few years the Lodi Sultans spent in Delhi they lived in Purana Qila and palatial mansions in Firozabad. Their armies moved with a large kitchen brigade to feed the foot soldiers and cavalry on the move but no details are available of the rations dished out or the special meals prepared for princely commanders. The Lodis chose discretion over valour and shifted their capital to Agra and left no imprint on the food of Delhi.

Four

Akbar's Dastarkhan and Its Legacy

A 16th century miniature painting depicts Babur at a banquet, where the menu included roast goose
Source: Wikimedia Commons

Babur, the founder of the Mughal dynasty, arrived in India with a small band of loyal soldiers after he had been cheated out of his patrimony in Fargana, Uzbekistan. He had spent some years in Kabul, and after defeating the Lodis in 1526 in the first battle of Panipat, as well as subduing the confederacy of Rajputs in numerous battles, he established himself in the Purana Qila. Babur was a gifted diarist, a keen observer of people and places. He enjoyed his food and his memoirs, the *Baburnama*, provide interesting glimpses into food in Delhi around that time.

Babur, a child of Central Asia, missed the sweet melons, plums and pears of his native land. The only Indian fruit he considered worthy of mention was the mango. To his mind, the Indian fish were 'bothersome'—presumably he could not handle the many bones in local varieties of fish. Babur does not mention any of the dishes that he sampled in Delhi, with one exception—a roasted rabbit served to him by a Lodhi queen whose husband he had defeated. The dish had been poisoned by the vengeful queen before being served to him. He was sick for many days and mentions that the dish, considered a delicacy, tasted 'off' from the beginning. He also lists the game that was hunted and used for meals while camping. Babur was given to drinking wine and did not hide his love for good-looking boys, but he swore himself off wine when Humayun was once suffering from a serious illness. He died, literally in harness, and was buried in Kabul.

Humayun, his son, who succeeded Babur, was of scholarly temperament, mild-mannered and a devout Muslim. In the event, he proved incapable of defending his empire against the invader from Bihar, the Afghan soldier of fortune, Shershah Suri. Most of Humayun's time was spent seeking refuge in neighbouring Afghanistan and Persia when he was harassed and chased out of Delhi.

Akbar, his son, who succeeded him, was born in exile in Umrakot. Some historians suggest that Humayun acquired a taste for the robust, rustic food of the villagers whom he befriended during this troubled period in his life. His fondness for *besan ki roti* and recipes prepared from millets dates back to this time.

Shershah Suri died in a freak accident during the siege of Kalinjar, when a rocket that was fired ricocheted off the walls and fell on a pile of explosives kept where Shershah was sitting. In the ensuing explosion, Shershah got badly burnt and he died soon thereafter. His plans for ousting the Mughals and founding his own dynasty in India died with him. Before he had embarked on the fatal expedition, he had started work on a new city, at the same location where the Purana Qila stood, designated as Shergarh. All that remains of the ambitious architectural project is the beautiful Qila-i-Kuhna Mosque that overlooks the Pragati Maidan today.

Humayun decided to complete the unfinished urban project, changing its name to Deenpanah. The poor man was not destined to realize his dream either. Responding to the muezzin's call for evening prayers, he tripped on his robe while climbing down the stairs of his library in a hurry and broke his neck.

Like Jahanpanah and Shergarh, Deenpanah remained unfinished and a capital in name only. These cities were all stillborn. Sundry surviving buildings like Sher Mandal or Humayun's Library can hardly give an idea of what was planned. These 'cities' were never home to settled communities.

All we know about the food in these cities is from stray references provided in the *Humayun Nama* and accounts of Shershah's reign. It was Shershah who repaired the ancient 'Uttrapath' originally constructed by Emperor Ashoka, which connected Patliputra to Purushpur (Peshawar). So long was the time-lag between the original infrastructural project and its repair that the British thought Shershah was the one who had built it. One of his claims to fame is as the father of the Grand Trunk Road. In course of time, the Grand Trunk Road became an imperial highway of great strategic and commercial significance. It was through this that merchandise and ideas from the

Silk Road trickled down to the heartland of India. Some of these imports were in the domain of food. These included the samosa which, surprisingly, originated in Kazakhstan, and was not always shaped as triangle but as a lumpy dumpling, steamed and baked and filled with whatever meats were at hand. Leavened bread, naans of all varieties, also came via the Silk Road from Central Asia.

Akbar inherited the throne at the age of thirteen and ruled from Delhi till he became a major. Behram Khan was his regent. After overcoming the rebellion of Hemu, in the second battle of Panipat in 1556, Akbar asserted his independence from Behram Khan, who was politely retired and sent off on a pilgrimage to Mecca, and he shifted the capital from Delhi to Agra.

Akbar himself led a less ostentatious life and was not a gourmet, but many of his courtiers like Abul Fazal were. Abul Fazal was a connoisseur, a polyglot, a jurist, a statesman and a strategist. Prominent among the Nine Gems (*Navratna*) in the court of Akbar, he took pride in a lavish spread at home. It is reported that over a hundred dishes were served for his pleasure at each meal. He is the author of *Ain-i-Akbari* and *Akbarnama* and it is from these works that historians have gleaned details of what the Grand Mughal ate every day and on special occasions.

Abul Fazal mentions that more than four hundred cooks from Persia and various parts of India were employed in the royal kitchen. This led to the merging of Turkish, Afghan, Indian and Persian styles of cooking. The kitchen brigade was hierarchically organized, with head cooks, official tasters and numerous administrative departments. He says that provisions were sourced from all across the land—rice from different regions, ducks and water fowl from Kashmir, and special breeds of chicken, hand-fed with pellets flavoured with saffron and rosewater, raised for banquets. Beef was rarely eaten by the affluent Muslims and pork was forbidden. The choicest produce from orchards and kitchen gardens in the palace ensured a wide variety.

A typical meal for Akbar, the Grand Mughal, consisted of dozens of dishes made from grains, rice, goat, chicken and fowl, fruits and vegetables. Indian delicacies such as *puri*, *khandwi* and *dal kachori* became part of the royal table. In addition to these accounts, *Ain-i-Akbari* lists the ingredients and ways of preparing various types of halwa, pulao, kebab, meat and vegetables.

The variety of breads baked for the royal dastarkhan was large: *Naan e tunak*, *naan e paneer*, *baqarkhani*, *noe digar*, *sheermal*, *naan e badam*, *naan e taftan*, *naan e besan*, *naan e jowar*, *naan e wari*, *naan e churma*. All these breads have survived to date.

The soups were called *aa'sh*. The list includes: *aash e keshtaleh, aash e bacardi*, *aash e lang barah*, *chashnidar*, *aash e sang sheer*, *aash e nakhudi*, *shore naked aab*, *shorba-e-gosht*. There are no detailed descriptions available of these dishes and we can only speculate about the recipes and the resultant flavours. The name *chasnidar* suggests that this could have been the Mughal version of sweet and sour soup.

The main course dishes were *qaliya*, *qorma* and *salan*. *Qaliya khaas do pyaza*, *chashnidar*, *nargisi*, *talvi*, *naubahar*, *nakhud kofta*, *sang sher*, *ghoora*, *kundan*, *safranı chashnidar*, *badana*, *khasa*. Sheep head was cooked and liver was served in a spicy, thick, sauce-like gravy (*Jigar pur masale, salan Shirazi qorma*).

The Mughal nobles vied with one another to display a mind-boggling variety of delicacies when they lavished hospitality on important guests. Badauni, the court chronicler, describes one such incident when a courtier, Pir Muhammad Khan, asked Behram Khan to have potluck with him. When the honoured guest rested under the tree, as if by magic, 'Three thousand drinking cups and seven hundred porcelain dishes of various colours were brought out from the travelling kitchen, which was accompanying entourage of the host.'[6] Badauni may have been exaggerating, in order to impress his readers with the opulence of his patrons, but it does illustrate that food played an important part in the imperial lifestyle.

Though Akbar may have shifted the imperial capital to Agra, the connection between Delhi and Agra was never completely severed. The Yamuna River provided a convenient channel of transportation through boats and even the road via Mathura and Ballabhgarh was well trodden. Delhi was not totally abandoned. High-ranking nobles, and rich traders continued to live here.

An interesting account of food consumed by nobles in Delhi is provided by Edward Terry, who had accompanied Sir Thomas Roe, the British ambassador sent by Queen Elizabeth to the court of Jahangir. Ambassador Roe was once treated to a fabulous meal by Asaf Khan, a relative of one of Jahangir's wives, a high-ranking noble in Delhi. Terry has described in Abraham Eraly's *The Last Spring*[7] the lavish meal served in a splendid setting.

> We sat in a Large room as it were in triangles, the ambassador on Asaph Khan's right a good distance from him. And myself below, all of us on ground…The Ambassador had more dishes by ten and I less than ten by our entertainer. Yet for my part I had fifty dishes. They were all set before us at once. Though all of them tasted very well…Now for the provision itself. For our larger dishes they were filled with rice dressed in many colours, flesh of several kinds…To these we had many jellies and culices, savoury meat jellies…rice flour ground with sugar candy, sprinkled with rose water, and eaten cold. Mingled with sweet almonds, flesh so beaten that it couldn't be discerned, finest wheat flour mixed with milk saffron and ambergris preserves of fruits.

Another feast organized for Roe by Mir Jamal al-Din Husain (a prominent Jahangiri notable) consisted of diverse dishes prepared with raisins, almonds, pistachios and fruits. The meal is described as dinner, though it was served much before evening had descended and could be called a late lunch. The 'dinner', the host informed the guest was only to whet the appetite. It extended into an early supper that was no less elaborate. The supper comprised, '*salletts* (salads) and meat *rost* (roast), *fryed* (fried), *boyld* (boiled), and diverse *rises* (rices).'[8]

Other European travellers who came to India during the reign of the Mughals have provided glimpses of the imperial repast. Pre-eminent among them is the French physician, Francois Bernier. His account of the emperor's spread mentions, in addition, a profusion of fruits: melons, plums, prunes, dried fruits pears, apricots, mangoes. Bernier was not very happy with the work of Indian bakers and shocked by the unhygienic conditions in which sweetmeats were made. Abraham Eraly quotes him in *The Last Spring*:

> There are many confectioners' shops in the town but the sweetmeats are badly made and full of dust and flies. The bakers are numerous but their ovens are defective, the bread, therefore, is neither well-made…others are not sparing of fresh butter, milk, and eggs, but though it be raised it has a burnt taste… In the bazaar there are shops where meat is sold but there is no trusting of their dishes composed for aught I know of the flesh of camels or oxen which have died of disease. Beef was often palmed of as lamb, capons are not available, though fowls are plentiful and cheap. Good fish is difficult to get by, pigeons partridges and ducks and hare were sold alive. Water in Delhi is a foul receptacle of all kind of filth.

One rich source of information is *Dastur-i pukhttan-i atima ke dar sarkar-i padishah shahjahan maahu wazn be amal amad*. However, no author or date of composition is recorded. It contains ten chapters, on *nān-hā* (breads), *āsh-hā* (pottages), *qalīyas* and *dopiyazas* (dressed meat dishes), *bhartas* (also *bhurta*; mashes), *zerbiryans* (a kind of layered fried rice), pulao, kabābs, *harīsas* (savoury porridge), *shishrangas* and *k͟h͟aginas* (Indian omelette), and *khichri*. The last chapter covers preserves (*murabba*), pickles achār, pūrī, sweets (*shīrīnī*), warm pudding (ḥalwā) and finally some basic recipes for yoghurt, the preparation of Indian curd cheese (panīr) and for the colouring of butter and dough.

Some of the recipes are tagged with the names of royal personages like the *Bakir Khani naan*, *zerbiryan-i Nurmahali*, *pulav-e-kabuli Mahavat Khani*, *kabuli Islam Khani* and *pulav-e-Shahjahani*.

Among the recipes listed are *naan-e-sarkar-e-shah Sahil al-Din* and *masala kebab-e-sarkar-e-Nawab-Hikmat-Panah*. The most interesting among these is *shola-e-sarkar-e-Shah Zahir al-Din Muhammad*, a dish cooked with rice, meat and beetroots.

Other recipes have a 'geographical indicator', prefixed or suffixed, such as *qaliya Shirazi*, *zerbiryani Rumi*, *pulav-Shiraz*, *halwa-e-Rumi* and *halwa-e-Firangi*.

In addition, some dishes were identified according to the cooking techniques employed. The words used in this context are *dum pukht* and *zerbiryan*. The main ingredients that lent a distinct identity to a particular dish were also used to name some delicacies.

The last set of dishes includes recipes for rice dishes like pulao, and shola along with accompaniments—spiced pickles of turnips etc. For most of these recipes, only the ingredients and quantities are listed and the method of cooking is missing.

Bayaz-e-Khushbui is an encyclopaediac work comprising forty chapters, each devoted to a particular category of dishes. The first deals with breads and others cover a range of *qaliyas*, *dopiyaza*, kebab, *zerbiryani*, khichdi, pickles and sweetmeats.

The recipes here also only mention ingredients with weights and measures but cooking steps are omitted. Certain spices figure repeatedly in different recipes as do the spice combinations. One can suggest that this text gives us a fair idea of what the Delhi palate preferred during this period.

The common spices mentioned are *darchini*, *zira*, *qaranful* (cloves), *ilaychi*, *filfil* (peepli or black pepper), *adarak*, *kishniz* (coriander), and *zard chub* (turmeric). These in most recipes were used along with fried onions.

A caveat is in order here. The recipes recorded in Persian cookbooks shouldn't be seen as representative of what the majority of people ate in Shahjahanabad. These are gleaned from the royal spread. At the same time, it may be reasonably concluded that the culinary influences filtered down to the eateries in the market place, catering to commoners.

This process was, most likely, not uni-directional. For instance, the,

Khulasat, a compendium of recipes during this period, has a recipe for *qima kabab tarah-e bazaar* (bazaar-style mincemeat kebabs). The same recipe is also found in the *Nuskha-e-Shahjahani*. The *Nimatnama* also records recipes with similar titles suggestive of popular or rustic origins: *mahi rusta-e-ganwari* (rural style fish) and *rusta-e-sabzi* (rural style vegetables).

The fortunes of Delhi revived after a gap of thirty years when Shah Jahan decided to build a fabulous capital for himself, a city more resplendent than any in the world, the city that would be called Shahjahanabad, and make him immortal. This was the high noon of the Mughal Empire, which may not have lasted more than a quarter century, but for this shining moment, it could claim with justification that here in Delhi, there existed paradise on earth. These are the lines inscribed on the walls of Diwan-e-khaas, where the Peacock Throne, wrought in solid gold, was kept. '*Gar firdauss bar rue zami asto, hamin asto, hamin asto, hamin ast.*'

People from different parts of the country came and settled down in Shahjahanabad bringing with them their foods, ingredients and cooking styles. Some were invited by the emperor to form the original pool of master craftsmen, skilled administrators and others who came in search of prosperity. They came from the Punjab, Kashmir, neighbouring Rajasthan and today's Uttar Pradesh. The Mughals had tried to extend the limits of their empire to Gujarat and till the borders of Bengal. Shah Jahan was keen to make the new capital a cosmopolitan one.

Refinement of cuisines is discernible here in contrast to the rustic and robust fare that even the royals enjoyed during the period of the Sultanate. Until the drastic change after the advent of the Europeans (post-1803), food in Shahjahanabad remained a part of its distinct identity—for commoners and nobles.

Shahjahanabad was built according to a well-thought out blueprint. The main road from the Red Fort that ran from Lahori Gate to

Fatehpuri Masjid (built by Fatehpuri Begum, one of the wives of Shah Jahan in 1650) led to Chandni Chowk—literally the Moonlit Square. This was a beautifully designed, public plaza of peerless elegance. Shah Jahan's favourite daughter, Jahanara, had taken great personal interest in its design and construction. The spacious square had a circular pool of water in the middle that reflected soothing moonlight and justified its name.

With the passage of time, the path connecting Chandni Chowk to Fatehpuri Masjid came to be known as Fatehpuri Bazaar. Ballimaran, a mohalla close to Chandni Chowk, got its name from the wooden balli (poles) that were made here for use in the construction of the Red Fort and Jama Masjid.

The stretch from Lahori Gate to Kotwali was called Urdu Bazaar, as a detachment of soldiers guarding the palace were stationed here. This is where *lashkari khana* (*nahari-paye,* robust *barra* and *boti kebab*) was popular.

> The walled city of Shahjahanabad sprawled over approximately 1500 acres and the Red Fort formed its core—virtually a city within the city. The walls enclosed the grand Jama Masjid, and the landscaped Chandni Chowk that comprised the throbbing heart of the imperial Capital. Aristocrats had mansions in Daryaganj, on the riverfront. Commoners populated in surrounding villages that covered thousands of acres of land—some of it covered with forest. By the time Aurangzeb died, the outlying suburbs included areas like Mughalpura, Paharganj, Rakabganj and Sabzi Mandi.
>
> The fortified heart of the city was surrounded by sprawling suburbs that were an integral part of the landscape. Almost half of the population lived in the suburbs, and these areas provided living space for the surplus population that could not be accommodated within the walls. They also served as suppliers for many of the city's needs. They were entwined with the city's food life.[9]

Many historians have explained the manner in which the city could be envisioned with the palace-fortress as the head, the central bazaar as the backbone and the Jama Masjid as the heart. Smaller streets 'represented ribs knotting themselves into the backbone of the main bazaar.'[10]

A number of streets branched off from the main road. These were called *kuchas*. These were residential-cum-commercial zones occupied by people who shared common attributes and practiced the same profession or trade. The kuchas were named after these occupants. Kucha Chelan was where the disciples of the emperor resided and gardeners lived in Kucha Maliwara.

Kuchas were subdivided into *katras*—blind alleys—that had one-room apartments built around a courtyard. A narrow entrance, secured with a heavy gate that could be locked at night for additional security, provided the ingress.

The kuchas were almost self-contained, and most of the food in the Hindu households was cooked at home. The Muslims bought the *khamiri naan* or *tandoori* (leavened bread)—from the naanbai (local baker). Even the *roomali roti* (bread as fine and wide as a handkerchief) was bought at a shop. It was called *chapatti*, as the glutinous flour was flattened and stretched with the hands, quickly cooked on large, upside-down pre-heated tawa.

Kebabs, grilled or pan-fried, were also bought from the neighbourhood shop. Only the gravy dishes—*qormas* and *salans*—were cooked at home. The menfolk ate out at a friend's house or at a mushaira where these delicacies were cooked by professionals. Biryani sellers also plied their trade on the streetside.

Looking back, one can't miss noticing that Shahjahanabad had a distinct food divide in the residential areas. The Muslims would have only halal meat, which was not considered kosher by those Hindus who were non-vegetarians. One must hasten to add that this division was not hostile in nature or one that led to sectarian conflicts. Residents respected each other's dietary prohibitions and prescriptions. Vegetarian food could be shared without reservations. Particularly sweets. Noteworthy is that this was not an issue related to pork and beef. High-caste Hindus abhorred pork as much as their Muslim neighbours and the upper-class Muslims considered beef fit only for the poor. Most of their meaty delicacies were prepared with goat.

We come across references to game and game birds like quails and partridges which were caught and sold for cooking. Strangely, fish doesn't figure prominently in Delhi menus and items prepared with it seem to be included only to increase the number of dishes in a royal spread.

It would also be wrong to conclude that Muslims sustained themselves only on meat. It's true that a small measure of meat was indispensable even in vegetarian dishes and lentils. For breakfast, the Muslims, like the Hindus, had *puri*, aloo and halwa.

It is worth pointing out that when Shahjahanabad, the then 'New' Delhi, was being built it did not suffer from the congestion and the squalor that we encounter today. The poor were settled outside the walls and whatever was ugly was well hidden. The havelis, home to rich nobles, courtiers and jagirdars from districts neighbouring Delhi, were located in the space adjacent to Chandni Chowk that was considered posh and upmarket due to its proximity to the Qila Mubarak.

The haveli was a large mansion, with a large courtyard, surrounded on four sides by spacious rooms; and often there was another walled courtyard around the exterior. Most famous of the havelis that have survived to our times is the Chunnamal Haveli in Katra Neel. Ghalib ki Haveli in Gali Qasim Jan, in Ballimaran, is built on a much more modest scale. The haveli still exists as a protected monument but in a state of neglect.

A street, named after royal treasures, called Gali Khazanchi, is a long tunnel that connects the Khaẓanchi haveli and the Red Fort, so that money could be transferred safely.

Naughara Gali, off Kinari Bazaar, gets its name from nine grand mansions built by rich Jain traders in the eighteenth century. The facades of these Jain havelis were decorated with brightly coloured paintings and floral designs.

As late as the middle of the nineteenth century, the area around Jama Masjid was considered quite posh and many of the members of the royal household had mansions in this locality. These served as secondary residences, outside the confines of the Red Fort, where privileged individuals would spend time, unfettered by protocol or the scrutiny of forever conspiring courtier-informers. These were pleasure retreats. Even Begum Zeenat Mehal, the favourite youngest wife of Bahadur Shah Zafar, had a haveli here.

Wholesale grain merchants lived in the suburban areas of Patparganj and Shahdara, and supplied raw foods to the city.

Delhi, in its various incarnations, has always been a city of stark contrasts. Shahjahanabad was no exception. As K.A. Nizami writes in *Delhi in Historical Perspectives*:

> Affluence and heart-wrenching poverty, stoic asceticism and ribald rivalry existed side by side in this city. Humble thatched shanties existed on the peripheries of magnificent palaces and mighty forts, opulent durbars, and elegant gardens. Dancing and singing establishments flourished close to mosques and sacred shrines. Its colourful bazaars, khanqahs (tombs of saints), madrasas, serais (inns), and recreational facilities together presented a picture that would enrapture hearts.[11]

The khanqahs, at times, provided food and shelter to the abjectly poor and needy, old pilgrims, and also housed young disciples of the pir.

The city was struck by plague, soon after the capital was shifted from Agra. According to some estimates, almost half of its population perished. The emperor was very concerned to revive the economy and invited *saudagars* (traders) to come and settle here. One such family was that of Sadaulla—a *sarakkai*-speaking businessman from Multan. He was accompanied by 350 of his kinsmen and retainers. The family had converted to Islam under the influence of a Sufi Pir.

They settled down in the tract of land granted to them near Kauriya Pul that stretched up to Kashmiri Gate. The clan prospered, despite the political violence and social unrest that the city experienced after the death of Aurangzeb. Post 1857, some members of the clan bought Bara Hindu Rao and an Englishwoman's bungalow near the Ridge, in the Civil Lines.

Shah Jahan's invited expert cooks from Persia, Afghanistan and different regions in India to train the kitchen personnel employed in the Red Fort. The influx of diverse gastronomic influences can be traced to this period. Princess Jahanara was an aesthete and connoisseur of food. She commissioned a luxurious serai that could be compared to the deluxe eateries of today. This is where she held court and organized her salons.

Afghan and Persian culinary influences had reached Delhi before the time of Shahjahanabad. The Turko-Afghan sultans had introduced robust foods and rustic flavours, favoured by them, to the city. These included some dishes that had travelled along the Silk Road. Humayun, during the years spent as a refugee in Afghanistan, had acquired a taste for local staples. Empress Noor Jahan was a Persian, and under her influence Jahangir's court had turned pronouncedly Persian. What these immigrant experts did was to recover some of the overlooked culinary elements and refine pre-existing recipes.

Five

The Downslide: From Heaven to Hell

Ghantewala, Chandni Chowk, Delhi (2012)
Source: Wikimedia Commons

It would be a hundred and fifty years before the sun finally set on the once great Mughal Empire. Its decay and disintegration, however, convulsed the imperial capital for decades.

Dara Shikoh, the eldest son of Shah Jahan and his favourite, designated heir-apparent, was the last in the line of great Mughals to take a serious interest in arts and letters. He was also fond of the good life, as testified by the delicacy named after him in the Kashmiri repertoire *Darashahi Kaliya*, with a nuts and dried fruits enriched sauce-like gravy, bearing the Mughal imprint. Dara, the aesthete and connoisseur, lost to Aurangzeb in the fratricidal struggle and was executed by him.

Aurangzeb, a puritanical Muslim, had little interest in cultural activities as he believed that 'devotion to duty left no time for festivity.'[12] In 1668, he banished music from the court, though the practice of *naubat*, ceremonial beating of drums announcing the arrival of the Emperor at the main gate, was retained. Aurangzeb's correspondence with his estranged son, Prince Akbar, however, sheds interesting light on his food preferences. The aged emperor was fond of khichdi prepared with meat, dried fruits and nuts. He asked his son for the cook who had in the past prepared this delicious dish for him. The son, known for his cussedness, expressed his inability to spare him. The father then requested at least an understudy to be spared. Clearly, he had not forsaken all pleasures of the palate! We do not know if the son obliged, but Salma Husain has included the recipe for *lazeeza*—the delicacy that found favour with Aurangzeb—in her book *The Emperor's Table*.[13]

Soon after this incident, Aurangzeb left Shahjahanabad on a military campaign in the Deccan, never to return. He passed away in Central India of old age. Nominally, Delhi remained the capital, but, for all practical purposes, it was abandoned. For a little over four decades, no reigning Mughal emperor set foot in the city. This sorry state continued till the assassination of Alamgir II in November 1759.

After the death of Aurangzeb in 1707, Delhi was continuously ravished by predators. The city suffered from political instability and this in turn effected trade and commerce.

A succession of weak emperors followed. They were soon overthrown and some of them even assassinated. Often they were manipulated by powerful and ambitious courtiers. Delhi passed through turbulent times, when neither princes nor paupers enjoyed any respite.

There are hardly any references to the food during this period. The only exception is of a young sweetmeat maker coming to Delhi from neighbouring Jhajhar to set up shop in the city. This shop endured for more than 225 years, braving the vicissitudes that the city went through. With the passage of time, the shop became the famous 'Ghantewala' in Chandni Chowk.

Hopes that the new emperor, Jullandhar Shah, would restore the prestige of the monarchy, protect the prosperity and influence of the nobility as well as reduce the plight of the impoverished subjects by ensuring the regular supply of food grains were belied. What made the new regime unpopular from the start, was the high price of food grains.

According to an account in Ahmed Ali's *Twilight in Delhi*, 'The calamities of death and fire and the scarcity of food grains reached a limit that nobody had ever seen or heard of in the past. A widespread epidemic raged, following the famine. Owing to the great famine and epidemic, scores of common people and imperial troopers died in Delhi for want of bread, and became carrion feed for kites and crows.'[14]

Mir Taqi Mir, the great poet-predecessor of Ghalib, who recognized his genius, was heartbroken by the tumultuous events.

Chor-ucchakke, Sikh, Marhatthe Shah
o Gada Azkhwaawan hain.

Chaiyn mein hai wo jo kuch nahin
rakhte, Fakr hi ek daulat hai ab.

(Princes or Paupers, Sikhs or Marathas
all are reduced to the same state.
Only those have peace of mind who
have nothing to lose)

When Muhammad Shah came to the throne, in 1719, people hoped that they might have some respite from the turmoil of over a decade. The new ruler was fond of dance and music, cross-dressing and other pleasurable past-times that for him signified the 'good life'. He soon came to be known as 'Rangila', the Merry Monarch. Though an incompetent administrator, whose reign saw rampant corruption, Muhammad Shah was a generous patron of arts—particularly music. He was trained in classical music by the great ustad of the day, Niyamat Khan, whose pen name was Sadarang. There are many beautiful compositions attributed to him which continue to be sung by classical musicians.

Nizam-ul-Mulk, Asaf Jah I, the subedar of Hyderabad, and one of the Emperor's most trusted aides, spent a little over three years in Delhi, on an extended visit from June 1738 to July 1741. Travelling with the Nizam was his official chronicler, Dargah Quli Khan, who kept a detailed record of his travels with the Nizam and called it *Risala-e-Salar Jung*, which was re-published in 1926, as a travelogue titled *Muraqqa-e-Dehli* (literally, Portraits of Delhi).

The *Muraqqa* leaves us in no doubt that the hedonist ruler indulged extravagantly, almost recklessly, on sensual delights. His days and nights were spent enjoying music, poetry and dance. He had no inhibition about appearing in public attired in women's costumes and matching footwear. He was also fond of watching elephant and partridge fights. Performances by the city's best courtesans, jugglers and mimics were organized for his entertainment in the privacy of his chambers. On a whim, the Emperor would take off on hunting expeditions.

There's another valuable contemporary source that supplements this information. Anand Ram, whose pen-name was Mukhlis, was a well-educated Hindu Khatri, who spent a major part of his life in the Walled City during these years. A high-ranking bureaucrat in Mughal Delhi, he was a writer of elegant prose in Persian, necessary for his profession, besides being a poet, memoirist and chronicler of his travels. He has left behind a detailed account of life in the city in his travelogue *Safarnama-eh-Mukhlis*.

Anand Ram describes Emperor Muḥammad Shah's expedition to Garh Mukteshwar, to chasten the local jagirdar, Muhammad Khan Rohilla, and the food served to the Emperor in camp. He also recounts the other meals that he had enjoyed with his companions there, that seamlessly blended what may be simplistically considered as 'high' and 'low' cuisine.

Early on in the narrative, he mentions an enjoyable meal of khichdi and *do pyaza be masalih* (braised meat cooked without spice). Foods such as khichdi, naan as well as preparations of seasonal gourds and greens are mentioned repeatedly throughout the narrative, alone or alongside other rich dishes made with meat.

Game birds were abundant in that area, on the banks of the River Ganga. Bird-hunting expeditions undertaken by members of the upper class often turned into occasions of gastronomic experimentation with the game. Anand Ram recounts an incident of going on a hunt with some friends, when they bagged nine *durraj* (partridge) and one *charz* (bustard?). Some of these were distributed, with four durraj and one charz remaining in the bag.

Anand Ram had the durraj prepared in dum pukht style—slow cooking in a sealed pot—and enjoyed the charz as do pyaza. He adds that 'the flesh of the charz is considered [the] best fowl meat.' In a meal at the house of one Hatim Ali Khan, a *raan* (hind leg) of venison (*ahi*) was served.

Qahwa khanas or coffee houses were a major attraction of Shahjahanabad in the eighteenth century. Anand Ram describes these as places where people 'sit and make merry and drink' [coffee]. The word *qahwa* alone is used in the verses of many poets for qahwa khana. He mentions that coffee houses, very elegant and graceful, were common in Vilayat (Middle East and Central Asia). High-ranking nobles would go there and make merry.

'Men of taste, eloquent persons, poets, [and] men like nightingales assemble there.' Anand Ram tells us that in Shahjahanabad there were one or two shops in Chandni Chowk where the city elite retired to engage in poetry recitation and lively conversation over an expensive cup of qahwa. He himself enjoyed the setting and the beverage. 'I also used to go there during my youth, and enjoyed the company of these people. While my other friends used to take qahwa in the market, my servants used to prepare it in my house and I took it with them.'

Dargah Quli Khan's journal, *Muraqqa e Delhi*, provides independent corroboration of what Anand Ram describes. He also mentions the existence of many qahwa khanas 'where eloquent poets are to be found reciting their verses.' Chandni Chowk according to him was 'the most beautiful and profusely decorated passage in the city. It is a centre of recreation for the pleasure seekers and a gallery of rarities for interested buyers.' Until then, the city had not yet decayed beyond repair.

The time of reckoning wasn't far. The revelries were interrupted by invaders, who descended on Delhi to plunder it ruthlessly, one after another, for the next three decades.

Muhammad Shah wasn't interested at all in administrative matters, strategic threats to his throne or diplomacy. He sat on the Peacock Throne for almost three decades (1719-1748) before the invasion of Nadir Shah, ruler of Persia, cruelly ended the charade of happy times in Delhi.

Nadir Shah's name has become synonymous with the *katl-e-aam* (genocidal manslaughter) he carried out in Delhi.

Michael Axworthy has graphically reconstructed the gruesome affair in his book, *The Sword of Persia: Nader Shah, from Tribal Warrior to Conquering Tyrant*.

> On the morning of 22 March, Nader mounted his horse and rode from the palace to the Roshan-od-Dowala mosque [the former name of Sunehri Masjid]. As he arrived there with his men about him, some people threw stones from balconies and windows around the mosque, and a shot was fired, killing an officer beside him. He had already made up his mind, but this final insult may have added fury to Nader's frustration. He went to the roof of the mosque and stood by the golden domes, looking out over the houses, shops and roofs of the Chandni Chowk district. He ordered that no one should be left alive in any part where any of his soldiers had been killed, and then drew his sword as a signal that the massacre should begin.[15]

Nadir Shah went back with plundered booty, never to return, but the misfortunes of the city continued unabated. Extortionist expeditions of other brigands continued. A large number of poets, artists, respectable citizens and artisans were compelled to leave Delhi to seek refuge or patronage elsewhere. The situation worsened in the years to follow. The Jats were lurking on the sidelines, waiting to raid and claim leftover riches.

The decade after the death of Mohammed Shah was relatively uneventful, with lack-lustre weakling emperors installed on the throne—Ahmed Shah and Alamgir II. They made way for Shah Alam I. He could never live down the ignominy associated with the shrinking boundaries of the Mughal Empire during his reign. As the derisive quip has it, 'Sultanat-e- Shah Alam az Dili te Palam.' Literally, that the Emperor's writ ran only between the Red Fort and Palam Village, on the southern outskirts of the city.

Shah Alam II ascended the throne in 1759 and 'ruled' virtually as a puppet manipulated by his ambitious minister Nazaf Khan. It was during this period, 1759–1806 that Jats, Rohillas and Sikhs attacked Delhi repeatedly, demanding ransom/protection money from the Emperor. He had earlier fled from Delhi, virtually abdicating his throne, to live in comfortable, self-imposed exile in Oudh, where he idly dreamt of returning to Delhi at some point in the future. The quarter century that followed witnessed the irreversible decline and disintegration of the Mughal Empire and political power slipping from them into the hands of Sikhs, Jats and Marathas. The last to enter the scene but to benefit most were the British.

The line of Grand Mughals was not extinguished immediately. The gradually weakening flame continued to flicker for some more time.

Six

The Lull before the Storm: The City At the Turn of the Nineteenth Century

Colonel James Skinner holding a Regimental Durbar (1827)
Source: Wikimedia Commons

As Percival Spear, the pioneering historian of British India, has observed in *Twilight of the Mughals*, when the British occupied the city after decisively defeating the Marathas, Delhi was 'a confusing aggregation of contending sovereignties of Nawabs, Sardars, Jagirdars and swashbuckling brigands.'[16] He doesn't include in this list the Seths—wealthy Baniyas and Khatris—as well as scholar-scribes, mostly Kayasthas, direct descendants of courtiers in the Mughal court. They seldom called themselves Seths and preferred to use honorifics conferred on them by the sovereign. They played no significant role in Delhi's life during these tumultuous times. They occupied important administrative posts and largely remained loyal to the British during the Mutiny for which they were amply rewarded. The manipulators of power behind the scene were bestowed with titles like Rai Bahadur, Rai Sahib and, in exceptional cases, Raja.

Though the decadent Muslim aristocracy harboured illusions of grandeur, they were powerless to cause any distress to the Englishmen.

Reminiscences of contemporaries and works of fiction help us recreate the life in the palace and mansions of nobles during this period. Among these the most valuable resources are the memoirs of poet Ghalib, an eyewitness account of the Great Revolt by the 'standard bearer', and the historical fictions penned by Shamsur Rahman Faruqi, *Kai Chaand The Saare Aasman*,[17] and *Zikr-e-Mir*[18] by Mir. These provide glimpses into this dying world of make-believe, where poetry and pursuit of pleasure mattered more than statecraft, and aristocratic aesthetes spent their days and nights lusting for beautiful boys and enchanting tawaifs, oblivious of the stench of surrounding squalor. The weak flame in the lamp was flickering before its extinction.

Metcalfe commissioned Mazhar Ali Khan, a renowned Delhi artist, to paint a series of images of the monuments, palaces and shrines in the city. This album came to be known as 'Reminiscences of Imperial Delhi' and was compiled by Metcalfe in 1844, and sent to his daughter Emily as she headed to join him in Delhi, after her schooling in England. The volume had an explanatory text and evoked the landscape and life in that period in a unique manner.

The British routed the Marathas in the battle of Patparganj and General Lake effectively took over administrative control of the imperial city in 1803. The British appointed an Agent to the Mughal court and also stationed a Resident to look after the day-to-day administration. The character of the city as well as the landscape began to change.

Even in 1803, there were a number of white men and women residing in Delhi—English, Scot, Anglo-Indians of mixed blood, mostly soldiers of fortune, who had settled in and around Delhi. Many had adopted the style of dress and manners of the native nobility. The most colourful among them were Begum Samru, Major General David Ochterlony, Col. James Skinner and William Fraser.

Begum Samru, as a young woman, had married a French soldier of fortune and converted to Christianity after her husband's death. Others had married Indian women (mostly courtesans) and even raised their children as Muslims. These are often referred to as the 'White Mughals'. It is interesting and useful to cast a close look at the lifestyle of this small group as their interaction significantly influenced the foods and flavours of the elite in the city.

The girl who was destined to become famous as Begum Samru was born and raised in a poor family in Kashmir in 1753. Named Farzana Jebunnisa, circumstances forced her to become a nautch girl in her teens. At fourteen, she caught the eye of Walter Reinhardt Sombre, a French mercenary, forty-five years older than her, who subsequently married her. After her marriage, she assumed the name of Joanna Nobilis, but history remembers her as Begum Samru (a corruption of 'Sombre').

The French mercenary governed his jagir at Sardhana with the airs of a sovereign. After his death, his widow became the ruler of Sardhana and administered the large estate ably. She commanded the troop of mercenaries trained by her husband, and adroitly switching sides to help the highest bidder, she played a crucial role in military skirmishes and diplomatic arrangements between the Mughals, Marathas and the British.

Though short-statured, she displayed extraordinary courage on the battleground and led her band of ruthless mercenaries from the front, displaying great strength of character.

Her marriage to a white man, her Christian faith, and charismatic personality combined to create a powerful mystique around her. At the peak of her power, she controlled a large tract of land from Sardhana, near Meerut, to Gurgaon, and wielded substantial influence in the affairs of Delhi. It was her intercession that saved Shah Alam from greater humiliation at the hands of the British, infuriated after the murder of Resident William Fraser. Fraser was an eccentric, one of the early White Mughals who fraternized with members of Mughal aristocracy in Delhi. He at one time had acted as a guardian and mentor of his friend, the Nawab of Firozpur Zirq's son, but later the two fell out as a succession dispute surfaced. It was also rumoured that Fraser had tried to win the favours of the young Nawab's sister who hired a professional killer to assassinate him.

After the fall of Aligarh in September 1803, she was left with no choice but to surrender to the British forces led by Lord Lake and afterwards lived on good terms with the British.

In the years to follow, she hosted high ranking dignitaries like Reginald Hebbar, Bishop of Calcutta, and Lord Combermere, Commander-in-Chief of the Indian Army. In 1808, she built an imposing palace, with a large garden, in Chandni Chowk, and entertained them there in grand style.

Seema Qasim cites A. Deane in her essay, 'Time Present and Time Past', in *City Improbable*. In his *A Tour through Upper Provinces of Hindustan* (1823), Deane has described a party hosted by Begum Samru in Delhi:

> (At her palace) We found thirty persons of rank assembled, and a splendid banquet in the European style. This ended, she arose and threw over the shoulders of each of the ladies a wreath of flowers… then strains of soft music were heard, and the two folding doors of the saloon flew open as if by enchantment, discovering a number of young girls in the attitude of dancing a ballet, or as it is here termed a "noch".[19]

She died at Sardhana at the age of eighty-five, in January 1837 (the year when Bahadur Shah II was crowned the Emperor), leaving behind a huge fortune, estimated at billions of rupees in current prices. After the Mutiny of 1857, her palace was bought by Lala Bhagirath Mal, a Hindu banker, and the place today bears his name.

Another colourful character was David Ochterlony, popularly called General Akhtar Loony, the Commander-in-Chief of British forces in Delhi. Miniature paintings show him sitting cross-legged, supported by a bolster, puffing a hookah, enjoying a nautch. He had adopted the manners of the Mughal nobles. He was rumoured to have no less than thirteen Indian concubines who were pampered as wives. Every evening, he used to take all thirteen of them on a spectacular promenade around the walls of the Red Fort, each perched on the howdah of her own elephant.

Mubarak Begum, the mother of his youngest child, was his favourite. Unfortunately for her, Mubarak Begum failed to endear herself either to her compatriots or white 'relatives'. She assumed pompous titles like 'Qudasia Begum' and 'Lady Ochterlony', only to invite ridicule. She could never live down the infamy of her low birth and concubinage to an Englishman. She was rumoured to dominate her patron Ochterlony to such an extent that she was at times referred to as Generalli Begum. But the epithet that struck to her was of *randi*—a whore.

James Skinner, a swashbuckling soldier of fortune, was a child of mixed blood. He established the Skinner's Horse that continued in the Indian Armed Forces as a cavalry regiment. He had a highly successful career as a mercenary and amassed a large fortune. He owned a large estate in Hansi (in present-day Haryana). In his estate, Skinner was addressed as 'Sikandar Sahab' by his 'subjects' and had no inhibition about emulating the ways of native chieftains and princelings. Like Begum Samru, he also adopted the airs of a sovereign. In Delhi, he liked to project himself as an Englishman, though he was not accepted as an equal by most of them. Some of them who enjoyed his lavish hospitality referred to him behind his back as a 'nigger'.

A prominent building erected at this time was the St James Church. The entire expenditure on this building was from the personal resources of James Skinner. Legend has it that as he lay gravely wounded in the battleground, he had vowed that he would build a church if he survived. He lived to fulfil his vow. It is estimated that a sum of Rs 95,000 was spent on this building. The church was vandalized by the rebels in 1857 but repaired and restored after the British recaptured the city. St Stephen's Church was built at Fatehpuri only in 1867, ten years after the Mutiny.

William Fraser, like some of his contemporaries, had enthusiastically embraced the ways of native nobility. He built for himself a large house that stood close to the Ridge, and mingled with the members of the local elite and frequently entertained them at home. Shamsur Rahman Faruqi has based his novel, *The Mirror of Beauty*,[20] on the fascinating life of this Englishman and his love-hate relationship with Shamshuddin, the young Nawab of Loharu. Fraser was a close friend of Shamshuddin's father and in the beginning treated him like a nephew. However, after the death of the old nawab, the two fell out due to a property dispute in which Fraser supported the rival contender's claim.

Faruqi describes a dinner at Fraser's house to which many of the notables in the city were invited. Fraser was offering sherbet and kebab to his guests. It is reasonable to assume that, keeping in mind the dietary code of Muslims, the kebabs were prepared with halal meat. Shamshuddin and the lady were both present that evening. Pleasant banter was exchanged and poetic verses enjoyed. However, the patch-up did not last long. Fraser was murdered by an assassin, hired by Shamshuddin, in 1835. The murderer was caught and confessed to his crime. Shamshuddin's complicity in the crime was exposed and the chieftain was arrested and summarily hanged. This incident ended the honeymoon between the white men in power and the aristocrats who had no real means to resist or strike back.

By the time Independence dawned, the British had started leaving India. Those who had left to fight the enemy on the front didn't return, like Dr Baker, IMS, my father's predecessor at the Indian Veterinary Research Institute in Mukteshwar, where he had found temporary employment to substitute for the Englishman. Slowly, the trickle became a stream. Those who remained or were left behind were the Anglo-Indians. I have fond memories of them from my growing up years in Mukteshwar. Most prominent among them in this small colonial outpost was Mr Atkins, who was identified as 'PA Saheb' (the abbreviation stood for personal assistant to the director). He was considered more powerful than the AO (administrative officer) who was stationed at Izat Nagar in the plains. Mr Atkins was fair-skinned and of ruddy complexion—just like the departing gora sahib log. He was a bachelor, kept to himself, and never mixed with the brown Indian officers. He owned powerful binoculars that he sometimes kindly lent to people he liked, to bring the snowcapped mountains within touching distance.

Then there was Mrs Chapman, an Anglo-Indian lady who dressed smartly in tartan-patterned skirts, well-stitched blouses, and jackets in the winter. She, no longer young, was the gregarious stenographer who never lacked admirers. Clicking her high-heeled shoes, she walked back in the company of chivalrous officers to her bungalow, hidden in a grove of cedar trees close to the PWD dak bungalow. She lived alone, and no one knew anything about Mr Chapman. The khansama she employed cooked *angreji khaana* for her—soup, salads, boiled vegetables, roasts and occasional curries. His memsahib was never invited to parties, nor did she extend her hospitality to anyone. She had once sent bread and milk pudding by her bearer to our house to share some good news.

Another charming Anglo-Indian was a gentleman known only by his nickname 'Cuckoo Babu', who had returned to Mukteshwar after surviving the war as a navigator-gunner in the Royal Air Force. He was as fair as PA Saheb or Mrs Chapman and always wore the leather jacket favoured by the aviators of that vintage. Cuckoo Babu was a jolly fellow who had found employment as the manager of the co-operative store, which pretended to be a departmental store catering to the British. It stocked tinned meats, cheeses, butter and coffee, as well as more expensive brands of soaps and toothpastes, not to forget Brylcreem. He spoke excellent English peppered with army slang and impeccable Hindustani. We visited the store often to buy table tennis balls, shuttlecocks and chewing gum when in stock. As I look back, I feel more than a little regret that we never bothered to find out Cuckoo Babu's real name. What lingers is the warm memory of a person more Indian than Anglo. But weren't most members of the Anglo-Indian community like this?

Signature Anglo-Indian dishes like Murgi Roast, Shepherd's Pie, and cutlets continued to keep their memory alive in Mukteshwar. Atkinson Sahib's cook was out of work when he left and sought employment as the cook in the Visiting Officers Bungalow reserved for high-ranking officers. He took great pride in the soups, stews and custards he could rustle up at short notice.

Anglo-Indians in Delhi had relations living in Agra, Meerut and even more distant Kasganj and Dehradun. The descendants of Colonel James Skinner owned large tracts of land in present-day Haryana. These colourful people with fair skin and blue eyes congregated in the capital to celebrate X-mas and Easter until the middle of the

1980s. Till the imperial capital was shifted from Calcutta, the largest concentration of Anglo-Indians was in the railway colony near Kauriya Pul and in areas around Kashmiri Gate and Mori Gate. By the mid-1920s, Anglo-Indians began pouring into the city from all around. Among them were two of the tallest leaders of the community—Henry Gidney and Frank Anthony.

Traditionally, most Anglo-Indians worked in the Railways, Post & Telegraph and Customs departments across the country. But in New Delhi, the community was also at the heart of the new capital's Western culture scene: most pianists and crooners at the city's clubs, restaurants and hotels were Anglo-Indians. With their impeccable English and refined social skills, they soon cornered the city's hospitality industry. Some musically inclined youngsters played and crooned in live bands in classy hotels. They preserved their distinct identity, and though they professed the same faith, their food and lifestyle was very different from those of other Christians living in Delhi.

Sydney Rebeiro, an Anglo-Indian retired professor of Delhi University and chronicler of the community, has reminisced that his mother, Mary Issacs, headed the Mori Gate post office during the war years, which had been an all-male bastion till then. Anglo-Indian women were the first ones to go out and work in the city—mostly as secretaries, teachers, nurses, stenographers and telephone operators, both in the government and corporate sectors.

The Gidney Club in K Block of Connaught Circus was the centre of social life for the Anglo-Indians in Delhi. It was here that births and marriages were celebrated. Gala events marked Christmas and the New Year. Sometimes families travelled to railway colonies in towns nearby to share joyous festivities with kinsmen and close friends.

Breakfast was hearty—bacon, ham, sausages, eggs and buttered toast. Kedgeree was for special occasions. This anglicised khichdi was made from rice, eggs, smoked fish, and curry powder, a far cry from the desi vegetarian dish. Everyday lunch consisted of pilaff rice, 'doll' (dal), and mutton mince cutlets. Popular tea-time snacks were croquets, curried puffs and sandwiches. Fish sticks, *ajwain*-cheese straws, and sausage curry are Anglo-Indian creations. The dinner time array of dishes was no less mouth-watering—soups like pepper water (mulligatawny), minestrone, stews and pies—Shepherd's and Yorkshire. On Sundays, *kofta*-inspired curried mince balls were served tongue-in-cheek as the 'bad word' curry (the risqué name for it being ball curry). For festive and celebratory feasts, the menu was lavish, with the inclusion of dishes that required patience and skill—roast leg of lamb, Murgi Roast and 'Double Onions meat', the Anglo-Indian take on *do pyaza*. Even the tables in modest homes were overladen with homemade jams, jellies, chutneys, assorted preserves and condiments.

Iconic dishes of the British Raj were the Railway Mutton Curry, Dak Bungalow Murgi Roast, Colonel Sandhurst's Beef Curry, Bengal Lancer's Shrimp Curry, Fish and Chips, Grandma's Country Captain or Capon. What they cooked and shared may be termed as the first stage in the evolution of pan-Indian taste. Chicken, Pork Bhuni, Banger's Crush, Devil Pork Curry and Jhal Farezi bear testimony to the *joie de vivre* of the Anglo-Indians and their creativity.

Brian Silas, a self-taught piano player, cajoled his keyboard to sing out enchanting Hindi film songs at Dum Pukht, the elegant ITC restaurant at the Maurya, from the 1980s onwards. So melodious was his offering that the diners often stopped in the middle of their Awadhi nawabi meal to enjoy the fare prepared by S.D. Burman, O.P. Nayyar and Salil Chaudhari. There was never a mismatch between Lucknow's delicate food and the music that subtly accompanied it. Wasn't it Cliff Richard, a Lucknow boy, that had put Great Britain on the international Rock-n-Roll map before the Beatles appeared on the scene?

Young Anglo-Indian writers were rising stars of the capital's literary scene in the 1960s and 1970s. Ruskin Bond freelanced and was a regular columnist in the *Hindustan Times*, and R.V. Smith, an immigrant from Agra, carved a niche for himself in *The Statesman* as an archivist of 'Purani Dilli' and *angrezon ki virasat*. Blending legends, folklore, excerpts from memoirs and newspaper articles with his own interviews with old-timers, he recreated the ambience of a world inhabited by his kinfolk about to disappear.

By this time, the numbers of this always minuscule community in Delhi had already dwindled to a little over a couple thousand from the peak of forty thousand at the time of Independence. The older generation, if they had independent means, preferred to stay back in India rather than embark on a journey to an imagined homeland to start all over again. Those who were more adventurous, young, restless and apprehensive about the future emigrated to Canada and Australia. However, they left behind the sparkling gems from their kitchen repertoire. These have become staples in clubs, officer's messes in the Army, dak bungalows, circuit houses, railway dining cars and canteens, and in residential public schools all over the land.

An interesting feature of some Anglo-Indian classics is that the recipes vary in different regions. Railway Mutton Curry in Chennai tastes quite different from what is served in Kolkata and Mumbai. Praveen Tripathi, a management consultant, who, owing to a childhood spent on a railway compound, has been obsessed with everything connected with Indian Railways, ordered it specially for me to sample at the Royal Yacht Club in Mumbai. The flavourful dish didn't share anything other than the name with what I had savoured just before the devastating Covid lockdown at the Tollygunje Club in Kolkata. Decades ago, while travelling with Jiggs Kalra, the journalist and foodie, shooting the television show *Zaike ka Safar,* I had sampled yet another version in Bangalore and Chennai.

As the excitement of centenary celebrations commemorating New Delhi built up, popular interest in Raj-era food was rekindled. Concept restaurants were launched with menus exclusively showcasing food served in clubs, dak bungalows and on trains. Marut Sikka, who had worked with Jiggs, started the Club House, and Michael Swami launched Anglow in Khan Market. As we enter the second quarter of the twenty-first century, the Anglo-Indian culinary legacy in the capital has proved to be enduring.

Seven

Angrezon ki Dilli

A view of Wenger's window in the 1930s
Courtesy: Atul Tandon

The officers of the Company who succeeded the White Mughals did not approve of the ways of their predecessors. Persons like Metcalfe believed that to assert their superiority the white men must maintain a distance from the natives. There should be no mingling at the social level to convey any sense of shared status. Unless superiority was signalled unambiguously, it would become impossible to exercise power. The idea was to dominate the minds and will of those who had been defeated and subdued.

The buildings that were erected by the Company officials were meant to serve as symbols of power far greater than the Mughals could claim. These edifices were inspired by classical European architecture—Roman and Gothic. Churches with large domes, mansions with imposing colonnades were intended to dwarf the decaying monuments in the Walled City. The Agents and the Residents no longer ate local foods or dressed up in the native manner.

English settlements came up beyond Kashmiri Gate, outside the Walled City at Alipur Road, Rajpur Road, Court Road, Ludlow Castle Road, Flagstaff Road (leading to the top of the hillock), Bara Hindu Rao (once Fraser's kothi), Racquet Court Road and Chauburji Road.

Thomas Theophilus Metcalfe arrived in Delhi in 1813, just eighteen years old. Charles, his elder brother, was the Resident at Bahadur Shah's court at that time. 'Theo' was to spend the next four decades of his life in the city. He made steady progress and served as Agent to the Mughal court after the murder of William Fraser in 1835. In 1842, Theo was appointed Governor General's Agent to the Mughal court, and from then on until his death in 1853, from suspected poisoning, he was regarded by many as uncrowned king of the territory of Delhi.

In 1830, Thomas Metcalfe commissioned an imposing residence for himself—a mini castle—on the outskirts of Delhi on land acquired from Gujjars. Local construction workers and sundry domestic servants found it difficult to correctly pronounce the name of the man who was their master so Metcalfe House became Matka Kothi. It was a spacious mansion set amidst verdant lawns framed with colourful flowerbeds. Exotic trees lined the property and the marble floored verandah afforded a tranquil view of the river flowing past to the east. This is where he parked his library that boasted 25,000 volumes, a rich art collection and substantial memorabilia.

His daughter Emily was just as fond of the castle as her father, who used to recount in between puffs of the hookah, the merits of the way of life he led in his country retreat and the entirely different one of the 'fastidious Englishman' at Metcalfe House, where his daughter and son, George, also stayed when they visited from England. Thomas led a well regulated life, compartmentalized for work and leisure. Emily writes in a journal she kept:

> He rose at five o'clock precisely and, after eating a light breakfast on the verandah, walked up and down in his dressing gown while delivering orders to his servants. At seven he went to bathe in his swimming pool; then, having dressed, he attended prayers in his oratory before eating his main breakfast at eight. After breakfast he would quietly smoke his hookah for half-an-hour and then retire to his study to write letters until 10 o'clock when his carriage was brought beneath the portico by his coachman. He then drove away to return at two o'clock for dinner at three. After dinner he sat reading for a time before going down to the billiard-room. A game of billiards was followed by two hours spent on the terrace contemplating the river. Then it was time for a light supper and the evening hookah. Immediately the clock struck eight he stood up and went to bed.

Metcalfe, a widower, lived alone, and strictly in the manner of a gentleman in England. He imported suits tailored in London to his specification 'sober but fashionable English clothes', by Pulford of St James's. However, he couldn't resist the seduction of tobacco, smoked in a silver hookah, like Muslim nobles. Even this indulgence was strictly measured. The puffing after breakfast never extended beyond half an hour.

His daughter has recorded her father's peculiar way of punishing and disciplining a servant who failed to meet his expectations. Metcalfe would call for a pair of white kid gloves.

> These he would pick up from their silver salver and slowly pull on over his delicate white fingers. Then, 'with solemn dignity', having lectured the servant on his failing, he proceeded to pinch gently but firmly the ear of the culprit, and then let him go, a reprimand that was entirely efficacious.

When the rains came, Thomas retired to 'Dilkusha', his sojourn in an area which was the traditional retreat of the Mughals for the monsoon. The first floor of the tomb of Mohammed Quli Khan, was converted into a mini-castle, with a study and ample residential accommodation for the Metcalfe family.

Percival Spear has made an interesting comment in *Twilight of the Mughals* about the first crop of officers of East India Company who presided over the forced transition of power from the Mughals to the British: 'If Ochterlony was the Babur and Charles the Akbar of British Delhi, Thomas Metcalfe was its Shah Jahan.' Obviously, the learned professor is getting carried away a little. With the advantage of hindsight, not only nationalist Indian historians but even revisionist English historians would consider the comparison as not very accurate.

Brown Sahibs and Seths

From the beginning of the nineteenth century, Delhi ceased to be one city—a settlement protected by the rampart of walls and nestling under the shadow of the Red Fort and the majestic Jama Masjid. As decay set in, the British influence steadily expanded not only in the domain of the emperor in the provinces but also within the imperial capital.

The British did not like to live in the congested squalid confines of the Walled City. They chose to maintain a reasonable distance from the 'Hindoos' and others, the not always trustworthy, Muslims. They set themselves up in the suburb beyond the Kashmiri Gate. A green buffer provided by Qudasiya Bagh and Roshnara Bagh separated this settlement from the old city.

Residents and Agents like James Fraser and the Metcalfes—father and sons—built imposing mansions for themselves in the tract of land in the proximity of River Yamuna, then covered with fruit-bearing trees. On the other side, the land was girdled by the Northern Ridge forest. This area later developed into the Civil Lines—the White Man's City (*Angrezon ki Dilli*)—replete with churches, clubs, hotels and palatial houses built in classical European style.

Some of the earliest buildings that stood in marked architectural contrast to the havelis in the sheher were St James Church, Metcalfe House, the palatial compound of Bada Hindu Rao and the bungalows built by Fraser and other senior officers.

Each community had its well-defined place of residence, like the caste groups of the city, and together they made up the civil and military station. The lives of residents intersected at different levels, but the two cities maintained their separate identity.

High-ranking British officers often entertained in the manner of Muslim gentry, with recitals by Indian musicians and performances of nautch girls marking the climax.

Bakeries mushroomed after the British took control of the city. The locals didn't take long to acquire a taste of buns, biscuits and rusks. Nanbais continued to bake a supply of traditional unleavened and leavened breads, *chapatti*, *tandoori*, *khamiri*, and special breads like *sheermal* and *roghani*. The bakeries in the beginning may well have been started by junior members of the family or apprentices branching off on an independent course. Their main line remained biscuits and rusks. They catered to the residents of the Walled City. The bakers who supplied bread, patties, pastries and cakes to European patrons were based in Kashmiri Gate and the Civil Lines.

The nanbais in the Walled City who had baked a variety of breads on a clay or iron tandoor much before the advent of the British were quick to learn new skills from the bakers in Kashmiri Gate who catered to the British, Anglo-Indians and Indian Christians. After Independence and Partition, many bakeries came up in the vicinity of Jama Masjid. Some still exist and specialize in rusks and biscuits, others have thrived selling buns and patties. In the past decade, a new crop of bakers has arrived in the city who specialize in baking Afghan or Kashmiri breads. These anonymous bakeries operating in Lajpat Nagar, Gurgaon and Noida have carved a niche for themselves.

Eight

The Emperor's Last Banquet

Bahadur Shah Zafar II
Courtesy: The History Collective Visual Archive

At the turn of the nineteenth century, Delhi lay ravaged and prostrate. By the end of its first quarter, the law and order situation in Shahjahanabad had become appalling. Thefts, robberies and armed assaults had become routine. As Khurshid-ul Islam and Ralph Russell have recorded in *Three Mughal Poets*, '…the city was swarming with thieves and robbers, who go unpunished because the police are in league with them; the danger of assault is always present so that men go out in the evening to a mushaira fully armed, as though they were going to a battle.'[21]

Regardless, some denizens of the city preferred to stay here rather than emigrate.

Dil-o-Dilli donon agar hain kharaab
Pa kuchh lutf is ujde ghar mein bhi hain

(My heart and my Delhi may both be in ruins
There are still some delights in this ravaged home.)

By this time the British had extended their influence from Bengal to Awadh and beyond. Shah Alam had granted the Diwani (collection of revenue) of Awadh to the East India Company, encouraging the Company's officers to set their eyes on the 'crown jewel'—control of Delhi. For all practical purposes, the British were the paramount power in northern India, though the Mughal Emperor in Delhi continued to claim sovereignty.

The large constellation of poets in Bahadur Shah Zafar's court presents a lop-sided picture of the flourishing cultural milieu. The Emperor was dependent on the pension received from the British and hardly in a position to patronize even distinguished poets generously. The resources at his command were very limited and stretched, barely enough to meet the expenditure on essentials—salaries to soldiers, the royal household and traditional ceremonies.

The favourite children of the aged Emperor led comfortable lives and a few, with protective mothers, senior queens in the harem, had the means to indulge in their interests. The rest of the blue-blooded brood were doomed to a wretched and miserable existence. The impoverished grandchildren and great-grandchildren and great-great-grandchildren of previous monarchs numbered over two thousand and were confined to a cordoned off area in the Red Fort.

Zafar, burdened with problems of his own, lost in poetic reveries, had no time to involve himself with the sufferings and misdemeanors of princes who were condemned to live as wretched prisoners. They were a cause of embarrassment to him, no more.

The first few high-ranking British officers appeared in Delhi in the last decade of the eighteenth century. After the acquisition of the Diwani of Bengal, the East India Company posted Agents and Residents as its representatives in the Mughal Emperor's court. Besides, there were English soldiers of fortune commanding mercenary armies, offering their services to the highest bidder. David Ochterlony, William Fraser and James Skinner belong to this lot, as chronicled in the preceding chapter.

Some Englishmen took a keen interest in the foods of India. When posted in Delhi, more than one officer of the Company had commissioned the compilation of recipes they enjoyed and got Persian cookbooks translated into English. These are an invaluable source of information about the preferred foods and flavours in the city through the eighteenth and nineteenth centuries.

Some of the recipes are referred to as 'Muhammad Shahi', which indicates that the text was probably either contemporaneous to the Mughal Emperor, Muhammad Shah or was written shortly after his reign.

Murder at the Mushaira, a novel by Raza Mir, recreates the milieu in Delhi in the years just before the cataclysmic events of 1857. Although a recent work of fiction, the author has relied on primary sources to give the readers an authentic feel and flavour of the life then. The food served to eminent poets and hangers-on in the court is described in some detail:

> He (Ramchandra) looked grumpily at the gulawati kebabs, sniffed at the Kashmiri Pulao, and checked out the lababdar murgh from a few angles before moving despondently to the vegetarian dishes. Even there he had found no relief. 'These Mughal chefs had found a way to ruin even the baigan and bhindi, stuffing them with masala until they were undistinguishable from the meat dishes, leaving them over-spiced and promising a night of uncomfortable acidity. The less said about the desserts the better, with their saffron and butter and crushed nuts.' All he could eat was some dahi with a roti although the roti was oily enough to upset his stomach on its own.[22]

The imperial boundaries continued to shrink and by the time Muhammad Shah's son, Akbar Shah II, ascended the throne, his writ was restricted to the Qila-e-Mualla and its neighbourhood. He had been badly scarred by the humiliation and deprivations suffered as an adolescent.

When Bahadur Shah II succeeded him, in 1837, at the age of sixty-two, the British had encroached into his domain even further. The enfeebled old man was not even free to accept *nazar* or distribute *khillat* without the permission of the British Agent. Though Charles Metcalfe, the Resident, appeared friendly and observed the protocol prescribed, he had no inhibitions about demonstrating who was in control and really exercised power. Stinging rebukes and humiliation were not unusual. The Emperor was resigned to his fate and devoted himself to the pursuit of poetry. The *umra* (aristocratic courtiers) lived in delusions of past grandeur, cut off from harsh reality.

Poet Sauda, who lived through these hard times, lamented, '*Is zamaane ka jo dekha toh hai ulta insaaf / Gurg azaad rahein aur ho shubaan pehre mein*' (Justice in this age is turned upside down, wolves roam free and shepherds [are] under arrest). We must keep in mind that Sauda was born and lived in Delhi's Kabuli Darwaaza, which was an upmarket neighbourhood back then, inhabited by the city's elite and connoisseurs of art; apparently no part of the city was safe.

As a young man of twenty-four, Sauda was an eye-witness to the siege of Delhi by Maratha forces led by Bajirao I. These bitter realities stared him in the face, but he expressed his desolation with an effortless elegance that would resonate with anyone, high or low, young or old:

> *Shaam hi se bujha sa rehta hai*
> *Dil hua hai chiraagh muflis ka.*
> (My heart is like a lamp in the poor man's house about to die,
> its weak flame unable to dispel descending darkness.)

An eye-witness account is provided in *Dastan-e-Ghadar*[23] by Zahir Dehlvi, a survivor. The author of this work, was appointed in his adolescence as *Darogha-e-Mahi-Maratib* (Custodian of the Order of the Fish). While the position was largely ceremonial, the office carried great prestige and provided the holder a ring-side view of the life in the palace. Zahir was not a historian or even an official chronicler, but a low-level courtier and an aspiring poet, staunchly loyal to the Mughal Emperor. Ironically, after 1857, his narrative is sympathetic to the British, although his own family had suffered a great deal due to their brutal repression. He constantly blames the *purabiya* (Hindu soldiers) who had mutinied and ransacked Delhi at the outset of the revolt. His prejudice can be partially explained by the fact that, by and large, the Hindu Baniyas and Khatris—traders and bankers—had escaped loss of property and persecution that the Muslim aristocrats had suffered. While mosques were deliberately desecrated and occupied by soldiers, and some turned into stables, Hindu and Jain temples mostly escaped this fate.

He describes the reprisals and restoration of law and order by the British following incidents of profiteering and black-marketeering as well as the reluctance of people to move out of their homes, as their families had lived there for generations.

He has little time to describe the plight of the poor menials who dwelt outside the city walls in slums that sprawled in the suburbs and the countryside, where starvation was rampant, and helpless people were left to cope on their own. Zahir himself was separated from his family during the mayhem, but was fortunately reunited with it later. Many members of the Muslim gentry had to seek the hospitality of their relatives and friends outside the city for long periods or make do with what the poor ate.

Daagh Dehlvi, who was a stepson of the Emperor, fared no better. In search of patronage, he wandered from place to place—Rampur and Hyderabad. He lived up to the ripe old age of seventy-five without complaining about his personal circumstances. Except for a minuscule coterie of imperial physicians and dwindling number of jagirdars/sardars, few could be sure of getting two square meals. The Muslim aristocrats and nawabs had to bear the ire of the British rulers after Fraser's murder in 1835.

We have a more detailed description of food in Delhi between 1830 and 1857 in Munshi Faizuddin's *Bazm-i Aakhir*,[24] published in 1885, almost three decades after the upheaval of 1857. He was a middle-level official, a scribe, who has written about the banquet and the royal repast served in the Red Fort during the reign of the last two Mughal Emperors.

They consisted of delicacies that commoners could not dream of. Even poets of aristocratic lineage, with access to the court, lived on meagre stipends that were whimsically granted and withdrawn. With these grants, they could anyway not afford to enjoy the haute-cuisine.

Munshi Faizuddin's elaborate description of the imperial dastarkhan lists dozens of delicacies prepared in the royal kitchen in the Red Fort. He titled his work *Bazm-i Aakhir* (The Last Banquet) as such lavish banquets ceased to be hosted after the last Mughal emperor was reduced to a pensioner of the British.

> The emperor washed his hands with gram flour and then with a sandalwood tablet. Finger bowls were provided. Pickles, hor d'oeuvres made with almond and pistachio, poppy seeds and aniseeds. Samose salone, aur meethe khajje, Shaakhain. Santare [orange], sharife [custard apple], seb [apple], anar aur ber [pomegranate and jujube].

The breads mentioned are those prepared with wheat and rice flour. Special breads—cake-like confections incorporating milk and eggs—were enriched with nuts and dried fruits. Some were leavened while others were not. Baking, too, could be done in tandoor or griddle. Many like *khamiri*, *chapattiyan*, *sheermal*, *bakarkhani*, kulcha, phulkey, paranthe and naan were traditionally cooked in the city by the local bakers, and continue to be so in Delhi till today. Other, more exotic breads, like *gauzaban* (literally ox's tongue) and *gav deeda* (bull's eye) are essentially Lucknow specialties and flakey *qatlam* belongs to the Kashmiri repertoire. Other exotic breads were created for the pleasure of the gourmet with slight variations on the original: *naan gulzaar* (shaped like a flower), *badam piste ki naan khatai* (a crumbly cookie laced with almonds and pistachios), *ghausi* (nothing is known about this bread). Some breads were made with vegetables like carrots, others were sweet in taste and incorporated sugar. Still others were stuffed with lentil paste and called *bervi roti*. *Naan bamba* was an exceptionally soft bread.

There was a great variety of rice dishes, mostly pulaos. *Yakhni pulao* was cooked with mutton or chicken stock, and *moti pulao* was garnished with pearls crafted of mince and covered with silver leaf. Raisins went into *kishmishi pulao* and *nargisi pulao* mimicked the beauty of iris/daffodil with a garnish of sliced, hard-boiled eggs. Green gram was what gave a distinct identity to *boont pulao*. Some pulaos were named after a person who may have first ordered these, like the *Noor ehal pulao*. Pistachios were the essential ingredient for *nukti pista pulao*.

Biryani pulaos were a separate category. In these pulaos, long-grained rice was first fried delicately to glaze the grains of rice before they were slow-cooked with marinated meats in layers.

The Mughals also relished plain rice dishes like *qabuli*, cooked with chick-peas, or a khichdi which combined rice and lentils and viands. *Tehri* was no less popular and it did not have lentils in it. Lots of seasonal vegetables could be added. *Pulao shola* continues to be cooked in the bylanes of Delhi, under the name of *shola khichdi* or *khichda*. It is a rustic dish and its inclusion in the royal dastarkhan indicates that street foods were not kept out of the imperial spread.

Qorma is the term used for braised meats that were cooked without turmeric and had a thick, sauce-like gravy wrapping the meat pieces. Meats were marinated for hours to let the flavours seep in. These were prepared with goat meat, venison (*hiran ka qorma*) and chicken. Do pyaza is a term used interchangeably in contemporary texts for *qorma*.

Kaliya was a dish with a thinner gravy that did not always eschew turmeric. Water or milk were added to the meat as it was cooked. *Salan* incorporated a vegetable in a stew-like preparation.

In the list provided in *Bazm-i Aakhir*, fish is scarcely mentioned. We do encounter *machhcali borani* but no details are available. There are some dishes that are enigmatic like *kheere ki dogi*.

Unsurprisingly, kebabs were an important part of the Mughal meals. In fact, even the Turko-Afghan sultans, who preceded the Mughals, preferred to make a meal of char-grilled seekh kebabs on skewers. The list of kebabs provided by Munshi Faizuddin mentions seekh kebabs as well as pan-grilled patties like *shami* kebabs. These were prepared with beef, mutton, chicken and game-birds like partridges and quails. *Khatai ke kebab* are mentioned as a Chinese recipe, but no details are provided. We can only hazard a guess. In Lucknow, there is a delicate crumble-to-touch kebab that bears the name *kham khatai ke kebab* inspired by *nankhatai*, which may have been replicated in Delhi. Or this kebab had a touch of some exotic souring agent.

Vegetables were usually cooked with meats, though some vegetables, particularly stuffed ones, were enjoyed on their own. *Dulma* were dishes that descended from Armenian dolamantes. There was *aloo ka dulma*, *baigan ka dulma*, and *karelon ka dulma*.

There were sweet pulaos—some cooked with goat meat—*muzaffer and muthanjan*—that were served as desserts. Kheer was commonly prepared with rice and milk, enriched with pistachios and almonds, and made fragrant with saffron. It was also prepared with *sevian* (vermicelli). *Phirni*, a kheer, prepared with rice flour, that had a soufflé-like texture, was set in small clay pots and served cold. Kheer was also prepared with fruits and vegetables like bottle gourd and carrots.

A number of preserves and pickles accompanied the meal. The last royal banquet included *murabbas* made with *karele* (bitter gourd), *seb* (apple), *aam* (mangoes), *baans* (bamboo shoots), *ananas* (pineapple), *badam* (almonds), *kakronde* (wild berries), *gurhal* (hibiscus).

Among the condiments, *paneer ki chatni* is mentioned. Interestingly, this is the solitary reference to paneer.

Most of the royalty had a sweet tooth and the royal cooks and confectioners created a variety of sweetmeats to cater to it. We have already referred to sweet-tasting pulaos, in addition there was saffron-laced *zarda*, mildly-sweet yellow rice, and frothy *nimish* (literally a blink), prepared by delicately collecting layers of froth from milk kept outdoors overnight 'to be chilled by dewdrops and moonlight'. It is called by different names—*malaiyyo* in Benaras, *makkhan malai* in Kanpur and *daulat ki chaat* nowadays in Delhi.

Halwa was prepared with a variety of ingredients. Besides semolina, wheat germ, carrots and bottle gourd were used. *Papri* is mentioned in the list of confections and was most likely a precursor of present day *son-papdi* derived from the Punjabi *patisa*. *Gondh ka halwa* incorporated edible resin that was believed to have heat generating properties. A laddoo made with *gondh* continues to be prepared by some halwais during the winter months. More exotic recipes incorporated dried fruits and nuts, meats and eggs.

Lauzaat was the term that covered a variety of dainty sweetmeats that were made with fresh seasonal fruits like *jamun*, *santara* and *falsa*. Among the many sweets mentioned in *Bazm-i Aakhir*, there are several that have travelled well across time. *Piste ki launji*, *imarti*, *jalebi*, *balu shahi*, *kalakand*, *faini*, *anarse ki goliyan*, *pethe ki mithai*, *barfi*, *moti paak*, assorted laddoos—*besan*, *khoya nariyal*, *til*, and *motichoor*.

One is tempted to suggest that some sweets with names resembling riddles, like *gehun ki baalin ki mithai*, made from ears of wheat, was perhaps a variation on the *jauzi sohan halwa* made in Awadh.

Such elaborate banquets were cooked largely by, and for, the benefit of the hangers-on in the innermost circle of retainers. Contemporary accounts of the affairs of the Qila-e-Mualla describe the plight of royal prince 'salateen' residing within the ramparts. They weren't allowed to take up remunerative jobs or engage in trade and commerce. Their survival depended entirely on the crumbs that fell their way or as petty pay-offs for participation in intrigues.

The question of who patronized poets and bore the expenses of lavish hospitality isn't easy to answer. It would appear that a small leisured class had survived the coming of the British, which had both the means and the desire to indulge in expensive tastes in poetry and cuisine. Circumstances changed dramatically after 1857. After suppressing the rebellion, the British ruthlessly wreaked havoc in revenge.

The life of Muslims in Delhi after the British crushed the rebellion in 1857 was hellish. Though all communities suffered, the Muslims were particularly targeted. Their shops were looted and houses reduced to rubble.

Muslims were denied permission to pray in mosques. For a while, rumours were rife that mosques would be converted into churches. Their compounds were used as stables and military stores. Fatehpuri Masjid was auctioned and bought by a Hindu Khatri banker—Chunna Mal. Lala Chunna Mal returned the Fatehpuri mosque to the Muslims only after he was compensated by the British with the grant of some villages in Nangloi and Gurgaon. The Jama Masjid, once the pride of the city, was handed back to Muslims in 1862, only after the intercession of Sikandar Begum of Bhopal with Lord Canning during her visit to Delhi.

The Hindus, particularly the affluent Khatri and Baniya merchants, escaped painful persecution and humiliation. They were allowed to buy properties of pauperised Muslim aristocrats that were auctioned. These included Haveli Hissamuddin Haider, Ahata Kaley Sahab and Baradari Nawab Wazir.

Aristocratic Muslims who had rallied around the reluctant leader of the mutineer sepoys were particularly targeted. Their mansions were razed, their places of worship desecrated. Properties were looted and later confiscated. Walls were broken down and residences with grounds flattened for strategic reasons. The aim was to clear the area of Muslims loyal to the Emperor as also to give the British soldiers occupying the Red Fort a commanding view of the 'field', to ensure that no guns could be placed there. During 1857, this area with its congested lanes and kuchas, had provided a safe haven to the rebels.

Families fled to save their lives.

It would take almost two decades before a semblance of normalcy could return to the devastated Walled City—particularly the katras, kuchas, and galis in the vicinity of Jama Masjid. Times were not favourable to indulge in palate pleasures or the muse of poetry. Patrons had perished and crafts persons scattered in the whirlwind. Eking out an existence was challenging enough.

Delicacies described in meals served at Mirza's Haveli in Raza Mir's *Murder at the Mushaira* seem to have a strong tilt towards Awadhi cuisine. This is understandable as after Delhi was reduced to rubble by the vengeful British, most of the skilled karigars and bawarchis had dispersed to sanctuaries in principalities like Rampur and Lucknow. When some semblance of normalcy returned to Delhi, the new technique of cooking and presentation they had acquired enriched the Delhi dastarkhan. Actually, the Awadhi influence can be traced to Akbar Shah's long sojourn in Faizabad and Lucknow, when he had fled the city ingloriously to escape invaders.

Contemporary literary works shed interesting light on street foods and eating habits of denizens of Delhi. Kebabs and *chaat*, sweets of different types and parantha became popular.

People ate at home and eating out was discouraged. The male members bought sweets and snacks to be consumed at home by family members—women and children were not allowed to step out. These snacks included kachori, samose, and jalebi. The khomche wala brought the moveable feast of *chaat-tikki* and *golgappe* to the doorstep.

This practice continued well after the Partition and Independence until the 1970s, when eating out came into vogue, the city expanded beyond Lutyens' Delhi and suburbs sprouted, severing the links between the Walled City and the city planned by the British. Food culture was bound to change with the cityscape.

When Bahadur Shah Zafar II ascended what continued to be referred to as the Peacock Throne, but was, in fact, a replica, he was already past his prime. Even if we concede that his voracious appetite had survived, it would be naive to believe that the dastarkhan before him could do him justice. Given the limited pension he received from the British, often irregularly, and the huge number of his dependents, it is difficult to imagine that expenditure on such lavish meals could be sustained. It is more likely that this was the repertoire of recipes from which the menu for daily meals was selected to suit seasonal requirements.

Nine

Traders, Treasurers, Scribes and Administrators

Khazanchi Haveli, Old Delhi
Courtesy: The History Collective Visual Archive

Muslims, Baniyas, Kayasthas, and Khatris who live in Old Delhi all trace their roots to times before Shahjahanabad was commissioned, in the mid-seventeenth century. The borders of Punjab touched Delhi, and almost three hundred years before the waves of post-Partition refugees came in, Punjabis, mostly from the Saudagaran community, comprised a substantial segment of the city's population. The Baniyas and Kayasthas were fewer in number, but these communities were well represented in the bureaucracy, trade and commerce. There was also a sprinkling of Kashmiris, Parsis and Christians. All of these communities have enriched the culinary repertoire of Delhi.

Not only professional cooks but traders and crafts persons, scholars and artistes, also gravitated toward the new city, full of promise. Besides them, members belonging to the above communities, also settled in the Walled City in the vicinity of the Jama Masjid. Dariba, a Baniya hub, shared with the Jain traders, was populated by jewellers, Sitaram Bazaar housed Kashmiri Brahmins, and a small square away lived their Muslim neighbours. Roshanpura was where the affluent Kayasthas were concentrated until the turn of the twentieth century. Many prominent Baniya families had their havelis in Katra Neel. Dharampura was an Aggarwal–Jain enclave. Raja Harsukh Rai, who was the imperial treasurer in the first decade of the nineteenth century, lived here and was granted permission to build a new Jain temple with a shikhar by Emperor Akbar Shah. Bazaar Sitaram, Kucha Patiram, Hauz Qazi, Chawri Bazaar, Kinari Bazaar and Paranthe Wali Gali were other Baniya strongholds. Many families lived on the upper floors and the ground floors were used for shops. Baniyas didn't reside in Ballimaran, Jama Masjid and Lal Kuan.

Members of a caste or profession clung together but shared the community life with 'others', their neighbours. The Jains observed stricter taboos. Potatoes, other tubers, roots and green leafy vegetables were forbidden. Most families ate the last meal of the day before sunset. However, deep-fried sweets and snacks that didn't contain onion and garlic could be shared. Many Baniya and Jain trading families intermarried. Baniyas and Jains originating from the Marwar-Jodhpur region were known as Marwaris, namely Marwari Jain or Marwari Baniya.

Prominent Kayasthas and Baniyas secured appointments as ministers, treasurers and royal bankers in Shah Jahan's court and helped to make Delhi a cosmopolitan city, where diverse culinary streams met. The city was never quite a melting pot but a place where many cooking styles coexisted harmoniously.

Lashkari khana like *nihari-paye*, robust kebabs grilled by legendary kebabchis like Maseeta and Gummi on the steps of Jama Masjid and sweets prepared by Shahi Ghantewala Halwai became synonymous with Delhi. Domestic kitchens preserved traditional Kayastha and Baniya cuisines. The flavours of Kashmir and Punjab happily coexisted with Baniya, Kayastha and Khatri tastes.

Food cooked at home was very different from the sumptuous, rich fare spread on imperial dastarkhans. We are afforded interesting glimpses on what the princes and their guests consumed at the high table and what sustained the underlings, masses without privilege, in the accounts of foreign travellers.

It is futile to assert that Delhi 'belongs' to any one community. When Sheila Dixit was the Chief Minister, an interesting advertising campaign was once carried out that proudly proclaimed '*Dilli hai dilwalon ki!*' This seems to capture the essence of who is a Dilliwala. The city, by whatever name it has been identified, has welcomed 'outsiders' who have chosen to make it their home. It has never imposed a straitjacket, that of a homogenized identity, on newcomers. From language to cuisines, it has celebrated diversity. Out of the many communities' cuisines, the Baniya, Kayastha, and Christian are the more easily discernible layers in Delhi's food.

Baniya Rasoi

My first Baniya meal in Delhi was a bit of a disappointment. My poet friend and mentor, Kamlesh, had raised expectations by lavishing high praise on the thali at the Marwari Bhojanalaya, Chandni Chowk. One sat on the floor and ate off the thali placed on a chowki. I found the offerings lack-lustre. They had a strong accent of *hing* and were much too rich for my liking, due to the generous helpings of ghee in the dal etc. The seasonal vegetables did not seem to have any distinct character. It seemed to cater to the price-sensitive customer, who was orthodox about observing the food taboos of his community.

Later, there were occasional invitations to eat at a Baniya colleague's house in the Jawaharlal Nehru University campus, where I encountered Baniya home cooking. Dr S.C. Gangal, a don, who loved food, eschewed not only meat but also onion and garlic. Mrs Gangal thickened the gravies with curd that was carefully cooked to prevent curdling. Generous quantities of coriander powder and cumin were used and the tempering relied on aromatic hing. Pickles of various kinds introduced the flavours of *saunf*, *ajwain*, *methi*, *kalaunji*. The range of vegetables used was limited to potatoes, colocasia (*arbi*), pumpkin and gourds. There were dishes the guests were treated to which were labour-intensive, but barely a stunning dish that could match the spread of the Kayastha table. Decades passed before I was introduced to the Jain kitchens of Delhi.

Nandita Jain belonged to the illustrious Jain family that owns the *Times of India* and manages the Bharatiya Jnanpith trust. We became friends while working together on the Newspaper in Education (NIE) programme and I had the pleasure of many a meal at her house on Sardar Patel Marg. Nandita was exceptionally vivacious and always eager to share food-lore related to the Jain community. Thanks to her, I was privileged to share meals with her cousins, uncles and aunts—near and distant relatives. I realized that not all Jains were equally orthodox, strictly following the prescriptions and prohibitions about eschewing green leafy vegetables, tubers and roots or eating before sunset. However, it was the rare exception who strayed from the path of vegetarianism. I was gently educated that Jain foods—particularly of Jains in Delhi—had much in common with the city's Baniya cuisine.

There was a senior colleague at the Jawaharlal Nehru University, Prof R.K. Jain, an eminent sociologist, who had taught at Oxford University. Softspoken and gentle, he was a practicing Jain and seldom ate out. Kamlesh Jain in the Department of Chinese Studies at Jawaharlal Nehru University helped me get rid of many misconceptions about Jain diet. She helped me understand that social class, education, profession and generational difference impacted what a Jain ate.

The word Baniya is derived from the Sanskrit *vanik*—a businessman, merchant, trader, shopkeeper and treasurer. From time immemorial, members of this community have acted as bankers and financiers to kings and princes. They belong to the Vaishya caste and, according to the narrative in Rg Veda, were born out of the thighs of the Purush. The thighs sustain the weight of the body and this suggested, symbolically, that the community sustains the economic welfare of the society and, through savings and investments, safeguards its prosperity. Creators and owners of immense wealth, ultra-rich Baniyas were bestowed with honorifics like Jagat Seth and Dhanna Seth.

Scions of most prominent families in the city prefix their names with Seth. The word is derived from Sanskrit *shreshti*, members of a small elite, superior in status. Chettiars in southern India share this etymology. In early mediaeval India, the shreshtis organized guilds of skilled workers, led caravans and sponsored voyages across the seas and financed charitable works for public good. A number of Jaina temples in Rajasthan and Gujarat as also in present-day Karnataka were commissioned by them. They were generous patrons of arts, literature and scholarship. The most illustrious Baniya families are immigrants from Rajasthan, Haryana (then a part of Punjab) and adjacent districts of Uttar Pradesh. The title of Raja, prefixing their names, had been bestowed upon them.

Much like Indian royalty, the merchant princes of Delhi have traditionally intermarried in Baniya families of matching wealth and social status. The matrimonial alliances and common ancestry bound the community together in good and bad times.

Two of the most prominent Baniya families in Delhi trace their roots to Rattan Chand Aggarwal, a confectioner, who lived in Jhajjhar. He was a halwai, money lender, trader, rolled into one, who moved from Jhajjhar to Delhi in 1803. He welcomed the advent of the British who had restored law and order in the countryside surrounding Delhi.

In 1821, when the British had established almost complete administrative control over Punjab and Delhi, and emerged as the dominant military power, he sent his second son Budri Das to work as khajanchi (treasurer) in the Karnal Commissariat. The job title was high-sounding but the young man most probably functioned as storekeeper-cum-accountant. The British masters were impressed by the hard-working youngster and his integrity and promoted him as kotwal in Ferozepur Zirka in 1840. He was promoted and transferred to Delhi in 1854, where he bought a house in Kucha Mai Das. His star remained ascendant through violent upheaval in the city. When the British reclaimed the city, he was rewarded with 50,000 rupees and some land for his unflinching loyalty to the Crown. His eldest son, Bhagirath Mal, bought Begum Samru's haveli, with its palatial house and garden, while his grandson, Gopal Rai, founded the Delhi Cloth Mills. The descendants of Budri Das were popularly identified as the Kotwal clan.

There were other Baniyas who were men of substance and influence in the city in the late nineteenth century. Still other Baniya families engaged in different trades and businesses. They had started with humble beginnings but amassed substantial wealth through grasping emerging opportunities and diversifying from money lending and shopkeeping or wholesale trade in commodities.

Lala Bhanna Mal belonged to one such family. Starting life as a humble ghari saaz—one who repairs watches—he rose steadily to become a dealer in expensive watches by sheer dint of hard work and integrity. He established the New Friends Co. and became famous as ghariwale. His son, Mohan Lal extended the business and was known as importer of the best watches in the city.

Other prominent Baniyas of Delhi were known by their businesses, like Rai Bahadur Lala Pearey Lal, the first person to import cars into Delhi, who bore the suffix 'motorwale' to his name. Rai Bahadur Ram Rup, born in Sabzi Mandi in 1891, was unrelated to either the kotwal or khajanchi clans. He took charge of the family business at the age of fourteen. Ram Rupji had an elegant lifestyle; he usually dressed in sherwani and churidar pyjama and owned a ghora garhi (phaeton). Like his contemporaries, he was fond of poetry and attended mushairas.

Gunjan Goela, chef, author and food consultant, has written lovingly about her father, Lala Prem Chand, who was born in the family of Mohan Lal ghariwale, in 1913. He was married to 'Memo', daughter of Lala Sher Singh, who belonged to one of the most illustrious Baniya families in the city and lived on 22, Barakhamba Road. Gunjan was born twenty-nine years after her parents got married and was only thirteen when her father died. She fondly remembers accompanying her father to prominent Western-style restaurants like the Gaylord, Kwality, Standard, Embassy and Milk Bar in Connaught Place and Mira Bella (that later became Khyber) in Kashmiri Gate.

A typical breakfast in summer for a Baniya was *lassi*, *basi paranthe* (*basi* literally means stale, but in this case, prepared for convenience the night before) served with freshly churned butter. In Anglicised households toast and sweet buns broke the monotony.

Not all Baniya families totally eschewed onions and garlic. At dinner, for instance, when *pakki rasoi* was prescribed (the term implied properly cooked, that is, deep- or shallow-fried food, not boiled in water like rice or lentils), *pyaaz ki sabzi* made an occasional appearance in season. The dinner was cooked by a professional maharaj or misrain employed for this purpose. This gave women in the family, who cooked lunch, some respite. At dinner, the favourites were *khattee kachalu* and *aam ke katre ka hing wala achar*.

The summer season's delights were *papris* and *phulkis*, to be washed down with *thandai*, *nimbu adrak ka pani* or *phalse* or *bael ka sherbat*. One of the typical Baniya dishes was *undiya* prepared with raw banana, potatoes, brinjal cooked in *meetha tel* (sesame oil), tempered with hing. Another seasonal specialty was *kankaue ka pator*. *Kankaue* is a green, rarely found these days. Palak and other seasonal green leaves were commonly used.

Gunjan recollects the sweets that used to be prepared at home during her childhood days (in the early 1970s): *ghewar* (a round, multi-tiered confection with delicate lace-like edges), *feni* (coiled spirals of unsweetened, very fine sevian/vermicelli), *andarse ki goli* (marble-sized sweets prepared with rice flour, crusted with white sesame seeds), and *malpua* (pancake made with semolina batter, then soaked in aromatized syrup, and enriched with a little *khoya*). *Mithai* ordered regularly from Ghantewala included *posth launj*, a special soft burfi made with poppy seeds, *badam launj*, a burfi made of almonds, along with savouries like *dal biji*, fried spicy lentils with seeds, and *aloo ka lacchha* from Kanwarji. By that time, some traditional classics like *kali balushahi*, *ghiy ka lachcha petha* and *saunth tikiya* had become extinct as customers' tastes changed and recipes were lost.

Food in affluent homes was served on brass or silver plates—metal being considered pure and non-polluting. Bone china was tainted, due to the prefix that exposed the process of its manufacture. Glass, which would, with the passage of time, become a synonym for tumbler, wasn't commonly used at home. Delicacies were prepared with ghee, and enriched with dried fruits and nuts. Seasonal fruits and vegetables were relished. Food prepared at home was considered the best.

Gunjan Goela has documented in her book, *The Baniya Legacy of Old Delhi: Culture and Cuisine,* many interesting details pertaining to Baniya cuisine based on her interviews. She quotes Atul Gupta, grandson of Lala Bhagirath Mal:

> My mother would cook lunch herself sitting in the chownka. A typical meal in the afternoon would comprise *arhar ki dal*, *chawal*, *bhune alu* and another *sookhi sabzi* like *baigan* or *tinda*. Alternatively, there would be *kadhi-chawal*. No meal would be complete without *dhaniya-pudina* chutney. There would be *mooli ka kas* and *adrak ka laccha* accompanying the raita or plain curd or simple raita usually made of *bundi*. There would be halwa as dessert or we would have fruit cream, kheer or jave. Mother would always take out gau gras

> that would be served to the cow. Lunch was the main meal of the day.[25]

There were many ritual foods prescribed for different celebrations. *Sabut moong ki khichadi* was prepared for Makar Sankranti and only 'stale' food was consumed on Basora, observed right after Holi. As the name of the day marked for the ritual indicates, it was food cooked and kept aside to go stale, not leftovers.

Large banquets on occasions like marriages, with hundreds of invited guests, were contracted to high-caste, high-class professionals. Between 1940 and 1960, the most popular halwai caterers were Hariram in Kucha Patiram and Shibo Mal from Sitaram Bazaar. We know little else about them, as they are no longer in business. Others have stepped in, but these are not traditional maharajs. More like caterers for banquets specializing in some traditional Marwari dishes. Some of them claim to be descendents of the old masters.

The baratis were, traditionally, first served *kachoris* and two laddoos. This was followed by a *tashtari* (small plate, often an earthern or leaf plate) with three, five or seven varieties of sweetmeats. At times, a namkeen was placed in the middle, to balance the taste. The main meal had two or more dry vegetable and the same number of gravy dishes. The menu didn't have any paneer item. The most exotic delicacy was *raswali matar* with almonds. *Koonje ki barfi* (*kulfi*) provided the dessert finale. Water was sipped from an earthen *kulhad*.

Most traders were addicted to a substantial snack in the late afternoons. They would be hungry by then. The practice was for the menfolk to eat lunch, complete with dal, sabzis, curd, roti and pickles, around 9 o'clock in the morning, before setting out for business or to the office. Vendors with their khomchas (portable wickerwork stalls), held in hand or clasped by the side, would walk down the street with their treats—*moong dal chilla* (pancakes prepared with green *moong* lentils batter), *aloo matar ki chaat* (boiled potatoes and green peas *chaat*) or *phalon ki chaat* (assorted fruits sprinkled over with chaat masala), *kanji bada* (black or green *moong* dumplings, fermented in brine water with mustard and spices) and *kalmi bada* (re-fried Bengal gram flat cakes, cut in diamonds or squares)—and do swift business.

A number of fasts were observed by the devout—mostly ladies in the house—and on such occasions the family partook of *phalahar* (light snacks). The *satvik* fare included *bhune aloo*, *ras ke aloo*, *kotu ki puri*, *shakarkand ka halwa*, *makhane ki kheer*, *sitaphal*, *dahi pakori*, *saunf wale tinde*, *ajwaini arbi*, *chapte dahi bade*, all prepared without sea salt. Sea salt obtained by evaporation of saline water was prohibited on days of fasting as it could possibly contain residues of creatures living in the sea. Rock salt and black rock salt were considered kosher. Nibbling *gola giri*, *chironji*, *makhane*, *badam*, *mungphali* was allowed, though not favoured by the orthodox elders. *Thandai* slaked the thirst and fortified the fasting. *Gulgule*, *Gurh ke chawal* tickled the sweet tooth.

On Gobardhan Puja, performed the day after Deepavali, *chhappan bhog* (fifty-six ritual foods) were offered to the Lord. Fifteen sweets and fifteen savouries, along with varieties of khichdi, kadhi, chawal, and kheer made up the number.

Lauki ki lauj, *gajar ka halwa*, assorted laddoos, *gujjiyas*, coloured puris—naturally tinted with spinach and beetroot—*kaanji*, *namak pare*, *papdi*, *dahi bade*, *basi paranthe*, *besan papdi*, *zimikand* (elephant foot yam) curry were cooked for the Rang Pashe dinner before Holi. On this day, it was customary to sprinkle the guests with rose water from a silver gulabdaani or gulab-jaldaani (rose water sprinkler) as they entered—a kind of curtain raiser of what would follow the next morning.

Many seasonal specialties were common to Baniya, Kayastha and Khatri kitchens. Among these *kale gajar ki kanji* (black carrot wedges pickled in brine water with spices), and *kanji bada* were the most popular. *Gondh ke laddoo* and *panjiri* in winters were considered to be tonic food. At home, extraordinary care was taken by housewives to impart their signature on relishes like *nimbu ka laccha achar*.

In her book, Gunjan describes her father as a 'Baniya who was Not'—he belonged to the class of shaukeen (bon vivant) who loved meats. He relished not only kebab and *qorma* but also Continental and Chinese dishes served by relatively new restaurants in Connaught Place. He enjoyed chicken sandwiches and cutlets at Wenger's and Embassy. His favourite outlet nearer home was the Flora restaurant. He ordered food regularly from it and instructed the cook in advance about how he liked a particular dish. Mian Shujauddin, who started Shereen Bhawan, near Jama Masjid, was a close friend. Before Mianji migrated to Karachi, he gifted his traditional family recipe for *qorma* to Lala Prem Chand, since he loved that preparation. He was, indeed, an exceptional Baniya who was a practicing Master at the Masonic Club and took his family out for weekly picnics to Okhla Barrage, Lodi Gardens and Qutub Minar. For these outings, special delicacies like *choti pakori ka pulav* (pulao with tiny lentil dumplings) and *kali masoor ke kebab* (brown lentil kebabs) were cooked.

Most of these outings go back to the 1960s and Gunjan's vivid descriptions of them allow us to savour flavours that had changed very little from the 1950s in the twin cities of Delhi, Old and New—Shehar and Connaught Place. This non-conformist Baniya had no qualms about going to Bholenath at Mori Gate or Khush Dil on Church Road in search of a robust *shami* kebab. Truly a connoisseur of street foods, he had identified the 'best in the class' vendors who sold *chana jor garam* (roasted and spiced gram), *kalmi vada* near Hyder Quli (opposite Piru Haveli), and *kanji pakoras* (pakoras pickled in brine water and spices) outside Kucha Ghasiram. Bombay Restaurant, opposite the iconic perfumery, Gulabsingh Johrimal (established in 1816), near Kucha Natwa, was another of his favourites. He believed that Kucha Asharfi had the best pineapple and strawberry ice creams, with globules of fat floating on top. He greatly enjoyed breakfasting on *halwa-nagori* at Dariba Kalan and, at times, indulged in the rich *moong dal halwa* at the sweet shop in Katra Mahajani.

Gunjan recalls being taken to the dining-room, on the right-hand side of Old Delhi Railway Station, with its elegant, formal service—starched white linen and all, for fish fingers and chips. He could mingle with equal ease with princes and paupers. Bir Bhan, the roadside chaiwala, boiled strong masala chai that went well with hard-boiled eggs. Gunjan's father was the rarest of rare exceptions. Very few Baniyas dared to challenge the caste taboos or ate out.

Baniyas have left an indelible mark on Delhi's food scene by establishing the now ubiquitous and immensely popular *mishthan bhandars* that sell vegetarian savoury snacks, besides sweets. More often than not, the founders of these joints hailed from Rajasthan, and belonged to the Baniya/Vaishya community, well known for their entrepreneurial spirit. Serving a menu considered kosher by all communities, the format not only stood the test of time, but perhaps topped the class.

Mishthan Bhandars

The phenomenon of North American diners—set-piece restaurants found across United States, Canada and parts of Western Europe, serving similar items, mostly American cuisine (local comfort food) alongside bottomless coffee, and an archetypal aesthetic of a mix of colourful booths and counters, without necessarily being part of any franchise—finds its mutations in North India in the form of *mishthan bhandars*, literally translated as sweet shops. Much like American diners, they serve a similar spread of assorted local comfort vegetarian food like chaats, chole-bhature, pao bhaaji, samosa, pakoras and sweets. They follow their own archetypal aesthetic based on stand-up tables, in red-yellow-white colours, live chaat counters, and separate counters displaying a myriad sweets, all of it based around a self-service model. Most of them started as snack or sweet shops, which later expand to full-fledged restaurants.

Within the group of *mishthan bhandars*, many types have spread across the city, with clones across the globe. These include various independently-run Aggarwal Sweet shops and Bikanerwalas, and franchised chains like Bikanervala, Haldiram's and Om Sweets. Wherever you may be in Delhi, you can find one of these establishments within a 15-minute radius, to assuage your hunger with familiar flavours, without burning a hole in your pocket.

What's in a name? The magic of Bengal

Two of the most iconic such stand-alone establishments include the Bengali Sweet House, founded in 1936 by Bhim Sain and Banwari Lal Aggarwal, and Nathu Sweets, which was founded in the 1930s by Nathu Ramesh Ram.

Brothers Manohar Lal and Madhusudan Agarwal turned a traditional namkeen shop into a full-fledged mishthan bhandar chain, Haldiram's.

In the 1960s, the range of products was expanded and varieties of traditional sweets and namkeens were added. By this time, they were renowned as the top-of-the-line sweet shop in the city and supplying *rasmalai* to Air India, clubs and hotels.

The success of the Haldiram's model spurred others to emulate it.

Haldiram's

Gangabisanji Agarwal, also known as Haldiram, once had a small shop in Bikaner that sold deep-fried snacks in the 1930s. Over the years, he had built up a solid reputation in the desert city. Half a century passed before it opened its first outlet in Delhi.

Brothers Manohar Lal and Madhusudan Agarwal turned a traditional business into a full-fledged international one. They adopted hygienic, standardised hi-tech manufacturing methods to maintain quality in not only their packeted savouries and sweets but also the food served, reduced labour-intensive work, and scaled up production manifold.

After moving to Delhi, Haldiram's expanded at a feverish pace. Branches opened in Lajpat Nagar, Rajendra Nagar/Pusa Road, Paharganj, Sarojni Nagar, Rohini, Pitampura, Panjabi Bagh, and Connaught Place. It has a strong presence in malls across the city and has become an inseparable part of Delhi food.

Haldiram's not only grew in size but also diversified from restaurants to bakeries. It has signed a franchisee deal with the world's second largest bakery chain, Brioche Dorée. The French brand opened its first vegetarian bakery in New Delhi with the help of Haldiram's bakery arm, 'HR Bakers'.

Bikanervala

Just after Independence, two youngsters from the Lalji family in Bikaner made their way to the nation's capital to try their luck. They began by selling namkeens on the streets, made with family recipes. Soon they saved enough money to set up a stall in Paranthe Wali Gali in Chandni Chowk. The shack-like shop bore the signboard, Bikaner Bhujia Bhandar. Locals also referred to it as Bikaner Namkeen Bhandar, abbreviated by regular customers, to Bikanervala. In the 1960s, more products were added, mostly more varieties of traditional sweets and namkeens. Branches were opened in other parts of Delhi including Karol Bagh. Expansion gathered momentum when Shyam Sundar Aggarwal, the young successor, assumed control of the family business towards the end of the 1970s. He introduced mechanization, as he realized that this was imperative to meet the challenge posed by foreign fast-food chains.

Om Sweets in Gurgaon

Within a span of six decades, it has grown from a small mom-and-pop shop to a thriving chain, with a seventeen-outlet footprint in the NCR. It's famous for its *Doda barfi*, eggless cakes, *aloo tikki* fried in pure ghee, and chaat. Om's chole-bhature, kachori and samosa have a loyal patronage in Gurgaon.

There is a peculiar point about Aggarwal sweet shops, they are mostly found at the corners, in busy marketplaces across the city. Amazingly, they have managed to retain these prime spots, running even franchised outlets profitably, as testified by the crows thronging them. Many of those who come to these shops are repeat customers or regular patrons.

Kayastha Food

Kayasthas trace their origin to a myth, according to which they are descended directly from Brahma. As the primal ancestor was born of his body (kaya), they are called Kayastha. Spread across the country (but more so in North India), they bear surnames like Mathur, Bhatnagar, Srivastava, Saxena, Ambashth, Kulsreshtha, Sarin, Saran, and Sahay.

Todarmal and Birbal are counted among illustrious Kayasthas though some believe that Todarmal was a Khatri. The Kayasthas have always been difficult to place in the caste hierarchy. They are considered a sankar (alloy) caste that came into existence by inter-caste marriages. They claim a rank immediately below the Kshatriyas and above the Vaishyas, while some scholars suggest that they occupy a position just above the sudras. Kayasthas for centuries have bridged the gap between Hindus and Muslims. The Kayasthas were well versed in Persian, the court language, spoke Urdu fluently, and as scribes and administrators, provided the interface between Muslim rulers and courtiers and Hindu merchants and traders who had business dealings with them. Unlike the Baniyas, the Kayasthas ate meat, enjoyed alcoholic drinks and cultivated tastes of their masters. Like the Muslim aristocratic elite, they participated in mushairas and soirees of music and dance. At the same time, they were proud of their Hindu identity and participated in religious festivals with their Hindu brethren. Some of them gained prominence as English-educated lawyers and doctors, and civil servants and made it easier for others to follow the transition to modernity.

Their contribution to literature, music, scholarship and administration has been substantial. The list includes names like the revolutionary and freedom fighter Lala Har Dayal, poet Firaq Gorakhpuri, chemist-scientist Sir Shanti Swarup Bhatnagar, sarodist Sharan Rani, vocalist Shubha Mudgal and the long line of members in the Indian Civil Service (ICS), pre-Independence, and the Indian Foreign Service (IFS)/Indian Administrative Service (IAS) after 1947. All Kayasthas take great pride in that they are a caste-based community of scribes and scholars. But to return to Kayasthas in Delhi and their food.

Delhi's Mathurs, believed to have emigrated from Mathura, consider themselves superior to other Kayasthas, including their cousins from Rajasthan and Agra as well as moffusil towns and small jagirs in Uttar Pradesh. Old families quote a verse to support their intrinsic worth:

> *Museebat mein bhi Mathur ki sharafat kam nahi hoti*
> *Karo sone ke sau tukde magar keemat kam nahin hoti!*
> (Even hardship doesn't corrode or erode the gentlemanly grace of a Mathur,
> just like a block of gold, broken in small pieces, retains its value!)

According to Ravi Dayal, himself a Mathur, in an article in *Seminar*:

> One of the traditional conceits of Mathurs of Delhi is that they consider themselves the highest form of a high species—perhaps less flamboyant than the Mathurs once based in Lahore, but infinitely more refined as speakers of a tongue untainted by Punjabi; a cut above those in Rajasthan, who servilely served provincial rulers and said hukum; somewhat similar to members of the community in Agra and Lucknow, but free of the small-town smugness of urban U.P. The Mathurs of Delhi also considered themselves Dilliwallahs par excellence.

Raja Raghunath Bahadur, the most distinguished ancestor of the city's Kayasthas had immigrated to Shahjahanabad when it was being built. He had managed to secure the patronage of Asadullah, the then finance minister. He retained his position at Aurangzeb's court and replaced his mentor. Rai Jivan Lal, born in 1806, in this lineage, rose to the rank of mir munshi and honorary magistrate by 1857. His grandson, Raj Narain Bahadur, who later dropped Narain from his name, was born in 1868—eleven years after the ghadar—and died in 1950. Raj Narain Bahadur was the grandfather of both Shiela Dhar, writer and vocalist, and Madhur Jaffrey, who rose to international fame as both actor and chef.

Early in the twentieth century, some Mathurs—successful lawyers and upwardly mobile civil servants, with a sprinkling of promising college teachers—started moving out of the crowded kuchas and katras to the Civil Lines area. It had many orchards at the time and, since the Yamuna flowed close by, there was easy access to sweet melons in season.

Barrister Raj Bahadur, the paterfamilias of the Mathur clan, decided to move to the Civil Lines in the first decade of the twentieth century, in consonance with his growing stature and desire to live in proximity with the English rulers. Soon his brothers joined him. What facilitated this move was the 'rewards for loyalty' granted to the Bahadur family by the British.

The family was given a large tract of land in rural Delhi. From the sales proceeds of this, orchards were bought in the area adjacent to Civil Lines. Twenty-four large parcels were carved out for members of the joint family, to build individual residences. Members of the extended joint family occupied these houses. The stately mansions had exteriors resembling colonial bungalows but the interiors were designed like the havelis in the Walled City.

Madhur Jaffrey, born in 1933, has evoked life and food in the affluent household in an evocative memoir entitled, *Climbing the Mango Trees.*[26] She recollects that the family ate food prepared by servants under the supervision of ladies of the house. On special occasions, food was brought from eateries in the Walled City. Seekh and *shami* kebabs, *rumali* and *bakarkhani* rotis, not to forget *bedmi* and *aloo ki rasedar* sabzi.

The flood of refugees from Pakistan after Partition introduced the Punjabi—mostly tandoori dishes. Moti Mahal in Daryaganj was famous in the early 1950s for its *tandoori murgh*, *kali dal* and later butter chicken.

There was a large retinue of servants and while males ate meat and preferred to dine in English style, the rest of the family, women and children, mostly ate desi food. The women continued to visit relatives and their paternal homes in the Walled City and made frequent shopping expeditions for jewellery, saris etc. The menfolk ordered kebab/roti and even *bedmi/aloo ka rasa* and *methi ki chutney* to consume at home.

After studying in Delhi University, Madhur left for England in 1955. Homesick for Kayastha food, she asked her mother to share some simple recipes with her. The mother wrote back to her regularly (on onion-skin paper, in Hindi) beginning with mutton cooked with spices like bay leaf, cardamom and cinnamon, a no-frills cauliflower accompaniment, a quick fix but flavourful egg curry. Years later, Madhur published a selection of these recipes in her first cookbook. Although simplified, they give us a fair idea of what was put on the Kayastha table in the 1950s.

Another memoir that provides colourful insights about the culinary and cultural world of Kayasthas is penned by her cousin Shiela Dhar. A few years senior to Madhur Jaffrey, she dropped out of Lady Hardinge Medical College to join Hindu College, and topped the English (Honours) batch in 1950. She returned to India after acquiring a Master's from Boston University and taught for a short while at Miranda College. She finally settled down as an editor in the Publications Division of the Government of India. Shiela Mathur married a Kashmiri Pandit, economist and political adviser, P.N. Dhar, and was an accomplished classical singer. Her book, *Raga'n Josh,*[27] spiced with anecdotes about bureaucratic life and idiosyncrasies of musicians, describes in an engaging manner the lifestyle of the Mathur Kayasthas around the 1940s and 1950s.

Both Madhur Jaffrey and Shiela Dhar have left vivid accounts of the incredibly large dining-table that could seat all sixty-two members of the family, including children, at the same time. For this purpose, three separate tables were joined. The practice of eating together at 7 Civil Lines, in the house occupied by the head of the family, continued till Raj Narain Bahadur's death in 1950.

Ravi Dayal, the legendary editor-publisher, was a scion of another distinguished Mathur family. His short piece in *Seminar*, quoted above, is a chiselled, sparkling gem that beautifully supplements the accounts of Shiela Dhar and Madhur Jaffrey—close contemporaries. He confirms that when he was a student at St Stephen's College (1954–9) the 'Shehar' and the Civil Lines merged seamlessly. 'Moti Mahal was a premier attraction, and the bar and nightclub at Maidens Hotel the fanciest in town.' Of the four stylish hotels in Delhi at the time, three—Maidens, The Metropolitan and Swiss—were located in the Civil Lines.

The Anglicised Kayasthas of Delhi were a minuscule minority. The Kayasthas had many branches. Not all of them were equally privileged.

Some Mathur families were tempted by builders to move to Central Delhi, in the vicinity of glamorous Connaught Place, on Barakhamba Road, Curzon Road and Hanuman Road. However, the umbilical cord with the Walled City was not severed. The visits to relatives in the Walled City and the Civil Lines were frequent. Chandni Chowk and Kashmiri Gate remained their preferred shopping destinations.

The childhood memoirs of Madhur Jaffrey, Shiela Dhar and Ravi Dayal are enchanting and evocative. Nevertheless, their perspective remains that of a privileged adolescent or precocious youth and their narratives bear this stamp. As children they were sent to schools in Nainital and Mussoorie and returned to spend time in Delhi only during vacations. All three left for England or the United States right after graduation, Shiela Dhar and Ravi Dayal returned to live in Delhi, Madhur Jaffrey came only on visits. In the interim, the Delhi of their recollections had drastically changed.

Not all Kayasthas found places in the higher echelons of the bureaucracy or were successful lawyers or well-paid managers. Most found employment as lecturers in colleges and universities. Obviously, they couldn't afford the lavish lifestyle of their more affluent cousins. They traced their lineage to a famous ancestor in the princely courts but lived far more frugally. Meat was cooked on rare occasions and ladies took pride in seeing exotic vegetarian delicacies mimicking meat, such as *kathal ke kebab* and biryani, *kachche kele ki machli* and *lauki ke kofte*.

I was fortunate enough to gain valuable insights into the lives of Kayasthas of Delhi outside the elite circle of the Mathurs in the Civil Lines when I fell in love with Jyotsna Saxena from Kanpur. She had many close relatives who were settled in Delhi. I accompanied her almost every week to one or another of her brothers-in-law. One of them was Professor S.K. Saxena, the eminent musicologist and connoisseur of Kathak, who taught Philosophy in Delhi University. I was treated with utmost kindness and affection by Professor Saab, whose life was dedicated to scholarship and music.

He lived in a small two-room apartment, with a tiny barsati, in Roop Nagar, in the 1960s. He was married to Satto Jiji, whose father was a senior officer in the Income-Tax department. We called him Jijaji, as he was my friend Jyotsna's brother-in-law. K.S. Saxena 'Jijaji', who lived in hutments on Sikandara Road, was married to Matto Jiji. The difference in the lifestyle of the co-brothers-in-law could not have been starker.

Professor Saab, short-statured, frail and bespectacled, had a fixed daily routine—he ate little and never entertained at home. The menu was unchanging, *lauki* and *tori* with watery *moong ki dal.* He wasn't addicted to tea, coffee or alcohol. He spent most of his time reading and writing and though he was mild-mannered, none dared disturb him when he was at his old-fashioned work desk. His language was chaste Urdu; and only when he was addressing young men, would he use colloquialisms such as *launde badshah*. Manju was his only child. She had followed in his footsteps. After her Master's in Philosophy, she was teaching in a women's college. The space at the Saxena home was cramped, the furniture was basic—takhts with thin mattresses and a few cane chairs and a multipurpose table with many stools.

In the barsati stayed young Charan Girdhar Chand and Gullu, Professor Saab's nephew. Charan was a Kathak dancer of great promise, whose father had died when he was a child. The rest of the family stayed in Paharganj. Jijaji had taken him under his wing to ensure that he didn't fall into bad company and waste his talent. Charan had started giving tuitions to dance students. His younger brother, Tej

Prakash 'Tulsi', was a jovial prankster, who occasionally came visiting. He was then training to play the pakhawaj.

Jijaji's other passion was dhrupad. Every morning, he would shut himself up in a room and practice an alaap—a meditation of sorts. His brother was an accomplished tabla player. He would be invited to accompany legendary musicians when Jijaji organized a music festival. Satto Jiji often walked up to the barsati where I lived, very close to their house. She was fond of cooking meat and didn't mind a tipple on these escapades from the stern, ashram-like discipline of her own home.

K.S., Jyotsna's other brother-in-law, was very different. An upwardly mobile Indian Revenue Service (IRS) officer—he was an 'almost arrived' bureaucrat. Not in the most prestigious IAS, but in the next lower rung, the IRS, like his father-in-law. He dressed in smart suits and stylish ties. He carried a small baton on his morning walks. At that time, in the mid-1960s, he was awaiting the allotment of a proper bungalow or apartment, but the living room in the hutment had comfortable sofas, and a proper dining table. There was a small study, with an impressive book-case in which were displayed leather-bound classics and paperbacks.

Poonam, his only child, went to an English-medium convent and non-vegetarian dishes were regularly cooked at home. He wasn't given to smoking or drinking but did keep a few bottles of good whiskey to offer to guests. Jyotsna's brother, who was educated at Doon School, was serving as the general manager at a sugar mill. He would stay with K.S. whenever he was passing through Delhi. K.S. had no interest in classical or Western music.

Both the co-brothers-in-law were Saxenas and comparatively recent immigrants to Delhi. There were many like them who broke the stereotypes of the descendants of the Civil Lines or Daryaganj Mathurs. School teachers, clerks, not very successful lawyers, doctors, those employed in supervisory jobs, the lower echelons of the bureaucracy, and journalists, comprised the majority of them. It was in their kitchens that heirloom recipes were preserved.

The art of improvising innovative and stunning delicacies reached great heights in the hands of Kayastha housewives—many of whom maintained the household on shoe-string budgets.

Upper-class Kayasthas adopted the dining table and children were trained to use knife and fork, but what was eaten remained essentially Indian. Preeta Mathur in her cook book, *The Courtly Cuisine: Kayastha Kitchens Through India*,[28] has collected a number of traditional recipes from the Kayastha kitchen. Quite a few have two versions—everyday, home-style, and another more elaborate one for formal entertaining and lavish hospitality. For instance, the three *pasanda* recipes—*bhure pasande, khule pasande* and *badam pasande*; *keeme ke kofte* and *nargisi kofte*; *raan* and *sururi raan* illustrate this.

As inheritors to 'royal' cuisine of the Mughals, the Kayasthas laid great emphasis on meaty delicacies. Everyday fare, however, was lightened by inclusion of a variety of seasonal vegetables in *bawli handia* and having thin flavourful gravies in *khatta kaliyas*. *Shami* kebab and *bhuni kaleji* were popular non-vegetarian snacks. Vegetables and lentils were indispensable. The dum cooking style was used for fish, fowl and flesh (*khade masale ka gosht*, *dum ki machhali* and *murgh*), as well as vegetables cooked *musallam* or *bharwan* (whole or stuffed). There were also faux meat dishes like *gobhi ka musallam*, *gobhi keema*, *kele ki machhali* and *masoor ke kebab*. Many vegetarian dishes in Kayastha repertoire were popular with Baniyas and Khatris like *kanji ke bade*, *aloo ke kulle*, *chhuki matarphali* and *chatpate chhote aloo*.

The Kayastha penchant for stuffed delicacies wasn't restricted to vegetables called *dulma*. Many chicken recipes resorted to flavourful stuffings. *Tangri kebab*, *bharwan kesariya murgh* and *safed murgh* were lovingly packed with a melange of tasty ingredients. These preparations were time consuming and conveyed to guests the extraordinary effort that had been put in to please their palate. This also was an indulgence in culinary one-upmanship and witty exchanges between gastronomic connoisseurs.

Interestingly, the *sandali murgh* attributed to Pushpa Narain has no trace of sandal. *Chari* was the name given to a mutton or chicken dish cooked with just four ingredients—meat, ghee, chillies and salt—which brings to mind the *junglee maas* in Raja Sahib Saiana's cookbook. Other Kayastha recipes were family favourites like *murgh kalimirch. Chaar magaz* (melon, pumpkin, cucumber and poppy seeds) were extensively used in the Kayastha kitchen. *Char magaz ka bharwan murgh* and *chaar magaz ki khatti dal* are dishes rarely encountered nowadays. Slow cooking meats, in their own juices, were preferred and the vessel called lagan was used for this and other delicacies like *lagan ki bataer*.

The celebratory rice dishes included *yakhni pulav* and *kathal ki biryani*. Sometimes rice was substituted with *seviyan*. *Tahiri* was everyday fare. For this, the long grain rice was neither boiled in stock (*yakhni*) or fried like in biryani. In winters, sweet green peas enriched the tahiri. It was also cooked with potato or cauliflower. It was spiced mildly and turmeric was sparingly used.

Most of the sweets to conclude sumptuous meals or to welcome visitors were prepared at home. Kheer and *meethe chawal* were the most common. *Malpua* was reserved for special occasions. Halwa and *laddoo* were prepared for consumption at home. Nothing less than *piste* or *badam ki launj*, procured from the most reputed halwai, was added to the *mithai ki tashtari* for formal guests.

Lentils were used in myriad ways in the Kayastha *rasoi*. Unhusked *mash* (*kali dal*) was considered inauspicious and only *dhuli urad* was cooked. The most common recipe was *khilwan /sukhi urad*, garnished with fried onions and green chillies, redolent of hing, and tempered with ghee. Green unhusked *moong* was perfectly acceptable and often combined with spinach or other greens in *sagpaita*. Husked *moong* was considered easy to digest and the *dahi pakori, dahi vada* and *mungodi* were prepared with it. *Masur* lentils were favoured for many faux meat dishes—vegetarian kebab, *kaleji* and *kofte*. These were in the style of *dhoka* (trick treats).

Shabdegh, a Kashmiri delicacy, slow cooked overnight during winters, was greatly relished. Turnips, meat and other vegetables were put in a pot covered with a heavy lid and sealed with dough. By the time the pot was opened, the aromatic spices would have had ample time to work their magic. Professional cooks were employed to prepare this for parties in Kayastha homes.

Mrs Rajesh Dayal, an old-time resident of Daryaganj, has in an interview revived memories of varieties of Kayastha food in the 1940s and 1950s. Her grandfather was a civil engineer in Kota. He built a colonial style, double-storey haveli in Daryaganj. The construction was completed in 1935. Mrs Dayal, born in 1930, remembered playing in the foundations, when work was under way. The ceiling had several skylights, there were fireplaces in rooms and floors were paved with coloured stones. Rooms opened on a central courtyard. Muslim cooks were requisitioned from Ballimaran and Matia Mahal to cook for large parties. The joint family lived together in this residence. Mrs Dayal recalls a cook called Booby 'who made the best *shabdegh* ever.'

Baniya and Kayastha food in Delhi is a mosaic of culinary traditions and practices of the different communities who have made the city their home for the past five hundred years and more. They speak in different languages and have their own styles of attire. They have traditionally adhered to prescriptions and prohibitions in the realm of food. Perhaps this is true of all great cities that have served as imperial capitals. Their magnetic pull resulted in creation of a rich tapestry to which emigrants from different communities have contributed across centuries.

The debate continues. 'To whom does Delhi belong?' Or, to put it differently, 'Who belongs to Delhi?'

Ten

From Empire to Republic and the Shadow of Partition: 1857–1950

Jama Masjid, Delhi by Thomas Daniell
Courtesy: The History Collective Visual Archive

The protagonist of Ahmed Ali's *Twilight in Delhi* is Mir Nihal, a well-off Muslim, who was ten years old at the time of the tectonic shift caused by the revolt of 1857. Nihal lives up to (for those times) a ripe old age and experiences first-hand the changes wrought by time—historic currents, tidal waves over which individuals had no control. He lived in a joint family following traditional norms. When his son is attracted towards Western attire and mannerisms, he is offended and tries to admonish him. When this fails, he yields, albeit reluctantly. Mir Nihal is fond of keeping pigeons, watching kite-flying from the roof top like many of his peers. He maintains a mistress in a separate house, some distance away from home.

His life, though compartmentalized, is often stressful, being torn between emotional loyalties and conflicting responsibilities. Events small, and more significant, take place against the backdrop of daily life in the congested by-lanes of Shahjahanabad repaired and reconstructed after the destruction in 1857. *Twilight in Delhi* recaptures the milieu of the Old City at the turn of the twentieth century very effectively. The descriptions of food and pastimes vividly evoke the period—but with a poignant tinge.

As Ravi Dayal laments in his article in *Seminar*,

> Until the late 1950s, even those living outside the city walls knew [the] Shahar reasonably well. New and Old Delhi together still formed a comparatively compact unit, with New Delhi wallahs making regular forays into the Walled City. The cohesive, urban combine of New and Old Delhi no longer exists and while Delhi has grown into a vast city over the last few decades, different parts don't seem to make up a whole…The 'distinctive civilisation'was always a fantasy, a dream, mirage call it what you may.

Ravi Dayal would like us to believe that the area covered by Shahjahanabad appears to have reverted to what it was before it was built—a collection of disconnected villages, each with its own ways and mannerisms, and altogether more provincial than urban-cosmopolitan:

> Before the decision to transfer the capital from Calcutta was made public and before the outbreak of the First World War, the roads of Delhi were full of camel and bullock carts. Trams were a novelty. Life wasn't easy in changing times. '[The] Old was giving way but the New was not yet clearly in sight.' Ahmed Ali, in *Twilight in Delhi*, gives us a broad-brush picture of the city as it existed before it was transformed, even more after the work on the new city began, and life was interrupted by the outbreak of the First World War. "It was a terrible summer (1911). No one had experienced such heat. Aam ka Panna, the time-tested thirst quencher, and kulfi brought little relief. Beyond the Fort and Mori Gate workmen were digging in scorching heat preparing the ground for the coronation of a new and foreign king."

As the reader follows in Mir Nihal's footsteps as he walks through Ballimaran, now aged sixty-two, the old city's food-scape is slowly revealed. We first encounter Noor Ahmed in *Twilight in Delhi* selling mulberries 'sweeter than honey' by the roadside—a *paav* (quarter seer) for two paise.

> Just behind the southern verandah (of Jama Masjid) sat the kebabi[s] in their booths on the pavement roasting meat on their fire. And, the smell of the ghee, fat, and grilled oil and burning fat filled the air. As someone asked for kebab, the vendor turned the skewers round to warm the spicy minced meat which had been wrapped round them, held together by means of thread and grilled into delicious kebabs. As he took them off the skewers with a quick movement, he broke them into two, put them in a cupped leaf adding finely cut onions, ginger and chillies on top. Wrapped the whole into a neat hot parcel and passed it to the customer. Some of the shopkeepers sold big fat round loaves also baked in the oven and many bought

> them…or too hungry to take them home, ate inside the shops and filled their bellies. Other vendors were selling small round kebabs fried in oiled, others still had fried fish or meat cutlets or pulao or vegetable cutlets…*Sherbets* prepared with season fruits were popular. Some liked their cold drink plain, others with jelly. *Sherbets* were drunk out of coloured China bowls broad at the brim and narrow at the base… The kulfi wallah sat on the steps of the grand mosque with a huge matka (earthen pot) placed in front of him and, as someone asked for it he dipped his hand inside the pot and took out a flat bottomed conical container tightly sealed with dough at the top. With the help of a sharp knife he would remove the frozen dough and prise open the cap to reveal the beautifully white, smooth surface of frozen condensed milk garnished with slivers of pistachio.

At another place, the reader finds Begum Nihal chopping vegetables—potatoes and pumpkins—for dinner. This suggests that even in Muslim households the fare was not all meaty. Children—boys—were given a few paise to binge on a snack—*aloo chole ki chaat*, or *dahi bade*. Interestingly, a fakir, who would force the violent bloodshed in the not too distant future, had requested for a meal of *paranthe* and *methi ka saag*.

Smoke Without Fire,[29] the memoirs of a young Muslim journalist, Abdul Rahman Siddiqi, takes up the story almost seamlessly from this point on. Born in 1922, he spent most of his childhood with his maternal grandfather and uncle who told him stories about life in the Walled City in times before his birth. As an adolescent, he was schooled in a madrasa, Delhi College (founded in 1792 as Madrassa Gaziuddin Khan), and after passing Intermediate privately studied, in St Stephen's College, in the newly established Delhi University. His elder brother, ten years older than him, and friendly young teachers were a rich source of information about what was happening beyond the confines of the Old City.

His maternal grandfather Haji Fazal Elahi was the proprietor of the largest and most famous general store in Chandni Chowk, H.S. Fazal-I-Elahi and Sons. The business was started in 1900, shrewdly anticipating the needs of the increasing number of White Sahibs. The signage proudly boasted that one could buy everything here 'from a needle to an elephant'.

The list of edibles stocked as recounted by Abdul provides an interesting glimpse into what the expatriate British ate. Cheeses and sardines, biscuits and chocolates, jams and jellies. Tins of Polson's and Lord's butter. Nothing desi, except Darjeeling teas like Lopchu, found a place on the shelves of this legendary store.

R.V. Smith, the grand old chronicler of Delhi, has published half a dozen volumes, based on reminiscences of persons interviewed by him in his long journalistic career. Some of them, when interviewed in the 1960s, were octogenarians. Those whose memories were intact, could recall incidents from their adolescence and early youth. Some of these recollections may have been embroidered in retelling or old memories may have simply been playing tricks, but the anecdotal information rendered in these accounts is very useful to supplement our knowledge of foods available on the streets of Old Delhi in the 1920s and 1930s. Some colourful characters come alive in the pen-portraits—the 'One-eyed' *kachori* seller, Kesho the *halwai* and bald-pated Mullaji, who sold *shami* kebabs that were delivered to the customers with rumali rotis from the stall next door at Sadar Bazaar.

Habib Miyan Al Diya, the storekeeper, was smitten by Raffo, the handsome lad who worked in a factory. The friendship with the youngster was nourished by 'the best milk and rabri money could buy' from Hardayal's shop. Raffo migrated to Karachi after the crash, breaking his elderly admirer's heart.

There were many small shops popular with the residents in the streets and by-lanes. Khan Sahib's shop below the steps of Jama Masjid was renowned for its delicious *pulav*. Itinerant traders from Afghanistan like the Paharhwala not only brought fresh and dried fruits *kandhari anaara, chaman ke angoor, kishmish* and *pista* but also were the main source of pickles and preserves. *Sirke mein pyaaz, karonde ka achar, seb, anjeer, ber* and *bel ka murabba* were in great demand.

Smith mentions delicious *halim* sold near Hindustani Dawakhana, which was opened in 1910. Favoured customers were served *halim* with a piece of tongue.

Smith also writes evocatively about Easter parties in Delhi Club on the Ridge that was reached via Ludlow Castle Road (Raj Niwas Marg). Such parties were also thrown by descendants of James Skinner on Nicholson Road. These were attended by distinguished Christian citizens like Sir Malcolm Hailey, Reverend Allnutt, Sir Maurice Gwyer and the 'Nawab of Kashmiri Gate'. Some eminent non-Christians were also invited.

The First World War and the Bolshevik Revolution in Russia were cataclysmic events. India, like other countries, could not remain unaffected by their impact. Gandhi on his return to India from South Africa had begun to transform the Indian freedom struggle from a reformist middle-class agitation to a mass movement. Never before had ordinary people been galvanized like this. Gandhi's call to support the Khilafat Movement (1919-24) may have ensured support of a section of Muslims for the nationalist anti-colonial struggle but it also unleashed sectarian fundamentalist forces that would lead to the partition of the country. The two-nation theory propounded by Jinnah struck a sympathetic chord in many Muslim hearts.

The unhealed wounds of 1857 were painfully reopened, infused with toxic rhetoric. The soul of Delhi was torn apart. Proponents of Muslim rights spread the canard that if the Congress came to power, Muslims would be reduced to second-class citizen or worse. Economic hardships embittered relationships. Gandhi's call to strikes, non-cooperation and boycott of British goods, civil disobedience hurt business. The milk vendor, the barber, the butcher and baker, the petty shopkeeper, no one was left untouched by politics. To many young and old, Jinnah appeared as the saviour and Gandhi the villain.

These fractious debates resonate in *Twilight in Delhi* and *Smoke Without Fire.* Fictional and real-life characters take on roles of partisans.

Dil-o-Danish,[30] a Hindi novel by Krishna Sobti, complements what we know from Urdu novels and memoirs. The protagonist Kripa Shankar is a successful Kayastha vakil who has a Muslim mistress. His life, like Mir Nihal's, is compartmentalized and equally stressful because the two lives intersect and spill over, refusing to remain confined to the invisible boundaries drawn. Kripa Shankar struggles to be fair both to his wife and children at home as well as to the mistress, Mahak Bano, and his children from her. He routinely buys *samosa*, *pakore*, *imarti*, and *kachori*, as well as *ras malai* in earthen pots, and gets them packed carefully in a wicker basket when he visits Mahak Bano. The description of foods that were cooking in his house refer to the aroma of frying of *kaleji aur chaap* that permeated different rooms. Children who were grown up enough to go out and buy snacks for themselves were given small change for getting *channa jor garam* and *churan.*

Many of these items are the same that find mention in *Twilight in Delhi* and *Smoke Without Fire.* Interestingly, even the recollections of an old Parsi about picnics in Connaught Place in the 1930s and 1940s mention *channa jor garam.* Some of these spicy nibbles have survived to date, and it seems that the Delhi palate is addicted to them.

Chaat and deep-fried snacks were especially popular among the Baniyas and Kayasthas but it is not as if the Muslim eschewed them. *Aloo chole ki chaat, dahi vada* were partaken by all.

When the 1911 Darbar was held in Delhi, schoolchildren were given coupons that could be exchanged at the snack shops for sweets or savouries.

Traders in the Old City came into windfalls during the wartime boom between 1914 and 1919. The shops catering to the British army personnel did good business during the War. But once it ended and peace was restored in Europe, these businesses in India suffered a setback.

The influenza epidemic of 1918 made life miserable in Delhi. The killer Spanish Flu was brought to India by soldiers returning from the war front. No one today is certain about the scale of this calamity.

It is estimated that hundreds of thousands of lives were lost in the crowded Walled City and the drastic measures taken to contain the infectious disease were traumatic as they involved breaking down some structures, improving sanitation and so on, which disrupted city life severely.

By the mid-1920s, the economic depression had set in. The War over, white customers, the sahib log, became a rare sight. Indians who thronged the markets were mostly window shoppers. They bargained for annas and pies (12 pies made an anna), getting on the nerves of shopkeepers, who were spoilt by the extravagant gora sahib customers. Their ranks had depleted and the purse strings had tightened. Strikes were frequent, following the call for non-cooperation given by Gandhi.

In *Smoke Without Fire*, Siddiqi's grandfather grumbled cursing the changed times and lustily abusing the Indian shoppers who wasted his time:

> Haggling for nothing. Shopping for the heck of it without a penny in his pocket. Farting more than actually shitting as it were. How can a down-at-heel, impoverished looking, bhooke [hungry] Bengali like him even dare think of English jams and jellies? They can hardly afford simple dal chawal…typical deshi log.

This extraordinarily perceptive account discloses the embryonic growth of communal prejudice in the Walled City where Hindus and Muslims had lived in peace and harmony for generations. He describes his walk from Urdu Bazaar to his residence in Ballimaran, Mahal Serai, Haveli Hissamuddin Haider, also known as Qutubganj. The entire route was divided in distinct sectors, by the smells of food being cooked in Hindu and Muslim kitchens.

These smells marked the territory in the lanes and by-lanes more clearly than any visible landmarks. 'The aromas that wafted in the air were varied. The pungency of the hot curries boiling on the cauldron was almost jarring. Walking along the streets, one was grateful that their sharpness was mediated by the sweet smell of fresh chapattis being baked on the tawa. Beyond Nazir Panwari's fancy shop, with a king-sized mirror mounted on the wall, the smells changed as one approached the Umami Dawa Khana and the Mohabbat Hotel, which was not really a hotel but a small tea shop.'

This was the invisible border where the dominant smell that entered the nostrils was the dal being cooked—more often than not, *urad ki dal*—in the houses in Charkhewalan, a predominantly Hindu locality.

Further down the path, Samman halvai's shop exuded a 'strong mix of buttery scent of desi ghee and condiments—cardamoms, cloves, pistachio, almonds and an impossible potpourri of several others. In the morning, the sweet smells were smothered by spicy vapours of puri–kachori and curried potatoes served with pickled mango and red carrot slices.'

Siddiqi has left vivid descriptions of food production and consumption on the streets of Delhi in his memoirs that deserve to be quoted at length. There is no other source that provides such detailed information about not only what people in the Walled City preferred to eat, but also provides names of the skilled craftsmen who enjoyed a reputation for their mastery in preparation of the delicacies they sold. That was a time when the area did not have an iconic eatery or two, claiming to be 'true inheritors of the royal cuisine of Shahjahanabad'; each street corner or a grand gate of a haveli had a competent kababia or a biryani maker.

> The chapattiwala sat at the extended front of a small shop 'quite oblivious of his surroundings, a plantain leaf *bidi* stuck between his lips' with a huge basin of dough and blazing tawa before him. He would flatten the dough into perfect chapatti shape and toss it up in air before catching it in his raised open palms and throwing them over the baking plate. He would go on through the act, softly humming some film tune almost like in a trance. Khalifa's nihari was the last word for the highly spicy Dilli dish. Its mouth-watering thick gravy, the huge slices of tender boneless beef, served with goat's brain and bone marrow, brought nihari lovers flocking to Khalifa's shop from the four corners of the city.

The description of the kebab maker at work reads like a film script and echoes Mir Nihal's account in *Twilight in Delhi*:

> The kebabchi dressed the spit with thick kebab paste, threaded it round to make it hold and place the spits on a tray of burning coal fitted with a hand operated fan. As his assistant operated the fan, Sharfu turned the spit several times over to give the kebab an even texture. Grilled to turn, he took the spit off the grill, peeled sizzling kebabs of the pit with a deft hand, placed it quickly in a leaf cup, adding lots and lots of finely peeled onion, green chilli and green mango lacings and handed it over to me. *Lo miyan tum bhi kya, yad kuroge Sharfu ke kebab ko*!

The end of the War was followed by economic slowdown. This was reflected in the changing lifestyle within the Walled City. Youngsters who studied in madrasas or in the Delhi College were exposed to the world beyond the walls. They were introduced to flavours unknown in the Jama Masjid neighbourhood. Of course, the prohibitions about haram food were observed.

Siddiqi describes a picnic with his schoolmates, escorted by a young teacher, near the end of the First World War. The packed lunch of *keema-parantha* made the day-long excursion to Mehrauli even more enjoyable. On the way back, the group stopped over at the Safdarjung aerodrome and the teacher introduced his wards to a friend who was a pilot and aspiring to join the Royal Air Force. The boys were treated to 'tea, pastries and sandwiches' after a conducted tour of the planes in the hangers. Other weekend outings to Okhla Barrage didn't require elaborate preparation.

Life changed for Abdul and others like him when they joined the Delhi University. The atmosphere at the University outside city walls was heady.

It would, however, not be right to treat this period as a water-tight compartment. The transfer of the capital from Calcutta to Delhi and the First World War and their aftermath spilt over and shaped these times. Both these events changed the lives of the people and marked the end of an era decisively.

Eleven

Food for the Traveller: Sarais, Dak Bungalows and Street-side Eateries

Maidens Hotel, Old Delhi
Source: Maidens Hotel Official Website

For centuries before the advent of Europeans, Indian travellers—traders and pilgrims, crafts persons and artistes—had relied on the system of dharamshalas and sarais while on the road. These traditional inns provided board and lodging and ensured security.

Delhi, outside the walled confines of Shahjahanabad, was dotted with sarais. The tracts of land where these inns were located continue to be identified by their names. Once upon a time, long ago, five sarais, adjacent to each other, occupied the large tract of land in South Delhi—en route to Mehrauli—where the campuses of the Indian Institute of Technology (IIT) and the National Council of Educational Research and Training (NCERT) are situated today. Legend has it that these were named after five sisters—Lado, Kalo (u), Ber, Jia and Katwari(a). The memory of these inns, however, had started fading by the middle of the nineteenth century. Ber Sarai and Katwaria Sarai abutted the Old Campus of Jawaharlal Nehru University that came up in 1969 on the land once part of Munirka Village. The memories of these old inns had already faded when Sir Syed Ahmed compiled a list of historic places in *Asar-us-Sanadid*, in the last quarter of the nineteenth century. He remarks that the existence of these five inns may be just local folklore. He believes that at least one of them may have been associated with a Sufi pir who lived there.

There are many other areas in South Delhi whose names testify to the presence of traditional inns and hostelries in years gone by. Yusuf Sarai occupies the stretch of land between AIIMS and Safdarjung Hospital to Hauz Khas. Green Park and Green Park Extension, as well as Safdarjang Development Area were developed in this area and carved out as upmarket residential colonies in the outskirts in the 1960s. Land where serais once stood was gobbled up by private builders. Only names of the old inns survived. Neb Sarai is just off

Saket in Maidan Garhi, near the IGNOU campus. Arab-ki-Sarai marks the site of another inn that was popular with pilgrims to the dargah of Hazrat Nizamuddin and was close to Kalo Sarai where the Nizamuddin Railway Station and the Interstate bus terminal have come up. Bhuri/Bhuli Bhatiyari ka Mahal or Sarai Sheikh Bu Ali, is a hunting lodge in the middle of a city forest. Its name is explained in folklore differently. Some believe that a woman with russet hair and dark complexion had set up a makeshift kitchen here for patrons who came here on a hunt. Others maintain that a Sufi pir, who exuded a magical aroma, once had his khanqah here.

The most glamorous of the sarais in Shahjahanabad was perhaps that of Begum Jahanara in Chandni Chowk. This is where the favourite daughter of Shah Jahan held a salon and entertained members of the ruling elite and lovers of good life.

The city gates were closed at sunset. Travellers who missed this deadline for entry had to seek shelter in the inns on the outskirts. Most of these were built on highways radiating out from Delhi to Punjab, Rajasthan, and Agra and into the heartland that comprised the Ganga-Yamuna Doab. Faridabad, Ballabhgarh, Palwal, Gurgaon/ Ghaziabad, Hapurgarh, Mukteshwar-Gajraula, Amroha, Moradabad, and Rampur.

The 2,000-kilometre-long Grand Trunk Road, at one time boasted of 1,700 sarais built as midway stopovers for weary passengers and troops on express march. These were built at intervals of 12–15 miles. Some were fortified for additional security, had wells for drinking water and arrangements to shelter horses and provide fodder for them.

A large part of the journey from Calcutta to Allahabad/Kanpur was completed on the river and that is perhaps why this stretch had few sarais. The road from Kanpur to Agra traversed Bareilly, Rampur, and Moradabad. Alternatively, the traveller could head towards Agra via Firozabad.

One can, with some justification, suggest that it was in the sarais that the style of cooking known as *Bhatiyari* developed. Travellers who spent nights at these inns had different tastes and varying requirements. Some travelled with a small retinue of attendants and had the means to ask the innkeeper to arrange special meals for them. The attendants subsisted on what was cooked as a staple for the not-so-demanding or affluent boarders. Like the present-day dhabas, sarais were a place where myriad tastes and cooking techniques mingled. The inns closest to a big city like Delhi offered on its menu recipes/delicacies imitating what was available in the bazaars in the city. Salman Rushdie and Shamsur Rahman Faruqi evoke the atmosphere of these inns imaginatively in their fiction.

In his novella, *Qabze Zaman*[31] (Time Compression), Faruqi has the protagonist checking into an inn that brings out the flavour of the places that catered to travellers of all kinds:

> I went to the mistress of the hostelry and explained to her that I was a traveller from Sind arrived here in search of opportunities of a better life and would like to stay in the caravanserai so long as I didn't find some settled appointment. She asked me my name which I truthfully told her. Oddly enough, she wasn't curious about my luggage, nor about the place in Sind where I hailed…I enquired about the rent: it was one and half paise per day for the room. Food would be prepared according to my wishes the price of which would be charged separately. For the toilette, there were many excellent bathhouses in Daryaganj nearby where I would be charged nominal fees.

The dak bungalows replaced the sarais in the nineteenth century with the coming of the East India Company's officials and, later, of the Crown, on the scene. They catered to a very different class of travellers—European officials on tours of inspection and their Indian subordinates. Accommodation, food served and other services for the new travellers were transformed.

The dak bungalows were also known as rest houses and travellers' bungalows. The first such bungalows were built in the 1840s, primarily as a night halt or staging post for mail. Dak bungalows feature prominently in travelogues and works of fiction about British India. The Nobel Prize winning English writer, Rudyard Kipling, who was born in Bombay and had spent many years in India at various times of his life, once wryly commented: 'A fair proportion of the tragedy of our lives out here acted itself in dak-bungalows…[and] many men have died mad in [them]…nothing is too wild, grotesque, or horrible to happen in a dak-bungalow.'[32] Rudyard's father, sculptor John Lockwood Kipling, the first principal of the famed J.J. School of Art, described them as 'about as handsome as a stack of hay' and forming a kind of "irreducible minimum" of accommodation.'[33]

Built at a distance of 12-15 miles apart, they provided free accommodation for government officials and, upon their permission, 'incomparably cheap' lodging for other travellers. Lodging charges were fixed by the government. As late as the 1920s, the charge for a dak bungalow was only 8 annas (half a rupee) per night for single occupancy and 12 annas (three-quarters of a rupee) for married couples. The essential staff comprised a caretaker-security guard, who doubled up as a makeshift cook-steward-attendant and had the grand designation of khansamah.

The early dak bungalows were Spartan, providing little more than a roof over the weary traveller's head and protection from the scorching sun or torrential rain and wild animals that lurked in the forest. With the passage of time, they became colonial outposts—symbols of British power—marking out yet another exclusive space inhabited by the White Masters. Over time, a distinct architectural style took shape. The facade of the building was imposing with massive pillars holding up the tiled roof. Steps led to the verandah in the front. In the centre was a hall that served as common dining area. Suites and rooms opened out on both sides. The kitchen and servant quarters were at the back, with a small kitchen garden.

Delhi had many dak bungalows in the nineteenth century, most of them maintained by the Public Works Department (PWD), like the ones at Alipur Road, Nizamuddin and Mehrauli. These had khansamahs who could, if required, cook a meal for the touring officer unaccompanied by a cook, the common fare being eggs and chicken dishes. The kitchen and servants' quarters were detached and located behind the main house in most instances. The bungalow was served by a retinue of Indian servants. The entire set-up reflected the sheer contrast of the lifestyles of the natives and the rulers. A small stock of provisions was maintained.

Lt Col J.K. Stanford, who was appointed to the ICS and served in India and Burma in the inter-War years, left behind interesting information about these traveller's shelters. He recorded that, before the advent of motor cars, officers often spent three weeks in a month on tour, living in these bungalows, with 7 rupees and 8 annas as a nightly travelling allowance that paid for the horse's feed, firewood, eggs, chickens, and paraffin; they did not have to pay for the accommodation.

Some of the dak bungalows of the British days were said to be haunted by the ghosts of sahibs long dead and gone. Then there were the spectres of 'native' women who had fallen in love with a passing firangi and died of a broken heart, when he left them in the lurch. Besides these, there were old khansamahs, whose spirit could not rest in peace, and who made an occasional appearance at midnight to surprise some young Englishman with a tray of whiskey-soda. Dedicated chronicler of Delhi, R.V. Smith, recounts, 'Once a sahib went looking for the khansamah and found him hanging from a tree. When he called out to him, the man just vanished.'

Smith states that at least ten PWD rest houses were functioning at the middle of the nineteenth century. These were numbered. The one at Mehrauli was number 9, while the one at Nizamuddin was identified by the number 6. Alipur was marked 3. The most famous was the Delhi Dak Bungalow, situated near the spot where the Mutiny Memorial was erected. It was close to the Delhi Railway

Station, Kashmiri Gate and Civil Lines, predominantly European neighbourhoods. Access to St James Church was easy. These dak bungalows influenced the city's taste almost invisibly but significantly.

If the officer on tour arrived late in the evening, or unannounced, he would have to be content with a frugal dinner of vegetable soup, egg curry and potato cutlets. Most often the dessert was bread pudding made with leftover baker's bread and milk sourced from the nearby villages. If the stay extended to few more days, the khansamah would procure meat from the butcher or slaughter a rooster to have a more elaborate menu. Long-staying guests, or those who were expected, were treated to more lavish meals—the standard dak bungalow fare of murgi roast, mutton curry, mince pie and caramel custard. Much depended on the skills and inclination of the khansamah.

R.V. Smith quotes an old overseer that 'as the times were cheap—goat meat was 5 annas per seer and a whole chicken could be had for 4 annas. Beef (buffalo) was 5 paise a seer—meat and poultry were procured daily from the butcher who did rounds of the Dak Bungalows.'

Dak bungalows were used not only by itinerant officials but at times by officers on transfer from one posting to another, accompanied by their wives and children. Sometimes Christmas and New Year were celebrated by these families in the dak bungalow. The fare on offer would have been much richer on such occasions.

As the city limits under British control expanded after the Mutiny, the Delhi dak bungalows fell into disrepair. With improved law and order and better roads, in most instances, officers could return home after a day-long inspection of the sites they had gone to.

The British, badly shaken by the events of 1857, took more than a decade to regain a measure of self-confidence. They continued to distrust their subjects, particularly the Muslims, who had all too readily rallied around 'their' Emperor. The British thought that it was necessary to convey to the Indian people unequivocally that the reigning British Queen Victoria was the real ruler of the land now. The power had passed from the East India Company to the Crown and there was no need to continue with the fiction of the sovereignty of the Mughal Emperor. As soon as some order was restored, an Imperial Durbar was organized, with pomp and pageantry, to drive home this point to the people of Delhi.

Preparations for the Durbar provided the initial impetus for construction of Western-style hotels in the city.

The first Durbar was organized in 1877 by Lord Lytton and was attended by the then Prince of Wales, who represented his father, Queen Victoria's consort, Prince Albert. The venue was the large maidan in Buradi and was designated the Kingsway Camp. It was announced grandly that Indians were subjects ruled directly by the British Sovereign—Queen Victoria of England, who had graciously consented to be the Empress of India. This event proved to be the catalyst for new settlements, irregular to begin with, but that would in course of time become permanent. Three decades later, Lord Curzon organized an even grander Durbar in 1903. It was held on a tract of land that ever since then has been known as the Kingsway Camp. Demolition of old existing structures in the Walled City was ordered to create space for imposing monuments testifying to British might.

When it was decided to shift the Imperial Capital from Calcutta to Delhi, the fortunes of the city got a new life. The transfer was announced at the Delhi Durbar, held from December 7–16, 1911, to celebrate the coronation of King George V and Queen Mary as Emperor and Empress of India. Work began on this ambitious project in 1912. The New City was to change the urban landscape and the lives of people who dwelt in the soon to become Purani (Old) Dilli dramatically.

The organization of three Durbars triggered an influx of hundreds of thousands of people from outside as labourers, skilled workers and craftsmen to be employed on these projects. The extensions of the railway line in Delhi also had the same effect. Many of these people did not return to the places of their original domicile as life there was harder than in Delhi. Delhi seemed to offer much better prospects for gainful employment. Law and order also was better than in rural areas in most princely states. The immigrants lived a life on the margins but their food habits slowly seeped into the food of Delhi, such as staples from Eastern UP, like *sattu*, and one-pot meals of *daliya*-like khichdi, cooked in a handi, *bajra roti*, parched gram in a flattened and spicy *chana jowar garam* incarnation. *Sattu* was adopted happily by denizens of Delhi to combat the scorching heat, and *matra* (dried yellow peas) were added to the chaat repertoire.

Hotels mushroomed to cater to the needs of an increasing number of itinerant Englishmen. Hamilton's, Courtney's, the Western Indian Commercial Associations Hotel and Mrs Benn's were all located in Kashmiri Gate, conveniently close to the railway station. The inauguration of the Maidens Hotel almost coincided with the pomp and pageantry of the second durbar. Maiden, a young soldier, landed in India as the nineteenth century was drawing to a close. After serving in the army briefly, he decided to resign, seeking to make more money. In 1900, he constructed the hotel that bears his name. Maidens was built on the site of the old Metropolitan Hotel and soon became the most sought-after and expensive hotel accommodation in Delhi. It opened its doors in 1903. Though there were other hotels catering to the British in Kashmiri Gate dating back to the 1840s and after the upheaval of 1857, none matched the stately elegance of the Maidens. A festive ball was held here in honour of the Prince of Wales, during his tour of the Empire. Edwin Lutyens, the architect-builder of the New Capital, stayed here as a guest for a long time when the construction of the city was going on. The Cecil Hotel came up the following year.

In the next two decades, other higher-class hotels opened in the Civil Lines after the Cecil—among them, Carlton's and the Swiss were prominent. Some advertised the provision of electric lights in the guest rooms as a special feature, while others boasted of a swimming pool as a major attraction. In its advertisements, Hotel Cecil emphasized the availability of 'Electric Light and Swimming Pool'. These Civil Lines hotels were keen to highlight how modern their hotels were in terms of facilities and comfort. Electricity had come to India only in the late nineteenth century, and that, too, first in Calcutta and Bombay. These hotels were probably among the earliest buildings in Delhi to have electricity. More than half a century later, on November 1, 1959, to be precise, the Cecil Hotel ceased to function. (The property was transferred to Delhi St Xavier's Society in December. St Xavier's School, Delhi, was inaugurated on January 6, 1960.)

Septugenarian D.N. Chaudhuri, in his *Delhi: Light, Shades and Shadows* says:

> Cecil was known for its homely environment. It had large apartment-like suites, which made it a favourite of many European families that visited India those days. Many foreign journalists had permanent suites in Cecil as well as in Swiss Hotel. But Indian businessmen and families, who visited Delhi often, stayed in hotels situated in the Walled City.[34]

It was decided even before the first Durbar to extend the railway line to Delhi, but this project had been suspended to punish the people of Delhi for the rebellion. However, the British soon realized that the railway line would facilitate the fast movement of troops in times when they were required. Land was acquired to build a railway station. The laying down of the railway track cut the Old City into two parts, severing age-old links between their residential colonies. Construction of a bridge dislocated more people. Those uprooted were resettled elsewhere but old residential areas near the station, including the Saudagaran Mohalla, where many Punjabis lived, were destroyed in the process.

The rich Punjabi merchants, most of them Muslims, bought properties that were available at a throw-away price on distress sales in the vicinity of Jama Masjid and relocated their families there.

The advent of trains triggered a spurt of construction activity. An impressive railway station was built, replicating the architecture of the Red Fort, and the British authorities commissioned other large public buildings, in the then prevalent European style. The Town Hall came up where Jahanara Sarai and the beautiful garden named after her once stood.

There was a large influx of outsiders who were employed on infrastructural development projects. This changed the demographic profile of the Old City and had a significant impact on the food business in Delhi. A number of small sweets and snacks shops came up around the Fountain installed in Chandni Chowk. It is during the three decades, between the first Durbar and the third, that many of the by-now legendary food outlets were set up.

Among the earliest is the Old Famous Jalebi Wala, which has been around since 1884. Sometime in the early 1880s, a young man migrated from his village in Agra to Delhi in search of a better future. His name was Nemichand Jain. According to lore, his family lived in a village near Agra and he came to the city with just eight annas (half a rupee)—all that he could afford to take with him from the small dowry he had received on his marriage to the eight-year-old Shobha Devi. Nemichand sold *rabri* from a khomcha before a kindly Muslim shopkeeper, Irfan Shamsuddin, took pity on the lad and let him set up his stall with planks on the pavement outside his shop in 1921. Frugal and hardworking, the Jain youth had saved enough money soon to buy a haveli in Khajanchi Mohalla. There was no looking back after this. The shop is now managed by the fifth generation descendants. Its *rabri-jalebi* are iconic.

The skilled craftsmen, *karigar*, toil daylong, pouring out fermented gram flour batter, squeezing it out delicately from a cloth bag covering the kadhai with boiling oil in a beautiful circular motion with intertwined spirals. As soon as the *jalebis* acquire a rich golden hue and begin to get crisp, they are removed expertly with tongs and soaked in sugar syrup placed on the side. The method of preparation has not changed ever since the shop was set up. No refined sugar is used in the syrup, only *desi khandsari.*

This was the time when adventurous and enterprising Bengalis, Madrasis, Sindhis and Parsis relocated to Delhi in substantial numbers. Christians and Anglo-Indian families from Agra also shifted base. All of these communities enriched the city with their flavours, cooking styles and traditional delicacies. Several culinary streams intermingled and transformed the eating habits of Dilliwalas.

Independence was not even a twinkle in the eye but it would not be an exaggeration to claim that a strong undercurrent of democratization was palpable. An embryonic form of a pan-Indian taste had already started making inroads into Delhi.

A number of iconic eateries in Shahjahanabad made their appearance only after the tumult and social unrest post the Mutiny had died down. Not all the 'legends' have survived and those who did weather strong winds have also changed, some beyond recognition, since Independence.

A number of parantha makers from Agra moved to Delhi in the 1870s, after the turmoil of 1857 was over and a number of shops had reopened in Chandni Chowk. One of the oldest outlets was opened by Pt. Kanhaiyalal Durgaprasad Dixit (established 1875) followed by Pt. Dayanand Shivcharan (established 1882) and Pt. Baburam Devidayal Paranthewale (established 1886). Onions and garlic were eschewed and the parantha were always served with sweet tamarind chutney, mint chutney, mixed vegetable pickle, paneer and potato curry, potato and fenugreek curry, and *ghotuwa kaddu* (mashed stir-fried) pumpkin. Till 1911, this area was identified as Dariba Kalan or Chota Dariba. The term Paranthe Wali Gali gained currency during the inter-War years.

Some shops closed down in the aftermath of the Emergency but the street has since experienced a strong revival due to the influx of Indian and foreign tourists. Most of the shops are being run by the sixth generation of the founding families.

Twelve

Durbars and Food

The Delhi Durbar of 1911 with King George V
and Queen Mary seated upon the dais
Source: Wikimedia Commons

Until 1857, neighbourhoods like Paharganj, Kishanganj, and Pahari Dhiraj, were separate pockets, whose limits were fuzzy. Shahganj was an extension of Paharganj, stretching towards the Jantar Mantar, touching Raja Bazaar. During the Mughal rule, Paharganj was the most prominent grain market in Delhi and the only one outside the city walls. Till the eighteenth century, grain was ferried across the river and stocked in warehouses here. Toll-tax collection chowkies (outposts) were set up just outside the Ajmeri Gate and at Shahdara and Patparganj.

A major impetus to the growth and diversification of food in the city was industrialization. The growth of Sadar Bazaar and Sabzi Mandi was directly related to this. In the early 1880s, there were no industrial establishments in Delhi to which the Factory Act was applicable. The karkhanas, which came nearest to the definition, in the sense that they employed a number of people in a particular job at one place, much as the karkhanas of the Mughals and their nobles had done, varied in size. Only ten were listed in 1885, varying from a textile factory at Bara Hindu Rao, owned by a Mr Wilson, employing two hundred men, to an ice factory in Kauria Pul, with twelve employees. But within five years, in 1888, the cotton spinning and ginning, and the flour mills were beginning to be mechanized. Delhi's advantage was her relative proximity to the cotton and wheat-producing areas in the Punjab.

The Delhi Town Planning Committee set up to finalize the blueprint for the New Capital submitted its report in June 1912. It proposed that Paharganj and Sadar Bazaar be included in the new imperial city. This would provide a link with the past. The suggestion was rejected by the Viceroy, when the cost of compensation for acquiring the properties was found to be too high. Paharganj and Karol Bagh were excluded from Lutyens Delhi.

Much before the transfer of the capital from Calcutta to Delhi was announced, seeds of another city had been sown. This was the glamorous faux city erected in honour of the Monarch.

The Temporary 'Tent City', the King's Camp (later known as Kingsway Camp) was spread over 72 acres. It had 2,000 tents to house over 2,000 VIPs. The royal couple were housed in a suite of six tents arranged in two rows. The Reception Tent was raised just below the Flag Staff Tower at the Ridge. The tents of the maharajahs and nababs extended along the Mall Road. This was a modern mini city. John Alfred Spender, the editor of the *Westminster Gazette*, who had been an eye-witness, records in his book, *Indian Scene* (quoted in *Delhi Durbar 1911: the Complete Story*):

> …the idea that you rough it [out]or suffer any hardship from camp life in the Coronation Camp is complete delusion…your tent is charmingly furnished, warmed with stove, and lit with electric lights, you sleep in [a] comfortable bed with spring mattresses, and have a Persian Carpet at your feet. Your servants have tents outside, and are always within call. The bathroom is thrown behind, and makes a separate room.[35]

For a week, over half a million people descended on this faux city and stayed there. Many of the original inhabitants, who were uprooted to clear the land for Coronation Camp, didn't return. The lucky ones were 'resettled' in barren land to the west of the Ridge or across the river. Businessmen with a sharp eye for quick speculative gains acquired tracts of land from innocent villagers and rented these to government authorities at exorbitant sums. Some went to the extent of 'developing' unplanned and unauthorized colonies where villagers had been resettled.

As Ghalib had observed in the aftermath of the mayhem of 1857, the only rich people who survived, were the sahukari moneylenders, of whom only three were Muslims, the majority were Hindus. The Muslims, who had pretensions of pursuing the good life, had become objects of ridicule, as a contemporary barb aimed at them shows:

'*Munh chikna aur pet khali, kangal bankas.*' (Impoverished dandies with smooth cheeks and empty bellies.)

Large open spaces created by the British near the fort and cantonment within the city reduced the living space. Mud houses were easily washed down by rains, rendering thousands of people homeless and vulnerable to diseases like malaria.

It was not only the rich Hindu moneylenders that prospered. Many enterprising Hindu immigrants were quick to take advantage of the changed circumstances. While Muslims who had fled the city in 1857 and the years that followed, to escape brutal repression at the hands of the British, weren't allowed to return for a couple of years, the Hindus faced no such barrier. First to open shop in the 1880s were the parantha-makers from Agra. The steady trickle of young Hindus continued. Some of them set up street-side eateries, catering to patrons with limited means, preparing and selling traditional sweet and savoury snacks, cooked before the eyes of the customers.

Shiv Mishthan Bhandar, situated in Kucha Ghasi Ram, close to Katra Neel, on the left side of the road leading to the Red Fort, was established in 1910, by Mohar Singh Yadav. It has a small menu and this has made it easier to maintain a consistent quality.

A traditional Delhi breakfast at Shiv Mishthan Bhandar comprises of *bedmi* (two large puris stuffed with lentil paste, served with *aloo ki sabzi*) or *halwa-nagori* and chole. The most popular item on the menu, the *bedmi* puris, are made using wholewheat flour along with *dal ki pithi*, spiced lentil paste, unlike regular puris. Methi chutney, tangy with a hint of bitterness, and freshly prepared pickles are served as accompaniments. The sweets sold with the above are *jalebi* and *imarti*, *gulab jamun*, *suji halwa*, *moong dal halwa* and *malpua*.

Nagori-halwa, a hot favourite, is prepared only for breakfast. The *nagori* is a mini puri, slightly larger than a *golgappa*. A small measure of *sooji* is mixed with the wheat flour dough to make them extra crisp after deep-frying.

Evenings were (and continue to be) samosa time with kachoris playing the second fiddle.

Proprietors of this Bhandar boast of an impressive guest list of celebrities like Indira Gandhi, Lal Krishna Advani, Atal Bihari Vajpayee, as well as many Hindi film-stars. Senior citizens recall Chaudhary Raghvendra Singh (founder of DLF) and his family regularly dropping in on Sundays for breakfast in the early 1950s.

There were other youngsters who were attracted by the magnetic pull of Delhi.

The second lot of legacy food outlets also trace their roots to the turn of the twentieth century. As its first decade drew to a close, an eight-year-old boy from Haryana strayed into the city with hazy dreams of a better life than at his place of birth. Little is known of his early struggles, when he trained with a halwai for about eight years. Kirorimal—that was his name—must have been exceptionally hard-working and talented because by the time he entered his teens, he felt confident to start off on his own. The beginning was modest. He sold *kulfis* in just two flavours on a pushcart. Business picked up steadily and his name was distorted to Kurhe Mal.

His son and successor, Manoj, could invest in a proper shop only in 1975. There has been no looking back since. The outlet today sells dozens of flavours—many fruit-based. Creamy milk is procured from a dairy in Hapur and saffron is source directly from Kashmir. Though *kulfi* continues to be made in the old-fashioned way, freezers have been introduced to store and freeze the pulp of fruits in season.

Marryam Reshii, author and food chronicler, has researched and documented the story of Haji Karimuddin, the founder of Karim's, in Gali Kebabiyan. He set up this shop only in 1911. Before that, he used to sell *dal roti–aloo gosht* on a pushcart on the streets in the vicinity of Jama Masjid. His successors claim that he belonged to an illustrious family of cooks employed in the royal kitchens of Shahjahanabad but it is almost impossible to verify the lineage. More than two hundred years intervene between the death of Aurangzeb and the appearance of Haji Sahib on the scene, at the end of the first decade of the twentieth century.

The Muslims in Delhi were targeted for brutal repression by the

British, post-1857, and many skilled crafts persons and artisans were forced to flee the city. Maybe Karimuddin's forefathers were among these refugees, who found sanctuary in Rampur and other princely states. Interestingly, though Karim's Nemat Kada was positioned as an eatery with royal roots, its menu was largely based on *lashkari khana—nihari-paye*, *barra*, *seekh kebab*, *raan* and *qorma* sans frills, popular with Afghan soldiers who had descended on Delhi with Ahmad Shah Abdali's armies between 1748 and 1757, and chosen to stay back in India, supplemented over time with dum pukht/do pyaza and the British inspired *ishtoo*.

By the mid-1960s, Karim's had become gentrified, like the Punjabi dhabas in Connaught Place. I remember going to Karim's in Gali Kebabiyan for lunch in the early 1970s, to fortify myself before a football match in Feroze Shah Kotla Stadium that was being played between East Bengal and Mohun Bagan. It was a treat courtesy my mentor and boss, Professor Sisir Gupta, a die-hard East Bengal fan. We gorged on *barra kebab*, *qorma* and *khamiri roti*. Bottled water hadn't captured the market and we quenched our thirst with Limca and Coke. Roghan floating on top of the bowl was a bit scary but the spicing was very different from the dhaba fare. The choices on the menu were wider. In subsequent years, visits to Karim's became regular as visiting friends and relatives had it on their must-do list. Neither the food nor service matched what I had experienced at the Flora restaurant in 1965-66. New Jawahar, next door, claimed that it had been named after Jawahar Lal Nehru, who was a darling of young hearts during the freedom struggle. He was married in this locality in the erstwhile Haksar Haveli in Sitaram Bazaar. Jawahar's food was less greasy and more mildly spiced. Most people got easily addicted to the taste of Old Delhi as unveiled by Karim's, just off the main gate of Jama Masjid, and soon branches of Karim's opened in Jorbagh and Basti Nizamuddin.

Nand Lal Sharma came to Delhi from Rajasthan in 1928 and set up a small dhaba in Paharganj. The roadside eatery was housed in a shack, unadorned by bricks or tiles. At that time, the Yamuna flowed a short distance away, and wild animals could be easily spotted. The river has shifted course since then, moving away, and so have the wild animals that once scared the residents and visitors.

There is no record of the dishes that Sharma served then but his business began to prosper when the Imperial Cinema Hall was built nearby and, as construction work on the new capital gathered momentum, there was an influx of new residents who moved in from villages adjacent to Paharganj.

It was only with the arrival of the Hippies in the late 1960s that Paharganj became the most preferred destination of backpackers looking for budget accommodations. Gradually, the hotels and guest houses spread to the neighbouring Ram Nagar and an area along Deshbandhu Gupta Road. This legacy continues even today, with its streams of budget hotels, cafes and restaurants, specializing in foreign dishes. Apart from that, Paharganj is frequented by the large number of Jewish and Israeli tourists, and has bakeries like 'German Bakery', named 'Ajay Cafe'.

Nand Lal Sharma's dhaba has given way to a glitzy multi-storied hotel, the Metropolis, with a fashionable roof-top restaurant that has a menu with no relic from the past. The roof-top restaurant has a retro menu very different from the earthy dhaba fare. It offers items like Chicken a la Kiev, Russian salad, shashlik, and chicken stroganoff.

Dozens of budget hotels catering to backpackers and price-conscious businessmen have sprouted like mushrooms in Paharganj over the past half century.

Compared to Sharma's dhaba, old mithai shops like Chaina Mal, the Sindhi halwai, may appear to be newcomers, but even this establishment has completed more than seventy-five years in the city. The original shop was opened in Lahore in 1901 and moved to Delhi just before Partition. It is famous for its *Sindhi halwa,* also called *Karachi halwa,* made with germinated wheat. Like most halwais in the Old City, this shop also claims that they prepare everything in pure ghee. Hari Gidwani, in his 1980s now, represents the fourth generation of a family of Sindhi halwais who migrated to Delhi in 1946. Mentored by Bishan Singh Bedi, he once dreamt of representing India in cricket. The young man flashed like a meteor before fading out but retains the love for cricket. He never forgets to send Virender Sehwag nourishing *Karachi halwa*, to provide him more punch.

Thirteen

The Christian and Parsi Communities and their Foods

SodaBottleOpenerWala, a Parsi cafe in Delhi
Source: Unknown

The Christians

Though Christian missionaries had been present since the time of Akbar, very few Christians were permanent residents of Delhi before 1857. Two Armenian Catholic churches were built during Jahangir's reign, one of them near the old Sabzi Mandi and the other near a slaughter house, which were destroyed during the invasion of Nadir Shah in 1739. A Christian cemetery existed in Delhi as early as 1650, when Shah Jahan ruled the city. It has been estimated that Delhi had a Roman Catholic population of about 120, which more than doubled to 300, nearly 120 years later, during Aurangzeb's reign. The early Christian settlements were in Sabzi Mandi, Civil Lines, Kashmiri Gate, Mori Gate, Turkman Gate, Daryaganj, Paharganj and, of course, Chandni Chowk.

After Lord Lake had 'recaptured' Delhi, defeating the Marathas, a church was built near the Red Fort in 1814 by the Baptist Mission. It was later shifted to Chandni Chowk. A few years later, James Skinner built his church at Kashmiri Gate, as has been chronicled in an earlier chapter, providing a rare link between the Delhi of the Mughals and the city cast in their own image by the British.

It was estimated that only 15,000 Christian families still lived in all of Old Delhi after the Christian basti in Daryaganj was sold out. Christians, who could afford to, moved to less congested areas. The main Christian colonies were in Daryaganj, near Cavalry Lines, where there used to be an Army chapel in Old Pataudi House, and Turkman Gate.

The Christians had no inhibitions about eating beef and pork—meats taboo for Hindus and Muslims. Eateries and butcheries that catered to them lost customers belonging to these communities. It was mostly the British who could afford to buy imported viands and condiments stocked by stores like Spencer's in Kashmiri Gate.

The Church of England helped start St Stephen's College near Kinari Bazaar. From 1891 to 1931 it operated from a building in Kashmiri Gate. The Delhi United Christian School for boys and the B.M. Gange School for girls were among the first institutions in the area. Queen Mary's school at Jama Masjid followed in 1912 and the Convent of Jesus and Mary at Raisina in 1919.

Professor Sydney Ribeiro's Anglo-Indian forefathers had come to Delhi before the Durbar of 1911, at which the transfer of the imperial capital from Calcutta to Delhi was announced. The family lived on Hamilton Road. The English and the Anglo-Indians preferred to live at a healthy remove from the congested squalid confines of the Walled City. Kashmiri Gate had developed as a fashionable neighbourhood for the new elite. In Sydney's words: 'It was considered by the residents as the Piccadilly Circle of Delhi. Carlton's and Wenger's—the famous bakeries—started here. There used to be a live band at Carlton's and across the road used to be a club that had the cabaret.'

Jacob, a septuagenarian, in the 1990s, reminisced in an interview with R.V. Smith, that there were a number of 'small, not-so-famous bakeries, where the not-so-affluent Christians bought items of daily need—bread, pastries and cake. The bakers in Old Delhi were very accomplished. Every Christian household would go to them with their cake batters before Christmas and get their cakes baked.'

The establishment of churches, educational institutions, and bakeries played a pivotal role in embedding the Christian community within the cultural and social fabric of Delhi, shaping its landscape over centuries. However, it was in the early 20th century that the city experienced a dramatic architectural transformation. This shift was spearheaded by British architect Edwin Lutyens, who reimagined the heart of Delhi, culminating in the iconic redesign of Connaught Place. As it evolved, Connaught Place not only became a symbol of the city's modern identity but also emerged as a vibrant hub of culinary delights, drawing people to its eclectic food scene.

Connaught Place Comes of Age

Lutyens had earmarked space for a grand hotel near Connaught Place. He envisaged The Imperial in New Delhi as one of the great hotels in Asia, and which would be equal to other great hotels in cities of the Empire—the Strand Hotel in Rangoon, Raffles Hotel in Singapore and The Great Eastern & Oriental in Calcutta. F.B. Blomfield, an architect working with Lutyens, was engaged to conceptualise the new hotel, which, like the melting pot that is India, was to be a confluence of three architectural streams—Victorian, Old Colonial and Art Deco. Pink marble was imported from Italy; silver crockery and cutlery came from London, chandeliers from Europe, chefs from France and Italy.

The Imperial Hotel came up in 1933 on Queensway (now Janpath), just after the work on Connaught Place had been completed. It primarily catered to the Europeans and a minuscule segment of affluent Indians who hung on to the coat-tails of the white ruling elite. This was before the passage of the Government of India Act and the formation of Congress governments in the states. Imperial Hotel's *1911* bar and restaurant has on view a number of Durbar photographs and lithographs on its walls, reminding the guest of its colonial legacy.

The hotel was named by Lady Willingdon, who also approved the Lion insignia. She took keen interest in the project, personally selecting the carpets, cutlery, and chandeliers, which were imported from Europe. The hotel was inaugurated with great fanfare in 1936. Lord Willingdon, the then Viceroy, was the chief guest at the glittering ceremony. A regal ball was organized for 1500 guests to raise funds for the development of the hotel.

The Imperial shone like a solitaire in splendid isolation for almost two decades, its grandeur unmatched. The hotel's pillared verandas were cast in the classical mould. It boasted plush dining rooms and elegant tea lounges, glittering royal ballrooms and sprawling lawns that would be suitable for elite, exclusive social gatherings.

Not many people travelled to New Delhi then, as there were no businesses or industries here. As the occupancy was low, the hotel let out its accommodation for offices on the ground floor. The room tariff was Rs 29 only. It was the tallest building in New Delhi in those days.

The Imperial took great pride in food served by it. It was exclusively Western fare. There used to be weekly dances in the Ball Room. This was the venue where members of the Anglicised elite—civil servants, army men and Indian princes and more—socialized. Strains of 'The Blue Danube' wafted through the place during lunch, and in the evening, an orchestra from London would invite everyone to the floor to conclude the evening after the candlelight dinner.

Pandit Nehru, Mahatma Gandhi, Muhammad Ali Jinnah and Lord Mountbatten also held parleys at The Imperial to discuss the Partition. The Imperial has witness history being made. It was here that Sir Stafford Cripps sat for lunch with V.P. Menon and Henry "Harry" Vincent Hodson, Reforms Commissioner.

In 1934, the Nirula brothers, who had for some years operated a hotel in Chandni Chowk, opened the tiny Hotel India in Connaught Circus, with just twelve rooms, a restaurant and a bar.

Hotel Marina, built in 1934, though less grand and imposing than The Imperial, didn't skimp on luxury. It had forty-six rooms and suites which could accommodate fifty-two guests. The hotel boasted no less than twenty-six garages for guests' cars and fifty-two servant quarters for accompanying attendants. It had a restaurant and a large ballroom. The hotel was initially managed by the 'Japanwala' family (called so because of their business relations with Japan). Later, an Italian family operated it till the early 1940s. During the Second World War, the Italian family went back and the management of the hotel was taken over by Sardari Lal and Girdhari Lal—businessmen from Delhi.

Veteran hotelier, Virender Dutta, remembers that when he was serving at The Imperial in 1962, before the Sino-Indian War, the place retained the aura of colonial pomp and pageantry. When an Ice Souffle was ordered, the steward marched in, with the metallic tray held high proudly, to the live accompaniment of the roll of drums and strains of martial music!

I first crossed The Imperial's hallowed portals some time in 1970, when I had gone there to interview Mrs Vijaya Lakshmi Pandit, who used to stay here as a long-stay guest in the winters. The 'English' (not American or Indian) Breakfast, on the sunlit veranda, looking out on the lawn fringed by tall palms, transported one to a world of leisure and grace long gone by.

Hotel Ambassador in Sujan Singh Park was completed in 1945, as the War drew to a close, and Independence was imminent. Designed by Walter Sykes George, who had worked with both Edwin Lutyens and Herbert Baker, the hotel carved a niche for itself among the clientele of guests who wished to have a comfortable stay and found the Imperial intimidating and expensive. It had a night club called Jewel Box. Men had to wear tailcoats or tuxedos and women had to dress in elegant long skirts to enter it. There were racks for guests to deposit their hats and umbrellas. It was only decades later that the hotel opened an Indian restaurant, Dasaprakash, renowned for South Indian vegetarian fare. A.K. Damodaran, freedom fighter-turned-diplomat and a wonderful raconteur, who was my boss then, took me for a vegetarian lunch there once. I must confess that the experience was a little underwhelming. Part of the reason, perhaps, being that I was expecting to be treated to an exotic Chinese meal at this hotel.

These hotels catered to a very small segment of the population. Most of the patronage was provided by travelling businessmen—English and European. They also served as venues for informal high-level meetings between leaders of the Indian national movement and high-ranking government officials. The restaurants catered primarily to the Indian princes and their entourage.

Unlike New Delhi, Old Delhi was 'out of bounds' for GIs but full of other ranks, who were having a last fling before returning home.

On Sundays, the young Siddiqi would take a bus to Connaught Place and get off at the Odeon stop, to walk over to the India Coffee House on Queensway, at Scindia House. The Coffee House in Old

Delhi had closed down after registering its presence for advertising purposes. In *Smoke Without Fire*, he says, 'Wenger's and Nirula's were the top favourites after the India and the Royal Coffee House…an Italian violinist played tea time music at Davico's—more expensive and elegant than other restaurants…The Nirula's was famous for its lunches and dinners. Its lavish vegetarian thali (priced a rupee and half) was a gourmet's delight. Although it featured a fixed menu, you could on request have refills of your favourite item.'

Inflation was beginning to pinch, but in the Walled City, a sumptuous non-vegetarian repast of kebab and roti was still affordable when celebrating on a small budget. Siddiqi tells us that 'four anna worth of kebab' were enough to enliven a clandestine dinner party for young adults, like the author's elder brother, who once sent him out to fetch the stuff when his friend, who had joined the army, turned up with a bottle of Scotch to celebrate the end of the War.

No one knew how long this post-War euphoria would last. Those who had the means were splurging recklessly on food and drink. The mood fluctuated like a pendulum between euphoria and despair. The spectre of Partition caused serious apprehensions. Siddiqi comments wryly, 'Those who could barely afford Hafiz Hotel in Ballimaran (where one could feed oneself to satiation for less than half a rupee) were flocking to the Shahjehanpuri Hotel opposite the Fatehpuri Mosque.'

The 'All India Radio crowd' comprised regulars who came all the way from New Delhi to eat at Shahjehanpuri Hotel. The regulars included the Bukhari brothers, the officers in charge of All India Radio, poets Majaz 'Lakhnavi', Josh 'Malihabadi' and Saghar Nizami, and short story writer Krishan Chander.

These eminent writers would first stop at a local restaurant and bar—Mansarovar or Lakshmi, down a few drinks, and then proceed, suitably inebriated, to Shajehanpuri Hotel for a rich and hearty meal composed of exclusive Delhi dishes—biryani, *yakhni pulao*, *rogan josh*, *nargisi kofta, pasande,* seekh kebab and a large variety of other mouth-watering delicacies.

The owner and the head cook would personally take orders from customers and gruffly ask them to wait. No special consideration or favour was shown to these men of letters and the arts, who remained incognito.

Siddiqi's observations are not restricted to what the gentle folk consumed. He notes that Nakti Bashiran, an outcaste sweeper, was known for two things: her excellent vermicelli and unrequited passion for men. Her home-made vermicelli would be like soft thread—long soft, fine and delicious.

These details are corroborated by Lalit Nirula, scion of the family. He recalls that the table d' hote menu had a choice of two five-course meals, priced at Rs 2 each! It was not unusual for young cavalry officers in the early 1940s, posted in the Delhi Cantonment during the War, to ride powerful motorcycles down to NCH on weekends to escape the insipid fare dished out in the army mess and gorge on real food—'desi khan'. Nirula maintained a well-stocked bar. Nirula's had a non-vegetarian thali as well but orthodox Muslims, who only ate halal meat, passed it over.

Siddiqi's comments on contemporaries are interesting. Khwaja Hassan Nizami, a master of Urdu prose, was a man of many parts—an intriguing personality—an enigma to most in the Walled City. Some suspected him to be a mole spying for the British. He ran the affairs of the dargah at Nizamuddin and enjoyed unhindered access to huqqam a balan (high officials) from the District Magistrate to the Viceroy. The upkeep of the dargah was generously funded by the ruling princes, including the Nizam of Hyderabad. Khwaja Sahib played host to all and sundry to partake of the special langar—*bara khana* of sweet and salted rice dishes—biryani and *muttanjan*—and to listen to qawwali music. Nizami belonged to the last of the post-Mutiny generation representing the pre-Mutiny culture and tradition.

In the late 1940s, and until the mid-fifities, many more restaurants opened in Connaught Place—Kwality, Gaylord, Volga, Alps, United

Coffee House, and York, to mention just a few. It was quite common for the well-off to go out for dinner and dancing, as all restaurants had a live band, many with crooners.

Lalit Narula remembers an old employee telling him about a legendary gourmand, a very eminent, tall and rotund lawyer, who was a regular at this restaurant for lunch. He would sit at his favourite table and ask the butler, Jameel, what was being offered. He would select one of the full meals and many times, after finishing it, would proceed to enquire about what else was available as he was still a little hungry. He would then order the second meal and proceed to do justice to it as well.

Nirula's could sense that with the British preparing to leave India, the market was bound to change. They shut down their existing restaurant catering to primarily to Europeans and Anglicized Indians and replaced it with three new restaurants in the same space—a 150-seat modern cafeteria targeting the new middle-class, selling clean hygienic food prepared before their eyes, a 'brasserie' modelled on the ones in France, and the Chinese Room, the first deluxe Chinese restaurant in India owned by a non-Chinese.

The Second World War ended in August 1945. The city experienced a brief period of euphoria. The American GIs thronged the restaurants in Connaught Place and rejuvenated the commercial centre that had till then not quite lived up to its promise. The centre of gravity—political as well as cultural—was shifting from Shahjahanabad and Kashmiri Gate-Civil Lines to New Delhi. Connaught Place at long last was bustling with life, thanks to the presence of American soldiers and officers. Restaurants were doing brisk business.

The American GIs lived it up as they awaited transfer to the Eastern Front on the China-Burma border. Life in Delhi was for them an unending party with balls hosted by the Maharaja of Bikaner at Bikaner House, pool parties at the palatial home of Sir Shankar Lal on Curzon Road, watching the newest Hollywood releases at Regal theatre, dining at the theatre-restaurant Davico's, and surprising P.L. Lamba and his old friend, business partner and, later, brother-in-law,

Iqbal Ghai, with their prodigious appetite for ice-cream after late-night shows.

Major Habib Rehman, who started his career as a hotelier in a property owned by P.L. Lamba in Aurangabad, recalls that the old man used to reminisce about GIs ordering ice-cream—not slices but entire blocks, meaning not a slice but a whole brick. It is believed that it was a US Army veterinary surgeon posted in New Delhi who introduced Lamba and Ghai to the American-style commercial ice-cream production. Kwality was happy to add new flavours that the Americans loved—flavours like Cassata and the all-American Tutti Frutti. The American impact wasn't limited to ice creams. They left behind before their tour of duty ended, piles of tinned food—part of their K-rations—that made even affluent adolescents drool.

Kwality was one of their favourite haunts. The restaurant, was already famous for its spicy 'melt in the mouth' *Pindi chana* and piping hot *bhature*, whose recipes was provided by a halwai in Mussoorie, where Lamba spent the summers.

Kwality was started as an elegant eatery for the resident Europeans and affluent Indians in Delhi in 1940. P.L. Lamba had a natural flair for gracious hospitality, and he also owned the more expensive and exclusive Gaylord next door. At one time, he also owned and managed the Khyber Restaurant in Kashmiri Gate. Other members of the extended Lamba family helped out at Kwality. Some later branched out to open restaurants in cities like Jaipur.

In *Climbing the Mango Trees*, Madhur Jaffrey has recorded in her memoirs that the post-War Delhi was swamped by US army 'leftovers in the form of mysterious boxes known as K-Rations…my cousins and I tore them open as if they were Christmas presents, pulling out each carefully fitted tin or package with the greatest glee. Thus I was introduced to my first olive, my first fruit cocktail and my first taste of Spam. I rolled mouthfuls slowly around my tongue and pronounced each of them to be exotic and wonderful. I had never eaten tinned fruit or meat before.'[36]

The War thus acted as a powerful vehicle for spreading the American way of eating across the globe.

P.L. Lamba was a dapper dresser, who made dramatic appearances in bespoke suits, colourful ties and pocket squares. Those who have worked with him, like Habib Rehman, remember the boss's penchant for living larger than life as well as his razor-sharp mind and complete mastery of day-to-day detail of running the restaurants.

The Anglo-Indian Club, where tambola sessions were held twice a week, was yet another attraction.

The British who had built the new capital were not destined to rule gloriously over the Indian Empire for long. Soon after the War ended, the transfer of power to Indians was completed. The nationalist leaders, who had waged the freedom struggle against the colonial masters, became the inheritors of the grandiose architectural legacy of the Empire.

The Viceregal Lodge was perched atop Raisina Hill, flanked by the imposing South and North Blocks overlooking the Central Vista, stretching out to India Gate girdled by the hexagon studded with palatial residences of Indian princes. The Central Legislative Assembly (now the Parliament) was part of this vast public space. However, strict discipline was maintained by those frequenting this zone that housed the seat of Imperial Government. Common people could only sprawl on the lush green lawns under the shade of jamun trees, punctuated by shallow water bodies.

The stately Eastern and Western Courts on Janpath were built for members of the Central Legislative Assembly; and the rigidly-stratified city had bungalows for high-ranking officers on Ferozeshah Road, and Lodi Road. Spacious quarters were built on Panchkuin Road and Peshwa Square near Gole Market, to house supervisory and subordinate clerical staff, mostly Indians. Some private bungalows were built on Curzon Road and Barakhamba Road and Sikandra Road.

Tree-lined avenues radiated from Connaught Place, flowing past countless roundabouts, to the city's southern extremity via Willingdon

Park, Lodi Road to Willingdon Airport (later renamed Lodi Garden and Safdarjung Airport). The Race Course, Air Force Stadium and Gymkhana Club were within Delhi Imperial Zone Area (DIZA), but accessible only to members of the ruling elite.

The buildings were ready for occupation by the mid-1920s, but many aristocratic Indians preferred to reside in Civil Lines—beyond the Secretariat on Ludlow Castle Road, Flag Staff Road, and Racquet Court Road. This posh area was the exclusive neighbourhood of the rich Indians.

Maidens Hotel had during the years of the Raj catered to the British. Exchange Stores in Kashmiri Gate (named so due to its proximity to the Stock Exchange) stocked edibles and imported tinned delicacies. Kashmiri Gate was within reach to enjoy snacks at tea-time at Carlton's.

The city had expanded rather slowly in the 1930s, along the end of the northern spur of the Ridge. The establishment of Delhi University in 1922, with just three constituent colleges in Kashmiri Gate—St Stephens, Hindu and Ramjas, accelerated the process. Later, Delhi College and College of Commerce were affiliated to it. In course of time, Kirori Mal and Hansraj Colleges joined the cluster of older colleges. Spacious and imposing Halls of Residence were built and residential apartments for resident faculty were commissioned.

What came to be known as the Maurice Nagar Campus was bordered by Malkaganj, Kamla Nagar, Roop Nagar, CC Colony/JJ Colony (now Vijay Nagar).

The Ganda Nala marked the divide between Roop Nagar and Vijay Nagar. Shakti Nagar and Model Town were a short distance away. On another flank, ran the Mall Road, connecting the campus with Timarpur, the Civil Lines and Kashmiri Gate.

It was only in the 1950s, after the end of the War and India's Independence that the Delhi University came of age. The Delhi School of Economics, the Law Faculty, Institute of Economic Growth and Patel Chest Institute added substance to the nucleus of Delhi University.

Colleges had hostels and canteens that quelled the hunger pangs of youngsters away from home. St Stephens called its canteen The Cafe and served snacks that were supposed to be classier—kebabs, mince cutlets, sandwiches, rolls and patties. The dining room maintained a High Table where the faculty ate keeping an eye on the students eating on tables placed lower down. The College was a Christian minority institution and most of those admitted into undergraduate classes came from elite public schools. Celebratory dinners on special occasions were quasi-formal and more elaborate.

The meals in other hostel messes and canteens were lacklustre—patties, samosas, pastries and sandwiches, served with no fancy frills. For a change, one could drop in at the PRRM Coffee House that served *dosai*, *vada* with *sambar*, vegetable cutlets, omelettes and sandwiches. The coffee house near the Students Union Office on Chhatra Marg was more posh and frequented by the 'smarter' set of younger faculty. It was more expensive and the special treats on offer were jelly with fruit salad and ice creams. One could also sip slightly stronger coffee and cold drinks in greater comfort provided by rexine covered sofa-sets.

Popat Kaka ni Lodge, on Raj Niwas Marg, catered to the Gujarati traders who lived in Kamla Nagar. In the 1970s, it served *thepla*, sweet and sour dal, *karhi*, *khichadi*, *rotli*, *chundo*, *muthiya*, *oondiyo*, *dhokla* and more. The place was very reasonably priced and homesick Gujarati students—there were very few then—could relieve their nostalgia one or twice a month. My classmate Suvarna Bhatt had introduced me to Popat Kaka ni Lodge. The food tasted very different from what was served at the Sampats' house in Kamla Nagar. The Sampats were Suvarna's local guardians.

Most of the senior faculty teaching in colleges resided in accommodation provided by the college on its precincts and the younger teachers (almost all of them preparing for the Civil Service examinations) found shelter in shared barsatis or two-room sets with colleagues in Shakti Nagar, Roop Nagar and Model Town. Most availed of the services of part-time cooks. When feeling rich, one could undertake an expedition to Kashmiri Gate to pick up chilled beer or stronger stuff from Exchange Stores plus seekh kebab and tikka from the Khyber.

Parsis and their Food

There were few standalone restaurants outside Connaught Place. The average Indian only visited these restaurants on rare occasions, for celebrating a marriage or a community feast. The memoirs of a Parsi gentleman, Rustom Sorabji, published in a special issue of *The Sunday Standard*, on October 1, 2016, provide rich nuggets of information about the Bawa way of life in Delhi and sheds interesting light on the social life of this small Anglicised community in Delhi during this period. Usually, a cinema theatre was rented for a wedding. His parents had got married in 1929, in the Novelty Cinema (opposite the Dufferin Bridge), which was then owned by Madan & Co. of Calcutta and was available to the Parsis of Delhi for lagan, Navroze and community dinners.

His forefathers had moved to Delhi towards the end of the 1890s. 'My mother's maternal grandfather, Nusserwanji Mehta, had come to Delhi during the Industrial Revolution, in the 1870s or 1880s. It was also the time the Delhi Cloth Mills and Gadodia Textile Mills were being constructed.' Delhi was slowly recovering from the trauma of the revolt and its repression. The Mutiny Memorial had just been constructed on the Ridge.

Most of the Parsi children studied at Queen Mary's school, founded in 1910, run by English missionaries. They were admitted to the section where European children studied. Some later moved to Presentation Convent, situated between the Red Fort and Old Delhi Railway Station, and Modern School on Barakhamba Road.

Mr Fozdar was the chief agent of the first Parsi-owned bank, the Central Bank of India. Central Bank and Godrej had offices in Chandni Chowk. Dinbai Jal D.B. Irani was the first Parsi lady entrepreneur in Delhi, and owner of the Empress Aerated Soda Water factory.

Dr Shroff's Charitable Eye Clinic had opened on the first floor of a small house near Jama Masjid in 1914. As the clinic grew in popularity, prominent citizens of Delhi such as Dr M.A. Ansari, Hakim Ajmal Khan, Rai Bahadur Lala Sultan Singh, and Shri Pyare Lal became associated with it. A trust was formed in 1922 with the goal of building up a dedicated eye hospital. In 1933, the British government awarded Dr Shroff the Kaisar-i-Hind, a gold medal for philanthropy, and helped with getting the hospital equipped with amenities and equipment. It later shifted to Daryaganj.

Parsis in Delhi like in Bombay were strongly loyalist. The King Emperor and the Queen Empress were lovingly referred to as 'Apro Rajo and Rani' (Our King and Queen). Large pictures of the Sovereign couple were prominently displayed in drawing rooms.

Parsis were the pioneers who brought moving pictures to Delhi in the aftermath of the First World War, in 1920, just as the new Imperial Capital was receiving finishing touches. Parsis owned and managed most of the cinema halls like Roxy Cinema (opposite Kashmiri Gate), Novelty and Majestic in Chandni Chowk. Majestic, opposite the Kotwali, was one of the earliest cinema halls with a balcony.

Towards the end of the 1930s or, maybe the beginning of the 1940s, Plaza Cinema was opened in Connaught Place by the Minerva Movitone Company, founded by the Modi brothers Keki and Sohrab. The venue was made available to Delhi Parsis, twice a year, free of charge, to celebrate either the Jameshedji Navroze, Shenshai Navroze or Khordadsal.

The Parsis would meet and greet each other in the foyer of the cinema at about 9.30 a.m., savour some Parsi snacks and soft drinks from the Empress Soda Water Factory. The treat included a special movie screening. Parsi Badminton Club was inaugurated on the roof of Plaza Cinema and the seeds of the Delhi Parsi Social Center were also sown here. As the membership grew, the centre was moved to the Anjuman Grounds at Mathura Road.

The Singer Sewing Machine Company's signboard in Connaught

Place was a prominent landmark. It was somewhere here, opposite the Company's New Delhi show room, that for several years, Parsis met every Saturday till the mid-1940s. In this account in his memoirs, Rustom Sorabjee says:

> Every Saturday, the band, Brass & Bagpipes, played at the Connaught Place Band Stand. While the band played popular tunes, marches and the drums rolled, the bawas enjoyed traditional homemade snacks, *chana-jore-garam* from the many hawkers who used to go around the park, or fresh cream-rolls or pastry from the cakewalla who carried bakery products in a wicker basket. The meet always ended with the band playing '*Rule, Britannia, Rule the Waves*', followed by '*God Save the King*'. Many a time, during the long summer evenings, we also had dinner there. It was usually potluck arranged by families living in Connaught Place and Chelmsford Road railway bungalows. Traditional Parsi festivals or *jashans* like the *Navroze* (Iranian New Year) or *Khordasa* (Prophet's birthday) were celebrated with great enthusiasm.
>
> The Sethnas lived above the cinema. Sometimes during the intra-mission, his wife Tehmina, would send hot tea and bhakras for us Parsis.

The Parsis, though a minuscule community, have left a deep imprint on the city's food. Bhicoo Manekshaw was a Cordon Bleu chef, who provided consultancy to various high-end hotels from the Ashoka and the Oberoi to the ITC, and to the India International Centre from the 1950s till the early 2000s. Her dhansak was a signature dish at the IIC. She also successfully ran Basil and Thyme, a fine-dining restaurant, from the Santushti Complex, near Ashoka Hotel, for years. At the other end of the market there was the Parsi Anjuman on Bahadur Shah Zafar Road that catered to those who lodged in the guest house and walk-ins. Rustom's at the Parsi Anjuman added many more Parsi dishes to its menu like Berry Pulav, Ragda Pattis and cutlets. Over the years the Parsi food has acquired a loyal following in the capital. Delhites have tasted the joys of pure milk ice cream produced by Parsi Dairy and fruit-flavoured sodas and falooda. The 'sweet n sour' taste is no longer alien to the city's chaat loving palate nor do ragda pattis and cutlets and mince puffs look like strangers. When Anahita Dhondy opened SodaBottleOpenerWala in Delhi as a Chef Partner, it was a runaway success. Bhonu moved over from Parsi Anjuman to 31st Milestone in Gurgaon. Though it doesn't have an exclusively Parsi menu, some of the bestsellers are fusion creations, sharing a firm Parsi foundation. One is tempted to add that while at one stage the Parsis in Delhi acted as interpreters of 'Continental' cooking and Indian flavours, subsequently they modified their culinary classics to lure the chaat loving residents of Delhi and tourists. While SodaBottleOpenerWala remains true to Parsi traditional fare Bhonu always has a long line of customers, due to the tweaked fusion finger foods with a hint of Parsi. Keema ghotala and akhuri are ordered less than meaty dahi vadas.

Fourteen

Regional Identities

The Potbelly Rooftop Cafe in Delhi offering Bihari Cuisine
Courtesy: The Potbelly Rooftop Cafe

Amar Sonar Bangla

Bengalis and Delhi go back a long way. The earliest arrivals from the subah of Bengal to the Mughal court in Delhi can be traced to the reign of Akbar, who had begun the annexation of this outlying eastern province. A small trickle of messengers, envoys from the quasi-independent sultans, adventurous traders came as visitors, some to reside for months, but none to settle. The arduous journey to and fro by road and river took months and a long stay in the city was necessary to rest and recuperate after the business had been conducted.

It was only after the Battle of Plassey in 1757 that the East India Company gained control of the diwani (revenue collection) from Mir Jafar—the treacherous nawab they had installed as their puppet. After this, interaction with the Court in Delhi became more frequent. By the turn of the nineteenth century, the British had established themselves as the predominant political power in the land, and though the scion of the Mughals held court in the Red Fort, it was the Governor General in Calcutta who took all decisions as de facto sovereign. Bahadur Shah II appointed Raja Ram Mohan Roy, an eminent Bengali, as his vakil to plead his case for enhanced pension in England. After 1857, even the pretense of Mughal supremacy was given up and India became a Crown colony with the Queen Empress becoming the sovereign.

Calcutta became the Imperial capital. The Government of India moved to the cooler climes of Shimla in the Punjab via Delhi every summer. The city, however, had been deprived of any train connection as a punishment for its display of 'disloyalty' during the 'Sepoy Mutiny'. The train track finally reached the city only in 1864, reducing the journey time between Calcutta and Delhi and the risks en route considerably.

This encouraged some intrepid Bengalis to move to Delhi in search of profitable opportunities. The city destroyed in 1857 was being rebuilt and beckoned the professionals—doctors, engineers, accountants and lawyers as well as clerks and teachers.

The newcomers, as they slowly settled down, built shrines dedicated to goddess Kali (Kali Bari) that, traditionally, have served as spaces where the community could organize cultural events and host festive feasts.

By the turn of the century, there was a thriving Bengali population in the city. Swami Vivekananda, the famous disciple of the great mystic Ramakrishna Paramahamsa, was hosted by Dr H C. Sen when he visited Delhi. This physician had become a living legend and shutters were downed in Chandni Chowk when he died in 1906.

When the capital shifted from Calcutta in 1911, a large wave of Bengalis arrived in Delhi. Most of them were permanent employees of the Imperial government and had been transferred to Delhi. This lot came with their families. At first, they were housed in temporary accommodation in Timarpur. It took a little over a decade before they could move on to the quarters built for government servants in New Delhi in the vicinity of the Gole Market—at a short commuting distance from the Central Secretariat.

Annapurna claims to be the original sweet shop that introduced Bengali sweets to the city. The owners, the Mukherjee family, came from Lahore and set up shop near the fawwara (fountain), opposite Gurudwara Sisganj, in the market area. Annapurna Bhandar was established later, in 1929, by the late Purna Chander Modak.

Mohinimohan Mukherjee moved from Lahore to Delhi in 1920 to work for the Railways but, unfortunately, met with an accident soon after and lost one of his legs. He lost his job but not hope. In 1922, he opened a modest sweet shop to cater to the small Bengali community that resided in the area. In less than a decade, it had become iconic. The shop, when it opened, had interiors resembling a railway coach.

Today it is owned by the third generation of the founder's family and continues to be extremely popular. The menu includes items like *kheer kadam*, *Sita Bhog*, *Kamala bhog*, *sandesh*, *mishti doi* and, of course, the *rasagulla*.

It seems a little odd to me, that the refugees from Punjab have dominated the imagination of historians of Delhi. The over-powering presence of Punjabis has pushed refugees from elsewhere off the centre stage. For instance, the refugees from Bengal hardly find mention in writings of scholars like V.N. Dutta. None of them seem to have found it worth their while to trawl through the telephone directories to find how many Ghoshes, Boses, Chatterjees, Banerjees, Mukherjees, Sens and others have moved from a temporary home to a more respectable address. The Bengali doctors, lawyers, engineers, teachers, journalists, and administrators have always made Delhi their home and contributed to the cultural life of the city. It is not as if they were inactive in the economic life of the city either. Is their invisibility the result of their understated lifestyle? Was this because an average Bengali had little money to spend or had an ingrained distaste for showing off their wealth, if any? Was the Bengali Babu suffering a superiority complex about his cultural attainments and intellectual prowess?

The Bengali immigrants had started coming to Delhi as early as the first quarter of the twentieth century; and in large waves as refugees after Partition. The EPDP or (East Pakistan Displaced Persons) colony was allotted for them. The numbers of refugees increased exponentially after the 1971 liberation of Bangladesh. Hundreds of thousands of Bangladeshis settled down in unauthorized colonies, never to return.

The Bengalis refugees have also left a deep imprint on the food scene in Delhi. Even the non-Bengali sweet sellers prefix the word Bengali on their signage to attract customers. Bengali colonies have also spawned large fish and condiments market to cater to a captive audience. Small eateries set up in these clusters attract tourists and casual visitors from other parts of the city.

Irwin Road, Albert and Havelock Squares in New Delhi came to be recognized as Bengali neighbourhoods, with small clubs and libraries catering to the Bengali diaspora. Many shopkeepers in Gole Market catered to Bengali customers. Saraswati Book Depot sold

Bangla books and household goods could be bought at Kamala Bhandar. Kamalalaya Mistanna Bhandar was known for *chhena* and Mahamaya Stores was the place to visit for sarees and dhotis. The New Delhi Kali Bari and the Raisina Bengali School started functioning at about the same time, in the early 1930s.

The Basu Lodge, set up in 1931, near Gole Market, became the first choice of new arrivals from Bengal looking for temporary lodgings. Although most post-Partition refugees from East Bengal found shelter in Calcutta and other cities in West Bengal, some did find their way to Delhi.

Of these Bengali settlers, some had roots in what was now called East Pakistan. They realized that they would never be able to go back there. They identified themselves as displaced persons from Pakistan. Most of them were government servants, who had small savings, and they carried on a systematic campaign petitioning the government to allot suitable land in New Delhi for their rehabilitation. These efforts bore fruit when a tract of land was earmarked for this purpose, in the arid wilderness on the periphery of South Delhi, in the early 1960s. It came to be known as EPDP (East Pakistan Displaced Persons) colony and was later renamed as Chittaranjan Park or CR Park, which is now famous as a neighbourhood where the Bengali way of life has been preserved. CR Park boasts the largest freshwater fish market and many shacks and stalls that sell Calcutta-style street food—chops, cutlets, *kathi* rolls, *puchka*, and *jhaalmuri* etc.

The iconic Nizam's, from Calcutta, had come to Delhi in the 1960s, with an outlet in the middle circle of Connaught Place, next to the Plaza cinema. Its kathi rolls attracted youngsters on a small budget, movie buffs, and book lovers who frequented a well-stocked second-hand book stall nearby.

In recent years, the Bengali food in the city has moved beyond splurging and slumming on street foods. One can enjoy fine dining, savouring the delicacies prepared in genteel bhadralok households. Oh! Calcutta, came to Delhi in 2003. This restaurant is designed to recreate the ambience of an old-fashioned Calcutta club.

The menu is quite eclectic and showcases home-cooking from

different regions of Bengal, celebratory dishes of the Muslim community, bearing Mughaliya influence. There are also some opulent Western dishes like the Lobster Thermidor, a dish created in honour of the French Emperor Napoleon Bonaparte.

One can enjoy at leisure *hing diye aloor dom* and *luchi*, *bhaja moonger dal* and the crown jewel of a Bengali spread—the *bhapa Ilish*. You can end the meal with the *safedar payesh* or the *daber payesh* (made of tender coconut) and the *bhape sandesh*.

Bengali cuisine has for long remained confined to homes. Things have changed. Youngsters searching for their ethnic-cultural roots as well as others eager to try out various regional cuisines, different from their own home food, have been happily devouring Bengali classics like *rezala*, *kobiraji cutlet*, *kathi rolls*, *fish fry* and even the harder to handle *hilsa*.

The shacks of CR Park for many years served Bengali food to the homesick. But only when Bijoli Grill came to Delhi did it gain respectability. Their offering, however, was largely adapted to suit the North Indian palate. Babumoshai, which opened in a small way in 1999, started a trend with its new restaurant in CR Park. Two other sit-down places, Banzara and Amantran, and half a dozen takeaways, dabba services and catering services, have opened recently. Add to this a roll shop in Vaishali, an eatery in Mayur Vihar, and a takeaway in Munirka Vihar.

Of course, Sunil Ghosh's eatery in Mayur Vihar, which serves 'home-food' to students and young working people, is a budget option. Having spotted the trend, Sumit Banerjee opted out of a marketing career to start a takeaway from his CR Park home.

For all those from Kolkata who had been missing the Shiraz-type biryani, Shonar Bangla in Munirka Vihar offered some relief.

Bengali fare is now widely available.

Madrasis in Delhi

When the British ruled India and there were no signs that they would ever cease to do so, a joke used to do the rounds in New Delhi that anyone trying to do business with the government had to negotiate two hurdles—the chaprasi (peon)—the officer's gatekeeper—and the powerful 'Madrasi', who was sitting inside. Madrasi was a generic term, applied without discrimination, to anyone who was not a North Indian or a Bengali. For the North Indian, everyone from peninsular India was a Madrasi.

Even before the Imperial capital had shifted from Calcutta to Delhi, a small number of South Indians had registered their presence in the city. Every year in the summer, the government moved from Calcutta to Simla, and camped in Delhi. The first lot of Madrasis travelled with the government to Simla in the summer. Most of the 'Madrasis' were employed in clerical positions and served British officers as stenographers, typists, personal assistants and account keepers. Many rose to supervisory and middle-level administrative positions in government. The most dramatic rise was registered by the likes of V.P. Menon, who steadily climbed the ladder, from the lowly position of clerk-stenographer to the rank of a Secretary, through sheer dint of hard work, integrity and efficiency by the time India became independent. He became secretary to Sardar Patel and assisted him with the integration of princely states in the Indian Union. There were many others who had risen from the ranks. At that time, the higher echelons of the government were the preserve of the coveted, heaven-born Indian Civil Service.

In the inter-War years, there was only a sprinkling of Indian officers in the Indian Civil Service and most of them were posted as district officers in the provinces. Menon's case illustrates the qualities that made the self-effacing, hardworking Madrasi, of unimpeachable integrity, such a formidable obstacle for power-brokers and wheeler-dealers. Many British officers valued the advice of their Madrasi subordinates. There were dozens of hardworking, English-speaking, stern-looking, South Indian officers and clerks, who frowned on the fixers and contract seekers wanting to get access to the influential white officers.

Another South Indian, who had humble origins and made a name for himself was K.R. Narayanan. He served in the Indian Foreign

Service (IFS), and after retirement, joined politics. After winning three elections to the Lok Sabha, he became the Vice-President and, finally, the President of India.

Before joining the IFS, he had gone for higher studies to the University of London and London School of Economics. After he returned from England, he continued to lodge in modest hostelries and had his meals in nondescript Madrasi eateries.

V.P. Menon's biography, *V.P. Menon: The Unsung Architect of Modern India,*[37] written by his great-granddaughter, Narayani Basu, recounts through anecdotes the lives of South Indians in Delhi in the pre-War years. The origin of South Indian messes and hotels (providing boarding and lodging to unmarried government servants or those temporarily employed in banks and private offices) dates back to this period.

The building opposite P Block, in the outer circle of Connaught Place, was known as the Madras Hotel. South-Indian style meals were served here in a no-frills cafeteria.

Over the years Madrasi messes and cheap tiffin joints serving the standard fare of *idli-dosa-sambar* evolved and expanded into multi-layered specialty restaurants.

Madras Coffee House

Interestingly, the iconic Madras Coffee House was not opened by a South Indian immigrant but by an enterprising Punjabi, Hem Chand Jain, in 1935. With the passage of time, the Madras Coffee House has slid into anonymity. Only half-hearted attempts are sporadically made by its owners to spruce it up. Mayank Austen Soofi, a keen observer of Delhi's city life, was constrained to comment in his food blog, not long ago that, 'you must hang out in the Madras Coffee House because it is so aggressively shabby, so determined not to look attractive, so unwilling to please anyone...In the eatery's quiet environ, the dignified waiters stand behind a far-away counter. They are neither very cheery, nor rude, and this too is a relief.'

The coffee house has had many incarnations. It was, initially, a modest ice-cream parlour which was owned by the Hem Chand Jain family who moved from Punjab to Delhi. Then it became a Shanghai Restaurant and Bar which was a popular haunt for the British soldiers during the War. They brought over their lady friends, danced with them to music of a live band, ordered Chinese food, and sipped on their cocktails. Indians were not allowed in this restaurant, even though the owner was an Indian national. All this belongs to a forgotten past.

Post-Independence, the restaurant became a pure vegetarian milk bar, called Respo Bar. Owing to its prime location and popularity, Jain transformed it into a fully functional coffee house in the 1950s, the Madras Coffee House.

This restaurant today has retreated into a cocoon. In urgent need of a facelift, it continues to exude a seedy charm, drawing those who revel in reverse snobbery, where, as Mayank comments, 'You can spend hours here over a novel and endless plates of idlis—hearing the murmurs of vulgar commoners walking outside, fancy yourself to be a cool radical.'

The elegant South Indian restaurant Naivedyam, in Hauz Khas village recreates the serene ambience of a temple, with wood carved interiors, waiters dressed as devotees, and incense burning on the altar of a small shrine. There are South Indian eateries in all suburban colonies in NCR catering to different budgets and tastes. Most have built up a sizeable clientele of North Indians.

Sagar Ratna

The Sagar Ratna restaurant is an iconic Delhi haunt for South Indian food. Its founder, Jayaram Banan, still remembers the day in the mid-1960s when he fled from his home in Udupi (in Karnataka).

From earning Rs 18 per month, washing dishes at a canteen in Mumbai, to setting up the Sagar Ratna restaurant chain—with an annual turnover of more than Rs 70 crore now—the rise of Dosa King Jayaram, from rags to riches, has all the elements of a fairy tale.

The tide of fortune turned in his favour when he decided to shift to Delhi in 1973, where his brother worked as the manager of an Udupi restaurant. Banan won the contract to set up the canteen at CEL (Central Electronics Limited, a Government of India enterprise) in 1974, for an 'investment of under Rs 2,000'. He had to wait for twelve years to open his first restaurant in December 1986, in Delhi's Defence Colony Market, with a team of three cooks, by investing all his savings of Rs 5,000. He named his 40-seater outlet 'Sagar' and served South Indian staples like *idli*, *dosa* and *sambar*. According to Sagar Ratna's owner, 'Back then, one could only get Haldiram ka dosa in the name of Udupi cuisine in Delhi.' In fact, authentic dosas were only available at two fine-dining and comparatively expensive restaurants, Woodlands at the Lodhi Hotel and Dasaprakasa at the Ambassador. Just four years later, Banan bought out Woodlands, the restaurant he had once competed against. Swagath was opened in 2001, a short distance from his first Sagar restaurant in Defence Colony, that had in intervening years upgraded itself to Sagar Ratna. Swagath's *prawn gassi*, *fish fry* and *neer dosas* became cult hits. The restaurants were patronized both by the common man and by hot-shot politicians. Swagath serves exotic coastal cuisines from Mangaluru, Chettinad and the Malabar regions.

Dakshin

Saket Dakshin opened in 2001. Dakshin is unique for its presentation of southern Indian cuisine from Andhra Pradesh, Tamil Nadu, Karnataka and Kerala. *Urli* and *adukku* are dishes which originated in an earlier period, in an atmosphere epitomizing the diversity of South Indian cuisines. Dakshin offers dishes including pan-fried sole, deep-fried prawns, *nandu puttu* (crab meat tossed with onions, ginger and green chilies) and *veinchina mamsam* (lamb with onions, coriander, chillies and a mix of Indian spices). The ingredients and spices for each dish are authentic and sourced from their home regions. Dakshin even offers little-known preparations that are staples in homes down south but difficult to find in most restaurants. The must-try dishes include *meen moilee* (fish in coconut milk), *Andhra kodi biryani* (with chicken), *kori suka* (chicken tossed in a spicy coconut paste) and Chettinad chops (pan-fried lamb chops).

Today, Dakshin is known to serve some of the most authentic food from communities across Andhra Pradesh, Telangana, Tamil Nadu, Kerala, Karnataka and Puducherry. Some of their popular dishes such as the banana dosa, made with five varieties of bananas, are still made fresh from the Iyer's trolley during each meal. Then there is the Dakshin *yera*—deep-fried prawns, marinated in a house masala, which has continued to win hearts for its robust flavours and juicy texture.

Understandably then, the banana dosa and Dakshin *yera* feature right on top of the list, as do the *elaneer payasam* (kheer made with tender coconut) and *mukanni* ice cream (house ice cream made using three fruits: jackfruit, mango and banana).

The décor and general ambience at different outlets that serve southern fare is similar. There are wooden statues or inlay paintings recreating scences of Shri Krishna exhorting the Pandava prince Arjun to fight at Kurukshetra, inspiring him with Srimad Bhagvadgita. Food is served on gleaming thalis, lined with green banana leaf, by waiters dressed in traditional attire of white shirts and veshti. Only the prices vary according to the location.

Prompted by the popular response to Dakshin, other five-star hotels opened their doors to regional cuisines, at least, periodically, by organizing 'pop ups'.

My interactions with specialist home chefs like Mrs Pillai and Prima Kurien, both specialists in cuisines of Kerala, at such 'pop ups' have made me sensitive to what the diners in Delhi like and what they remain indifferent to. I encountered one at Saket Select City Walk and the other at the Oberoi Gurgaon. Both the ladies have serious other interests, including painting and Tanjore glass paintings, but as far as I am concerned, they have helped me appreciate how distinctly differentiated southern Indian foods have become in Delhi in this decade, the 2020s. No longer is the label 'Madrasi' applied to eateries. It is not just that those who visit ethnic/regional eateries regularly articulate their preferences in terms of Tamil, Andhra, Kerala, and Karnataka cooking, but many are familiar with the sub-regional distinctions. Non-vegetarian recipes are commonly encountered. The city today has a fair sprinkling of specialized outlets in almost the entire NCR.

The heated debate rages on: Who can claim to be an asli Dilliwala and what is the main culinary stream in the city? It is true that the original settlers in Shahjahanabad were from the Punjab, Kashmir, Baniyas from Rajasthan as well as Kayasthas and Khatris from present day Uttar Pradesh. Some members of these communities had served as high-ranking officials in the Mughal administration or were respected courtiers, but what about the residents of older Imperial cities who dwelt in Siri and Tughlakabad?

There are many other miniscule ethnic minorities who have shaped and are shaping the foodscape in Delhi—the Parsis, Biharis, Nepalis and people from the North East. Anahita Dhondy, the partner chef of a Parsi restaurant, recalls, 'I grew up in Delhi. There are 300 Parsi families here, we speak Gujarati, follow all Parsi traditions and talk a lot about food'. Kashmiri Wazwan is no longer exotic. The taste of paradise can be savoured from Delhi Haat and Chor Biazzare at Bikaner House to smaller outlets and takeaways like Mattamal in Gurgaon.

When the Asian Games were over, the flats and double-storied apartments were handed over to the governments and large corporations in the public sector. This area soon became the preferred eating out hub of the residents of affluent adjacent colonies like South Extension Part I and II. Defence Colony Market always had interesting options like Moet's, Colonels Kebab and Swagath. In the back lanes, kebab sellers and kiosks of chole-bhature/kulche cater to the needs of shop assistants, sales boys and girls, drivers and errand runners who frequent the market. One side of South Ex had jewellers, branded clothes, electronics and music shops. Across the road Ring Road from South Extension Part II, stood sari stores, stationers, bookstores and a few stores retailing electronics. The Bengali Sweets at the corner is the most popular eatery here. Like its namesakes in other parts of the city it sold chaat, snacks, and South Indian short meals besides sweets.

Assertion of the Bihari identity has introduced the capital's diner to sub-regional dishes like *handi*-cooked *Champaran gosht* and delicacies from Mithila's kitchens. Purvaiyya food festivals and pop-ups in restaurants have cleared many cobwebs.

Naga Kitchens, once the rarest of rare sightings, are not so uncommon now. The trendsetter at Green Park has a Naga thali which can be ordered with a bottle of beer. Pork is cooked with minimal spicing and interesting green leafy vegetables. For those who can bear the scorching heat of chili, there is *bhut jholakiya* lurking in the wings. Similar restaurants have come up in Vasant Plaza and Aurobindo Place.

Fusion and improvisation have lifted up the banal chow mein. It has found its way into parantha, samosa and the momo. Paneer dosai, hilsa chokha, sandwich dhokla have moved up the hierarchy from streets to food courts and even fine-dining restaurants.

Availability of once exotic vegetables and fruits like avocado and kiwi, a variety of fish, and imported wines and cheeses have transformed menus in stand-alone chef-owned or partnered restaurants that are concept driven.

The palate of youngsters has changed dramatically with the constantly changing demographic profile. Bihari, Nepali and the North Easterners along with Oriya, Rajasthani, Jharkhandi and Chattisgarhi, all have found a place in Delhi and NCR. The predominantly Punjabi refugee taste is slowly being diluted.

What we are witnessing is no less than a ferment of pan-Indian taste.

Fifteen

City of Refugees

Kake Da Hotel, Delhi (1976)
Source: Kake Da Hotel Official Website

During the Second World War, ugly asbestos-roofed hutments had mushroomed in the newly-built capital to house the Tommies (British and American soldiers), giving it the look of a sprawling slum. Despite the years of scarcity and suffering, political instability and social upheavals, Delhi never ceased to grow. It attracted immigrants from all over the land, who were drawn to Delhi with the hope that this was where fortune favoured the brave.

The city's infrastructure was therefore already under great stress on the eve of Independence when the country was partitioned. The massive influx of refugees hit the city like an avalanche that threatened to bury it. Delhi's population was just a little over 200,000 in 1901, it had swollen to 1.44 million by 1951. It was estimated that of this number, about 4,50,000 were refugees from West Punjab.

Scholars who have laboriously studied the demographic profile of the Punjabi refugees concluded that about one-sixth of the refugee population originated from Lahore. Almost 40,000 came from Rawalpindi, a little over 36,000 from Multan. Displaced persons from Shahapura and Gujranwala accounted for roughly 25,000 each. Most of the uprooted Punjabis came from cities and were engaged in trade and commerce.

There was scarcely a spot in Delhi that was not claimed by the destitute, displaced persons who kept flooding in from across the border. Kingsway Camp alone sheltered over 3,00,000 refugees. The number kept increasing and by 1951 the figure touched 4,80,000 refugees. Some were later moved to Irwin Road, Panchkuin Road and the renamed Queensway, Janpath. Within two or three years, a fortunate few were allotted small shops in Municipal Market and Shankar Market.

The government accorded top priority to rehabilitation of the refugees and innocent victims of communal carnage. A separate ministry was put in charge of this task and the Delhi District Administration worked around the clock on a war footing. Refugee resettlement colonies were planned in twenty locations in different parts of the city.

Thousands of acres of land were acquired for this purpose and refugee colonies came up in the southern part of the city. After the homeless were settled, four areas of the city emerged, that blurred the boundaries separating the different cities within Delhi. Malviya Nagar in the south, Rajendra Nagar, Patel Nagar, Moti Nagar, Ramesh Nagar and Tilak Nagar in the west, Gandhi Nagar in Shahdara to across the river on the eastern side, with the centre comprising the 'Old City'—Chandni Chowk, Bara Hindu Rao, Sabzi Mandi and Sadar.

By the 1960s, the limits of Delhi extended beyond Kailash and Qutub in the south, covering Faridabad in the south-east, Gurgaon in the south-west and well beyond Najafgarh in the west. In the east, Shahdara and Ghaziabad grew into densely populated colonies, an unplanned mess of industrial units and residential accommodation. Sarai Rohilla, Jhandewalan, Paharganj, on to Shakur Basti along old Rohtak Road, filled up to bursting point.

Old Rajinder Nagar is sandwiched between Shankar Road and Pusa Road. Original allottees were rehabilitated in asbestos-roofed hutments on 50 square yard plots on which a small courtyard and two tiny rooms were constructed. These stood in stark contrast with art-deco bungalows on Pusa Road. The inhabitants were in no position to eat out, so the colony had no fancy eateries even in the main market. Clay tandoors, sunk underground (on the pavement), did lively business selling hot *tandoori roti*.

Beyond lay Patel Nagar East and West, Shadipur depot, Moti Nagar, Raja Garden, Rajouri Garden and Punjabi Bagh. Villages like Shadipur, abode of puppeteers, jugglers and crafts persons, remained isolated and ill-connected with both Old and New Delhi.

Rajinder Nagar and Patel Nagar were avoidable wildernesses till 1950. The Indian Agricultural Research Institute, Pusa Institute, had relocated from Bihar to the countryside (Village Inderpuri) here, with hundreds of acres of agricultural land allotted to it. The road leading to the research station, Pusa Road, was named after it, but very little traffic passed on it. The large tract of wasteland that stretched between the Ridge and the Pusa Institute was earmarked for major refugee resettlements.

Sometime in 1971, I shifted from Roop Nagar to Old Rajinder Nagar, when I got a new job in the Jawaharlal Nehru University. I rented a barsati that had a kitchen, but lacking the skills and inclination to cook rotis on my own, I was dependent on a lady named Kushaliya who 'manned' a tandoor on the lane leading to the main market.

Many women in Old Rajinder Nagar sent children to her tandoor with dough kneaded at home to get the roti cooked at the rate of 2 paise per roti. If you brought some ghee along you could take back *tandoori parantha* that would stay soft longer than *tandoori roti*. One could buy rotis at 10 paise per roti and eat these with the bharta or dal bought from the same outlet.

I learnt a great deal about what the refugees ate when they first came to Delhi after Partition and how cooking changed as they struck new roots from Kunda Lal Talwar, my landlord in Old Rajinder Nagar. His brother, Bhagat Ram Talwar, had driven Netaji Subhas Bose across the Indian border to Afghanistan, when he escaped from house arrest in Kolkata. Talwar Sahab remembered very vividly what the family had suffered and how it had stayed together surviving by sharing what little could be brought to the table. Years later, when I was assisting Manohar Shyam Joshi in scripting the TV serial *Buniyaad*, I got an opportunity to work with the great author Krishna Sobti. She generously shared with me how refugees in Delhi had tried to preserve tastes of the homes they had left behind. It was not long before sub-regional identities merged under an overarching category of 'Refugees'. The dhaba may have asserted that it was Lahori, Multani, Amritsari or Peshawari, but the food was more or less homogenized.

There were other areas in New Delhi, some even in South Delhi, where tandoors by the roadside did brisk business. In 1968, when I went to the home of my friend, Prayag Shukla, in Greater Kailash II, Jyotiji cooked delicious *rajma* and the hot rotis were brought from the tandoor when we were ready to eat. In Hauz Khas and South Extension also, one could pick up a home-style meal of *dal-roti* supplemented with a seasonal *sabzi—bharta* or *aloo palak*—from one of these shacks.

Karol Bagh, where the Ridge tapered off, also became a major settlement of displaced persons. The first lot of settlers had come here when their villages were acquired to build the new capital. These were villagers who had lived for generations on not very fertile land near Sabzi Mandi and villages Madhopura, Jaisinghpur and Raja Ganj. A majority of them were Muslims who were butchers, shoemakers, weavers, dyers and carpenters. They were allotted land in Regarpura. The better off among the uprooted, who could invest a little money, set up shops and built houses in Karol Bagh, till that time known only for the Unani Medical College and the herb garden. The newcomers populated the Faiz Road, Anand Parbat and the New Rohtak Road. During the Partition, a large segment of Muslim population left for Pakistan and their properties were allotted to Hindu refugees or were occupied by them.

Food on the roadside in Karol Bagh catered primarily to the taste of shoppers who made a beeline for bargains at the stalls run by Punjabi refugees. To begin with, most of the roadside snack vendors sold *chaat, pakora* and *samosa* along with *lassi* and *kulfi.* Years passed and some assumed the form of a popular affordable 'Indian' style restaurant. The by-lanes branching off from the main roads housed some South Indian messes like the Rasan, which met the needs of the immigrants from peninsular India boarding in lodges in this area.

Karol Bagh was connected via Idgah and Farash Khana to Delhi University. As normalcy returned, real estate in Karol Bagh appreciated. The stretch of Pusa Road from the Western Extension Area to the roundabout, where it met the Shankar Road, attracted the nouveau riche, who began building large art-deco houses here. For decades, no proper eatery or restaurant appeared here.

The refugees who had managed to cross the border before or just after the Partition, with some of their savings and valuables, set themselves up in new colonies that were not as dingy and congested as the Old Rajinder Nagar or Patel Nagar. They bought plots ranging from 300 square yards to 2000 square yards in Punjabi Bagh and Rajouri Garden and built large houses there. The residents of these colonies tried to replicate the opulence of the posh residential areas in Lahore and other large cities in Pakistan that they had left behind. There were clubs, large parks and gurudwaras in these privately developed colonies.

Prithipal Singh Vasudev, better known as Vasu to his friends, gave me a conducted tour of this part of Delhi that had come up beyond the Ring Road. He had studied in the elite Aitchison College in Lahore before the Partition. The institution was set up to educate children of chieftains and princelings. Vasu was a playwright and worked as tourist guide for a living. He spent almost all his spare time in Sapru House, discussing theatre and films, politics and society with friends like us, in the lawns. His father was a chartered engineer, his brother served in the Indian Army and his sister was with Air India. The family had bought one of the larger parcels of land in Punjabi Bagh, next to the club and the gurudwara. Their neighbours also had spacious bungalows with lawns and kitchen gardens. One of my father's Sindhi friends from Mukteshwar, Mr Makhijani, had built a house in this locality.

I still remember the taste of the *sayal gosht* he had lovingly cooked for me himself on a rainy day, when I had descended on him, despite the roads being water-logged. Makhijani uncle welcomed me warmly with 'Aao Pushpesh jaani, I had lost all hope that you would ever show up.' Then, he quietly pulled up his pyjamas and walked through the slush to the nearby butcher's before I could protest or offer to accompany him. He returned with the mutton that he lovingly cooked himself, with his wife keeping a running commentary, trying futilely to supervise.

Beyond Rajinder Nagar and Patel Nagar, other settlements came up—Raja Garden, Ramesh Garden and Kirti Nagar. Another friend, Sharad Dutt, lived with his mother and uncle and his wife in Kirti Nagar, in an independent house on a much smaller plot, approximately 250 square yards. Sharad, passionate about music, literature, films and theatre worked as a producer in Doordarshan. As a government servant, he was allotted a flat in Bengali Market, which he used as a bachelor's pad. The family hailed from Jhang and was strictly vegetarian, though Sharad was an omnivore and loved non-vegetarian delicacies from Old Delhi. What was cooked in the Brahmin kitchen at home eschewed onions and garlic. His lunch box was lovingly packed by his aged mother with *bharta*, *saag*, *gobhi* and stuffed *karelas* that were irresistible. Kirti Nagar had not become predominantly a timber and furniture market till the 1970s. All these memories of meals in different houses come rushing back as I try to remember how the refugees from Punjab and Sindh had tried to preserve their food culture.

As the refugees made good, they shifted from these colonies in northern and western Delhi to southern and south-western Delhi. Many a family built Spanish-style large houses in Kailash Colony and Greater Kailash.

Professor V.N. Dutta has interestingly analysed the Delhi telephone directory of 1979 to show that Khatris and Aroras, with surnames such as Khanna, Kapur, Chopra, Tandon, Malhotra, Seth, Puri, Sondhi, Talwar, Sahni, Mehra, Nagpal, Chawla, Taneja, Juneja, Tuteja, Dhingra, and Grover, dominated business and services in the city. Many of them by now resided in upmarket neighbourhoods like Golf Links, Vasant Vihar, Greater Kailash, Lajpat Nagar, Defence Colony, Maharani Bagh, and Bungalow Road, moving on and leaving behind the memories of deprivation and degradation as refugees.

Even those who had not tasted spectacular success, did well enough to set up businesses like retail shops, stores for general merchandise and workshops. These establishments were concentrated in Chandni Chowk, Connaught Place, Ajmal Khan and Karol Bagh.

As the refugee rehabilitation and resettlement project was drawing to a close, the government began the work of building government offices and residential accommodation for government servants in independent India. The CPWD was entrusted with the task that gathered momentum. Massive office blocks to house ministries came up—Rail Bhawan, Krishi Bhawan, Udyog Bhawan, Vayu Sena Bhawan, Nirman Bhawan, Yojna Ayog and the Reserve Bank building. The construction continued to erect auditoria and convention centres like Vigyan Bhawan.

These government offices had canteens outsourced to contractors to provide lunch and snacks to hundreds of employees who worked their every day. No one gave thought to cooking nutritious meals with changing menus to cater to the subordinate staff. The officers seldom used these facilities that were poorly maintained. At lunch time, the low-level employees could be seen thronging the roundabouts in the winter sun and eating out of their tiffin boxes. *Khomcha walas* selling fruit chaat or freshly-cut vegetable salad did brisk business in spring and early summer, and during monsoon the lunch packed from home was carried to the canteen, with the request to an obliging waiter to heat it.

Provisions had to be made for housing the ever increasing number of government employees. For those occupying the higher echelons of bureaucracy, spacious flats were built with lawns surrounding apartment blocks in Moti Bagh and Meena Bagh. Most of the residents in these colonies had access to an official or personal car. Middle-level officers were housed in Kidwai Nagar, East and West, and on Satya Marg in slightly scaled-down flats that were still quite comfortable and had small lawns in front or at the rear. These had at least two bedrooms, a separate living and dining room, alongside a servant quarter. Some preferred to be allotted accommodation in Lodhi Colony, where double-storied flats had been built, as the area had much better access to markets and schools.

Vinay Nagar was marked out for clerical staff and at one time sprawled from Raj Nagar to the Bhikaji Cama Place. Over the years, it had been split into smaller sub-colonies: Sarojini Nagar, Netaji Nagar, Nauroji Nagar and Laxmibai Nagar. Peons, drivers and other menial employees had their one-room tenements at Sewa Nagar.

The town planners marked out space for a shopping complex in all these government colonies, but no provision was made for proper restaurants. Perhaps it was understood that the officer class would entertain either at home or at a club. The police officers had access to their messes, as did the Army officers. Those lower down the pecking order, it was believed, it seems, should be quite content with a 'sweet and a snack shop' in their market. It was only when there was a severe crunch on governmental accommodation and senior officers were constrained to accept accommodation 'lower than their entitlement' that these omissions became glaring.

There were some residential areas for government servants that enjoyed much better access to food outlets, restaurants and popular eateries. These were Rabindra Nagar, Bharti Nagar and Kaka Nagar due to their proximity to Khan Market, Lodhi Road and Pandara Road market.

The bungalows on Shah Jahan Road and Humayun Road, in the vicinity of the Sujan Singh Park apartment complex that was developed in 1945, had the advantage of easy access to Pandara Road. Respectable hotels like the Ambassador and the Lodhi were within reach.

Pindi, the oldest eatery on the block, started as a roadside shack in 1948. K.L. Wadhwa, a refugee from Rawalpindi, began selling *channa-kulcha* at India Gate for a living. He shifted to Pandara Road only in 1954, when allotted a small shop as compensation for the loss suffered during Partition.

It was not long before the small Pandara Road Market prospered as a food court. The restaurants, Havemore and Gulati, followed in 1959, and over the next few decades, they and Pindi propelled Pandara Road Market to an iconic status. After the 1960s, the India International Centre also attracted its members and their guests as a watering hole where one could enjoy a decent meal in congenial company.

The retired government officers kept a sharp eye on building a home in Delhi after they would have to move out of sarkari accommodation. Comparatively large plots were auctioned to retired government servants in the area that later developed as Vasant Vihar. This had from the beginning provisions for up-market shopping complexes with a sprinkling of air-conditioned restaurants, quality bakers, fruit shops and florists.

As property prices sky rocketed, many of these retired officials sold off their bungalows or partnered with a builder to raise multi-storied apartments. A number of the houses were rented out to diplomats and the owners moved out to other parts of South Delhi like Safdarjung Development Area and Safdarjung Enclave. Vasant Vihar has provided a captive clientele not only to the eateries in shopping complexes of different blocks—A, B, C and D but also to restaurants and fast food outlets in the Priya Complex.

Partition and the flood of refugees had left the government with no option but to make drastic changes to Lutyen's Imperial designs. Planned and unplanned resettlement of the burgeoning population remained for years a work in progress. What impacted on the foods and flavours of Delhi was the constant churn. The refugees as they prospered moved residences and shops from make-shift camps and colonies to better suburbs. Government servants also moved from smaller to larger accommodation, closer to the more central prestigious locations. However, they retained ties with relatives and friends who continued to populate the neighbourhoods they had left behind. Eatries selling snacks and sweets, bakeries, pickle and spice shops that strove to preserve a 'taste of home' retained old customers. The situation was akin to ties maintained between residents of the Walled City and those who had first shifted to the Civil Lines and later to New Delhi.

Sixteen

Enter the 'Dragon': the Private Developers

Select Citywalk Mall, Delhi
Source: Wikipedia

The Beginning and End of Urban Planning

In the year 1960, private real-estate developers in Delhi were permitted to build colonies. The New Delhi Administration's Master Plan for the city was proposed. The Delhi Development Authority (DDA) had been created in 1957 under the provisions of the Delhi Development Act 'to promote and secure the development of Delhi'. In the next decade, the 1960s, Delhi was developed by them at a hectic pace. Even the interruptions of the war with China in 1962 and with Pakistan in 1965 didn't dampen the enthusiasm and entrepreneurial drive of these builders.

The DDA's mandate was to provide housing primarily for lower- and middle-income groups, with a very small quota of flats to be built for the higher-income group. Even these were out of reach for many of the people being targeted. The allotment was done by draw of lots and the cost was recovered in instalments, spread over decades. Understandably, there was great demand for DDA accommodation in South Delhi (Hauz Khas, Vasant Kunj, Munirka, Saket, East of Kailash) or in areas that had good connectivity with central Delhi, or had access to public transport, education and healthcare. The far-flung developments like Rohini, Narela, Dilshad Garden, and Shalimar Bagh had fewer takers. There were issues about the quality of construction, poor design and also corruption in drawing of lots. The transfer of DDA flats by primary allottees on Power of Attorney developed into a regular black market. As DDA did not make adequate provisions for restaurants, sweet and snack shops, schools and hospitals, service providers set up their own establishments in the vicinity of these colonies.

DLF had the first mover advantage and built up a land bank of hundreds of thousands of square yards in Delhi and adjacent Haryana.

The company had developed residential colonies in different parts of South Delhi. Hauz Khas, Green Park, Safdarjang Development Area, South Extension I and II, Kailash Colony, Greater Kailash I, II and III were developed by DLF, including the fashionable M-Block Market in Greater Kailash. Not only were large plots demarcated but the real estate company built—as stipulated by government regulations—shopping centers, private schools and spacious parks within these colonies.

Defence Colony was earmarked for war veterans who had served in the armed forces and land was allotted to servicemen by the government. This semi-planned development catered to the needs of a more affluent class than the indigent refugees—retired government servants from the upper echelons. These 'upmarket' colonies had shopping complexes very different from the Sarojini Nagar Market that catered to residents of small double-storied flats—mostly clerks.

This residential area had a cosmopolitan character from the beginning. Many of the tenants were highly successful surgeons, doctors, dancers and professionals. Defence Colony's restaurants, Colonel Kebabs and Moet's, enjoyed a captive clientele that could afford to spend more than the government servants who had fixed emoluments.

These markets had specialty restaurants like Hong Kong in the M-Block market in Greater Kailash II, and a few years later, the Wall of China also in G.K. II, and the Imperial Garden, now relocated and renamed as Nanking in Vasant Kunj, all three specializing in Chinese cuisine. Bakeries offering more varied fare to discerning customers also came up.

By the mid-1960s, the development of an elegant diplomatic enclave, officially named Chanakyapuri, was complete. The stately Shanti Path ran from Teen Murti House to the Ring Road with Moti Bagh flanking it after the bridge over the railway line. The largest embassies were the American and the Chinese. Many smaller countries flew their flags in exotically designed buildings. The two driving lanes of Shanti Path were separated by a broad patch of lawn and flower beds. The intersecting roads evoked the heritage and principals of Nehruvian foreign policy—Panchshila Marg, Nyaya Marg, Kautilya Marg.

The neighbourhood soon established itself as among the most exclusive residential areas. Its south-western boundary, marked by Sardar Patel Marg (earlier Kitchner Road) that leads to the international airport, was flanked by the forest land of the Ridge. The Indians who built houses in Chanakyapuri in the diplomatic enclave were members of the old elite moving in from Old Delhi. These included Lala Shri Ram's extended family, Sahu Shanti Prasad Jain of Bennett Coleman Co., publishers of the *Times of India*, and others like the Dehlvi family, publishers of Shama and Sushma, and the Thapars—Romesh and Raj—who published *Seminar*.

Malvika Singh, daughter of Romesh Thapar, recollects in her book:

> Down the road stayed Clovis Maksoud, Ambassador of the Arab League, who entertained guests ranging from Indira Gandhi and Krishna Hutheesing, to journalists and film makers, poets and painters, socialites and bureaucrats, all [of whom] came together for an evening of good conversation, delicious Middle Eastern food and new connections. [The] wife of the Chinese ambassador taught my mother a range of wonderful unusual dishes, prawns tossed lightly in rice flour and then put into bubbling hot peanut oil for one minute flat. Not a second longer. Most succulent I have ever eaten. Chinese food at her table and later at my mother's table was nothing like the Punjabified Chinese cuisine at many restaurants in Delhi.

Sprawling, well-designed private residences of the ultra-rich came up in Chanakyapuri and a suitably sophisticated market place developed on Malcha Marg to meet their gastronomic requirements. Decent restaurants offering Oriental—Chinese and Japanese dishes—as well as traditional Mughal delicacies opened their doors: Fujiya and Mikado were the most popular. It was only after the deluxe hotels like Maurya were built towards the end of the 1980s, that their ethnic and specialty restaurants carved out niches as trend-setting fine-dining destinations.

The four clearly recognizable refugee areas changed the face of Delhi, as these colonies have acted as independent nuclei for further extension. The colonies were planned as self-contained units, each provided with a small market, places of worship, bank, police stations, schools, and post office. They remained islands, but not isolated from the life in Delhi. The houses were usually not multi-storeyed or spacious. On the main roads, there were larger houses, but within the colony single-storey hutments accommodated low-income families.

People in these colonies have tried to recreate their former lives. Walking in these areas, one feels as though one were in the Dev Nagar, Krishna Nagar or Ram Nagar colonies of Lahore. The Sindhis concentration was in Mayfair Gardens, close to Hauz Khas.

People expected that things would change with the passage of time, the construction of the Ring Road and improvement in the city bus service.

Changing Modes of Commuting and Food

The city spread dramatically and at great speed with the refugee settlements and development of colonies for government servants. This highlighted the problems of commuting from home to the place of work and also to negotiate longer distances than ever before for shopping, entertainment outings with family and so on. The introduction of new modes of travel within the city profoundly changed the manner in which the residents of Delhi, high and low, ate and entertained.

Before Independence, residents of Delhi were dependent on bicycles to commute from home to their place of work. Tongas were used to and from the railway station or for rare family outings. Taxis were rare and an extravagance. Very few cars were seen on the roads in the late 1940s and 1950s. When eating out, therefore, most people were restricted to their neighbourhoods. This is why eateries like Karnataka Sangh and Tamil Sangam in Moti Bagh and Ramakrishna Puram (R.K. Puram) started attracting residents. They offered vegetarian fare, mostly tiffin items like *dosa*, *idli*, *vada* and a fixed thali. The ambience was not overpowering like a Western-style restaurant where one felt constrained to be formal. Here the family could happily slurp and disregard spoons and use one's fingers. Few, then, could discern the differences in the taste of *sambar* or the texture of idlis at the two outlets. Proximity to the Swami Malai Mandir also contributed to a sizeable patronage provided by visitors to the shrine. I remember being treated to meals at both places by hosts who lived in government accommodation in these colonies but they did not become regular haunts which memories are made of! After a couple of visits, the food became monotonous. It had no nostalgic appeal for Delhites who didn't belong to the Tamil or Kannadiga diaspora.

The Delhi Transport Undertaking was established in May 1948 and connected far-flung areas with central Delhi—Connaught Place and the Secretariat. Commuters took some time to get used to the city bus service. The public transport system was not able to cope with the population growth post-1947. Motor transport was very limited and controlled by private operators.

The burgeoning city, bursting at its seams, contributed to the food culture in most unexpected ways. In the 1960s, the Ring Road project had just about completed girdling the twin cities—both New and Old—with a highway that boasted it would be unhindered by traffic lights and ensure smoother, unimpeded flow of traffic. However, hopes of connecting the periphery to the core were soon belied as the city continued to spill over and beyond the Ring Road.

Institutions like the All-India Institute of Medical Sciences (AIIMS) and the Safdarjung Hospital displayed an insatiable appetite for land. From the crossing on the Ring Road, AIIMS and Ansari Nagar extend up to Yusuf Sarai, with the roads on the side dotted with pharmacies, surgical supplies and, alas, for funerals. Thousands of patients visited the hospitals with their attendants/family member and small shops and kiosks mushroomed to cater to their needs.

Another major institution that came up was the Indian Institute of Technology (IIT), the premier engineering education establishment.

It could not get a single, contiguous piece of land and the campus area was split, with urban villages jutting in. Further down the road, land was allotted to the National Council of Educational Research and Training (NCERT). The whole area beyond this was also allotted to institutions. This encouraged the establishment of low-cost restaurants and food kiosks in their vicinity. Most of these specialized in paranthas, bun-omelettes and deep-fried snacks, to cater to the students, who dropped in around midnight, for a bite.

In 1969, Jawaharlal Nehru University (JNU) was set up on 1,300 acres of rocky wasteland, covered by thorny shrubs, adjacent to the IIT. Given these institutions, the area came to be known as an institutional area; and it contributed to the 'campus food' culture and intermingling of tastes that had never been experienced on the North Campus of Delhi University.

The first rector of the JNU, Professor Moonis Raza, was a gifted town-planner and closely associated with the Progressive Writers Movement. He planned for a mini-food court at the Kamal Shopping Complex of JNU, when the first generation of hostelers and faculty members moved in. There was a South Indian idli-dosa outlet rubbing shoulders with a roomali roti and seekh kebab joint. Kamal, that lent its name to the small market, sold the North Indian staples—puri-chole and samosa-pakore with hot chai. At one corner of the open-air rectangle space was a 'Chinese' eatery Kiacha. It was a welcome change from the monotonous fare of the hostel messes. The food in the hostels was also curated to provide a taste of home, at least once a week, to students who came from different regions of the country. Dosa-idli, chole-kulche, and jalebis were on offer by rotation regularly.

Outside the shopping complex, in the open air, there was the Ganga Dhaba. The name derived from the hostel that faced it across the road, this was the first bus stop after one entered the campus. When the JNU was temporarily housed in the old campus, built originally for the Lal Bahadur Shastri National Academy of Administration, the original dhaba was run by a kindly soul, Kashi Ram. The times were kinder and Kashi Ram kept bottles of chilled beer handy in a matka.

The beer bottles did not travel well to the new campus and the Ganga Dhaba acquired a reputation for giving students a high on weed-filled cigarettes that the paan wala made available. As years passed, other dhabas and mini-shopping complexes came up on the JNU campus near other hostels—Kaveri and Periyar, Nilgiri, Sabarmati and Brahmaputra. The university also experimented with the idea of a 24/7 food court and wanted to invite well-known names like Nirula's, but the move met with stiff resistance from the left-dominated Student's Union and was given up.

The eateries on the JNU campus have proved to be a major attraction even for people not residing there. Some of them operated by ex-students of the university have survived the vicissitudes of times. Mamu who runs an open-air eatery serving a Bihari thali was once a scholar in the School of Foreign Languages and had completed an MPhil in Persian. Similarly, the Mughal Durbar was started by another student, who after he completed his MPhil, opted for a career in catering rather than academics. Till Covid struck, these eateries provided intellectually stimulating conversation as well as affordable home-style nourishment.

Seventeen

Punjabi Tadka in Delhi

Pandara Road, Delhi
Courtesy: Indrajit
Pant

Even before the advent of the British and the Anglo-Sikh wars, years before the Partition, the Land of Five Rivers reached up to the borders of Delhi. When Shahjahanabad was built, Punjabis from different regions of that area had come and settled in the new city. A diversity of flavours brought by these immigrants enriched the city's kitchens at home and in bazaars.

It is, therefore, not surprising that Punjabi foods have always contributed substantially to moulding the taste of food in the city. These have never been monolithic. Those who came from the Punjab hailed from different regions and practised different faiths. They were Hindus, Muslims, Sikhs, Nanakpanthi, non-Sikhs, and even a sprinkling of Christians.

Post the Partition, the profile of the Punjabi population changed dramatically. The term 'refugee' erased all sub-regional identities—Multani, Peshawari, Bahawalpuri, Sarakkai and so on. The nuances in ethnic foods were forgotten in the struggle for survival and Punjabi food was of necessity homogenized.

Different shades of diverse culinary traditions that had simultaneously coexisted resurfaced as soon as a semblance of normalcy returned to the lives of refugees. For instance, the proprietors of Moti Mahal in Daryaganj projected a robust frontier identity, quite distinct from the genteel Lahori personality that was represented by Kake Da and Gulati in Pandara Road. With the passage of time, the Peshawari and Rawalpindi rendering of dishes found its way into restaurants like Pindi.

One can easily trace this trend from the establishment of 'proper' restaurants like Kwality and United Coffee House in Connaught Place, before the Partition, which included some recipes from Punjab in their menu, to roadside dhabas that mushroomed all over the expanding city in the 1960s. Rajinder ka Dhaba, conveniently abbreviated to Raju's, started off in Green Park against the rather depressing backdrop of the crematorium—but who cared? His boneless, deep-fried *surmai* and *singhada* fish sold by weight and, with tangy green chutney, was finger-licking. It was where tipplers, young and old, parked their bikes and cars. I vividly recall a winter evening, after the declaration of the Emergency in 1975, when a policeman on the beat surprised the two of us enjoying a bagful of bar-bites with a few nips from a hip flask. He sternly admonished us, but let us off with the warning that the least we should do was to hide the pouwa (quarter bottle) and not be so foolhardy in pushing our luck. *Patan nahi Imergency lagi hai!*

Moti Mahal

When three friends, separated during the Partition, met by chance at a theka (country liquor shop), all of them jobless refugees, it was but natural that the conversation focused on how life had changed and what they planned to do next. To cut a long story short, they agreed to join hands and resume what they did before the upheaval in Lahore. According to the apocryphal story, they used to work in a popular eatery in Lahore. What they knew best was to tend a tandoor, roast chickens and turn the ladle to cook large pots of delicious curries. This time they thought they would work for themselves. Somehow a princely sum of Rs 15,000 was arranged and a shop hired in Daryaganj. This was the birth of the legendary eatery Moti Mahal. From its inception, the eatery specializing in North-west Frontier cuisine became a rage. The partners had created the right ambience for their food. Burly moustachioed waiters in Pathani suits and turredar safas would greet guests and similarly attired qawaali singers would provide the entertainment during the meal.

The *tandoori chicken* from Moti Mahal was then considered something special, far more succulent and subtly spiced than what was served in other street-side dhabas. From the beginning, Moti Mahal had positioned itself not as a dhaba but as an ethnic restaurant.

Its food was ordered for guests at the Prime Minister's house and for other dignitaries who found it inconvenient to travel to the congested Old City. Another bit of family lore informs us that Maulana Azad once recommended the dish to the Shah of Iran, when he was on a state visit to India. His exact words, according to the proud owners were 'to have come to Delhi and not sampled Moti Mahal's *tandoori chicken* is like visiting Agra without having a look at Taj Mahal.'

Monish Gujral, now chairman of Moti Mahal, has provided a detailed account of his family's contribution to Delhi's cuisine in the years after Independence. According to him, it was his grandfather, Kundan Lal Gujral, who 'created' the *tandoori chicken* and 'invented' the butter chicken as well as the famous *dal makhni*. For good measure, he adds to this list of delicacies *paneer makhni*. The legend of iconic dishes being created in a flash of Satori-like illumination is too good to be true. No one knows if an apple actually fell on Newton's head or Archimedes ran out of his bathtub in his birthday suit yelling 'Eureka!' Great discoveries and inventions normally follow the path of gradual evolution and even serendipitous discoveries are possible when the path has been prepared by years of hard work. There are many cases where two or more individuals have simultaneously made the same discovery or invention.

Claims to parentage or priority of discovery can be settled only tortuously through patents and copyrights in the realm of science and technology, it is almost impossible to decide rival claims in the field of Indian cooking. The tandoor has a history that dates back to the Indus Valley civilization and the clay oven was widely used in undivided Punjab; it is highly unlikely that chicken had not found its way to this hot place before founding grandfather Gujral decided to try it out. Butter chicken was most likely created in post-Partition India at the same time by a number of dhaba owners, who faced the problem of what to do with unsold *tandoori chicken* every night. Giving the birds a new life, after simmering them in a spicy buttery tomato gravy did not require a rocket scientist's imagination.

This is not to detract from the contributions of Moti Mahal

to the cuisine of Delhi or to suggest that the butter chicken and *dal makhni* at this outlet were not outstanding—far superior to whatever was dished out elsewhere. However, it is only fair to point out that whatever has been in the public domain and is of a generic nature cannot be appropriated by creating a back story to spice up a marketing campaign.

The narratives mythologizing *dal makhni* are no less intriguing. According to Monish Gujral's retelling of his family food lore, copious quantities of butter were incorporated in the lentils along with tomato puree at Moti Mahal to give it a rich regal taste. The use of tomato puree and butter may indeed have been the original contributions of Gujral Sahab, but the velvety texture of the dal at various outlets results from extremely slow cooking and constant stirring and mashing with the ladle. Many a cook will tell you that 'makhni' refers to texture and not the quantity of the butter in the dal.

Chefs like Manjit Gill, hoteliers like Diwan Gautam Anand, and food writers like Vir Sanghvi seem to give credence much too easily to the story of the creation of *dal makhni* by Mr Gujral. *Ma choliye di dal*, made in many Punjabi households, is at times referred to as the *kali dal* or *mah-di-dal*, but never as *dal makhni*.

It seems that all these knowledgeable folk readily concede the claim of Mr Gujral, to avoid a potential dispute with his product and the ITC Hotel's iconic *dal bukhara*, which has become an international brand. They strenuously seek to distinguish and differentiate between *dal makhni* á la Moti Mahal and dal Bukhara as two separate products. Ironically, innumerable road-side dhabas, small and big restaurants, in countless towns and cities sell *dal bukhara* and *dal makhni* without bothering about the infringement of intellectual property of either party.

Gautam Anand conjectures that as the Punjabis of East Punjab and of Lahore did not make whole urad dal, this specialty of dhabas in Peshawar was introduced when refugees from Peshawar arrived in the city after the Partition. In Peshawar, dhabas (there were relatively few restaurants in those days) sold a black dal made with whole urad and served with a few rotis. When the Peshawaris came over after the Partition, they brought this dal with them. As many Peshawari Punjabis became restaurateurs, this was the dal they put on their menus.

Gautam Anand, Manjit Gill and Vir Sanghvi agree with Monish that it was Kundan Lal who 'invented' the 'latter-day dal makhni', though they suspect that it emerged out of a desire to do a *shahi* dal to go with the rich non-vegetarian food. Manjit is candid when he opines that without Moti Mahal there would be no dal Bukhara. Punjabi home cooking has no such dal.

But equally, there are important differences between the Moti Mahal dal and the Bukhara version. At most restaurants, *dal makhni* is cooked once a day and then taken off the fire. When you order it, they heat it up again and add cream and various other kinds of dairy fat and flavouring to tart it up before service. This is why black dal in other restaurants is often served much hotter than the Bukhara version. There are other differences as well. Because Moti Mahal was a way for refugees to stand on their own feet after Partition, all its dishes emerged out of improvisation.

Years passed and the Moti Mahal craze also subsided. Other eateries upstaged it. The partners went their ways and one branch of them decided to launch an upmarket version of Moti Mahal to keep up with the changing tastes of a different generation. Moti Mahal Deluxe made its forays first in South Delhi and then grew as a chain across the NCR, with outlets in various malls.

Children and grandchildren of another founder slowly branched out of the food business, some even migrated abroad. It was only after decades that Raghav Jaggi, one of the grandchildren of the late Kundan Lal Jaggi, one of the three founders, decided to reclaim his inheritance. He invited a friend, Amit Bagga, to open a restaurant with a menu largely based on what was served in Moti Mahal, Daryaganj. The new restaurant named Daryaganj opened in Aerocity and Ambience Mall, Gurugram. It proudly proclaimed its original creations of butter chicken and *dal makhni*. The proprietors of Moti Mahal Deluxe have not challenged or disputed this claim. Both Moti Mahal and Daryaganj bear testimony to the resilience of the Punjabi refugees.

Restaurants that opened in the 1980s and 1990s prefixed or suffixed Punjabi words to their name to leave the guests in no doubt about the fare that would be served to them. Pind Balluchi and its extended family, is one such outlet that has prospered and proliferated in Delhi/NCR. Park Balluchi was opened in 1992, in Pragati Maidan by two interrelated families who specialized in catering—the Chaddhas and the Ahujas. They had by then become quite popular for serving dishes from the Balochistan and Multan regions in banquets. The venue in Pragati Maidan—Vatika—had easy access and ample parking space. Having won the contract to operate their eatery from the exhibition grounds gave them considerable advantage over competitors.

Entrepreneurs with good contacts among politicians in power and senior bureaucrats could bend rules and get entry into space that was, in fact, a monopoly and excluded the entry of competitors. It certainly was not a level playing field but it cannot be denied that these restaurants gave their guests a different experience which combined informal alfresco dining with casual parties, offering imported wines and classy stewards.

Simultaneously, the company operated a restaurant successfully in the Deer Park, Hauz Khas Village, appropriately named Park Balluchi. The restaurant closed after decades when the Delhi Government changed its policy regarding restaurants operating in public parks. (The Lodhi in the Lodhi Gardens and the restaurants that preceded Fio in the Garden of Five Senses met the same fate.)

Punjabi By Nature, set up by the brother-sister duo, Arjun and Piya Puri, opened their first restaurant in Noida, in 1998, later expanding to Vasant Vihar, Raja Garden and Gurgaon in the NCR.

The Eros Group's hotel in Nehru Place experimented with Punjabi cuisine inspired by the princely kitchen of Punjab. Singh Sahib offered the diners a variety of little-known delicacies like Murgh Charga and Chippa Gosht, from undivided Punjab and presented them stylishly. Conceived by Jiggs Kalra, this restaurant positioned itself in a league very different from the dhabas that had popularized Punjabi food from different regions of the state in the aftermath of the Partition.

Kalra continued his striving to elevate kitchens of Punjab to the next level, elegant and fine dining, changing the perception for diners that Punjabi dishes were only robust and rustic, not refined and subtle. He launched the Punjab Grill in 2007, along with his son, Zorawar Kalra, conceived as a high-end, fine-dining restaurant serving sophisticated dishes, 're-built' on traditional foundations, with discernible elements borrowed from Awadh and Hyderabad. Equal emphasis was put on best quality ingredients and personalized unobtrusive service.

The Kalras sold their stakes in Wrapster (Punjab Grill's holding company) some years later to Burman's Lite Bite Foods, the company that also runs brands like Zambar, You Mee, Tres, Hahn's Kitchen, and The Artful Baker.

The father and son team launched Made in Punjab in Cyber Hub in 2014.

Their next venture was the modern bistro, Farzi Cafe, which sought to bring Indian cuisine back in vogue with dramatic flair. It started in Cyber Hub and has franchisee outlets in Aerocity and elsewhere. Farzi Cafe designed a menu that appealed to the corporate executives and youngsters on a modest budget, looking to try out what are touted as lost 'culinary gems'. Interestingly, most of the dishes served are pan-Indian favourites and the kebab repertoire is largely Awadhi. The innovative cuisine and mixology targeted the wannabe gourmet diner as well as the trendy youth, ever willing to try anything new.

What needs to be emphasized is that the Punjab is more than a bit confusing when it comes to food. Today, what is served under the garb of Punjabi food is not confined to the traditional dishes belonging to different regions in the undivided province of Punjab. The menus of Punjabi eateries have enriched their repertoire with food and flavours that are associated with the periphery of Punjab—Rajasthan (*laal maas*), Kashmir (*rogan josh*), Pakhtunwa (*burra kebab*) and in some cases even Uttar Pradesh (*dal tadka*), particularly Lucknow (*galouti kebabs*) and the Awadh region. The princely kitchens like that of Patiala had made the *dum ki Hyderabadi biryani* their own. Many items, like the *nihari*, belonging to Delhi/Shahjahanabad, have been appropriated by Punjabi cuisine. Punjab's claim to Mughaliya culinary legacy rests on the solid ground that Mughal emperors maintained two imperial cities—Delhi and Lahore. Hardly any specialized Punjabi eatery serves delicacies from home kitchens or seasonal specialties like *aloo badian*, *makki ki roti-sarson ka saag*, *bharta* or *paneer bhurji*, which seem lacklustre.

Today, Punjabi food should be interpreted as what the Punjabis eat, rather than what was eaten in Punjab of yore, or what sustained the first generation of refugees who came to India after Partition. Interestingly, this is not the case when a Bengali or Tamil/Malayali guest dines out at an ethnic restaurant serving regional or sub-regional specialties.

Eighteen

Fun 'n' Games and Food in Delhi

Delhi Skyline
Source: Wikimedia Commons

The arrival of the 'Age of Plenty' was heralded by the organization of the Asian Games in Delhi in 1982. The dark shadow of the Emergency had receded by then, though Indira Gandhi was firmly back in the saddle. Neither in Kashmir nor in Punjab had the separatist alarm bells started ringing as yet. The opposition parties were in disarray—dejected after the humiliating experience of infighting which resulted in bringing down a coalition government. It was time to organize a spectacle, announcing to the world that all was well with India.

An experienced civil servant, S.S. Gill, known for his no-nonsense working style and efficiency, was deputed to ensure that the work was finished satisfactorily in time.

To house participating athletes, referees and spectators, large-scale construction activity was undertaken in Delhi. The empty stretch near Siri and Shahpur Jat, overrun by wild growth, was acquired to build the Asian Games Village. Abutting it was today's August Kranti Marg, also called Khelgaon Marg, leading from Hauz Khas to the South Extension–Kotla Mubarakpur crossing.

Ansal Plaza, on the August Kranti Marg, started off as a fashionable shopping mall and had some stylish eateries. For some reason, they didn't quite meet guest expectations. Nor did the 'High Level' restaurant, opened on top of the concrete tower there. This was despite their proximity to posh colonies like Gulmohar Park, Niti Bagh, and Uday Park. The old war horse, P.L. Lamba of Kwality fame, now an octogenarian, was still active. He set up Angeethi and Chopsticks in the Asiad Village. Another Indian-Chinese restaurant, Golden Dragon, opened at the crossing of Khelgaon Marg and the road to Nehru Place.

The Games provided the government with the pretext for giving a boost to construction of luxury hotels. By-laws were amended post-haste to permit high-rise buildings in Lutyen's imperial zone, in order to oblige hoteliers who were supporters of the Congress Party and considered protégés of Sanjay Gandhi. The main beneficiaries were the Apeejay family, who owned The Park, the then Congress MP, Charanjit Singh, who owned Le Meridien, and Lalit Suri, who owned the Holiday Inn Crown Plaza. All of them secured permissions to build hotels just off Connaught Place.

Among the Indian Tourism Development Corporation (ITDC) properties, the Kanishka Hotel, established in 1982, shared some of the limelight. Next to it was the budget-inn called the Ashok Yatri Nivas. For a short while, it was famous for Coconut Grove, its South Indian restaurant that served non-vegetarian delicacies, besides vegetarian, from the southern states. This was when the ITC Maurya, and Taj Palace were built on Sardar Patel Marg in Chanakyapuri.

ITC Maurya from the beginning made Indian food an integral part of its identity. It chose to highlight two distinctive cuisines—Awadhi and North-West Frontier—in two restaurants: Dum Pukht and the Bukhara. A.N. Haksar, a Kashmiri Brahmin, domiciled in Gwalior, was the ITC chairman then. He was a lover of good food. During a visit to Lucknow to attend a marriage, he was impressed by the cooking of Imtiaz Qureshi, who was part of the catering team at Clark Awadh for the wedding banquet. Haksar brought Qureshi to Delhi and put him in charge of Dum Pukht.

The ITC had entered the hotel business with the international Sheraton hotel chain as a partner, as its management felt that the company lacked expertise in the hospitality business. Though the Sheraton collaborated enthusiastically, differences soon cropped up, as it became clear that ITC was nursing ambitions of going it alone.

The first general manager of ITC, Shashi Pancholi, used to be at the Oberoi. He brought Todarmal with him and Madan Jaisawal, who worked as a junior anonymous *comis* chef in the kitchen at that time at the Khyber in Kashmiri Gate, joined as his understudy. Manjit Gill, then a young graduate from Institute of Hotel Management, Pusa, joined the ITC after a short stint at the Oberoi. By the mid-1980s, he had risen to the rank of executive chef at the ITC Maurya.

The real momentum was generated when Major Habib Rehman joined the ITC Maurya as the resident manager and disciplined the agitating workers. Yogesh Chander Deveshwar, popularly called Yogi, was his boss and the duo created iconic restaurant brands in the hotel.

What the ITC did was to restore past glory to classic dishes, with uncompromising insistence on the quality of ingredients and standardized recipes and plating with flair, to deliver a consistent product every time. Adjustments were made in spicing and quantity of ghee/oil used to lighten the delicacies for contemporary palates.

Jiggs Kalra joined the team as a consultant and should be given credit for creating a powerful mystique to launch the Indian food. It must be pointed out that neither the Bukhara nor Dum Pukht showcased Delhi's cuisines. It was many years later that Gautam Anand, former Executive Vice-President of ITC Hotels, gave the push for Dehlavi khana.

Dum Pukht brought to the city the refined Awadhi versions of *shahi tukda*, *dum ki biryani*, melt in the mouth aromatic *kakori* kebab, *murgh qorma*, *nalli nihari*. Bukhara revelled in *musallam raan*, jumbo family naan, robust seekh kebab, *tikke*, tandoori vegetarian platter, satin smooth, creamy *dal bukhara*, and *phirni*.

Encouraged by the spectacular success of Dum Pukht and Bukhara, the Maurya added Dakshin, an outlet serving southern recipes. Unlike its street-side cousins, Dakshin wasn't a pure vegetarian eatery. It served non-vegetarian delicacies from all the southern states and coastal peninsular India with fine-dining flair.

This shouldn't give the impression that non-Indian cuisines were neglected. The rooftop restaurant, first West View and later 360°, specialized in Continental and pan-Asian cuisine.

Exciting developments in the Indian food space were also underway at the Taj restaurants. Haveli at the Delhi Taj popularized dishes that are now menu standards (*achar gosht*, for instance) and Handi focused (originally) on a small menu of classic, but rarely-found-in-restaurants, dishes that were simmered slowly. (This predated Dum Pukht by several years.)

Camellia Panjabi, who was in-charge of the Taj Group of hotels, was no less passionately committed to promotion of Indian foods. Born in Mumbai, she studied economics at Cambridge University in the 1960s. She came back to India and applied for a job in the Tata Administrative Service and quickly rose to the top. At the helm of the Indian Hotels Company (the Taj group), she was on an overdrive to transform the culinary culture at the hotels of the Taj group. The Taj at Bombay, the flagship hotel, had always prided itself on the excellence of its Western delicacies and service. The Taj hotels in Delhi—Mansingh and Palace—were conscious of this legacy. The Taj Mansingh has experimented with many European cuisines—French at Le Champs, Italian at Casa Medici, over the years

Orient Express, the classy restaurant at the Taj has had as fabulous a run as the legendary train. The original Orient Express—the train, ran on its inaugural trans-continental journey on October 4, 1883, from Paris to Giurgiu in Romania, via Munich and Vienna. At Giurgiu, passengers detrained and were ferried across the Danube to Ruse in Bulgaria to board another train to Varna. The final leg of the journey to Constantinople was completed once again by ferry. Over the years, routes changed and more services were added, yet the timeless romance of the Orient Express endured.

The restaurant commemorating the legendary train sought to recreate the magic—serving a fantasy of old world opulence. The a la carte menu was dazzling, with a deliberately strong accent on the exotic. Beluga, Ossetra or Sevruga caviar served with traditional accompaniments (30 grams for Rs 15,000 a pop), followed by an array of stunning starters: Cognac flambéed lobster, Dijon mustard touched fresh shiitake *Pithivier*, pecan nut; wild mushrooms, Camembert cheese soufflé, paprika sauce. Soups on offer were lobster *bisque*, *mousseline de langouste*, *Lyonnaise onion consommé* with smoked duck *agnolotti*.

Lamb from New Zealand, pork loin from Canada, sea bass caught in Chilean waters left the diner in no doubt that whatever was being placed on his plate was the crème de la crème of imports. This was fare that the richest of the rich treated themselves to in sun-kissed rivieras and the most fashionable restaurants in cosmopolitan capitals.

Both beef (center-cut steak with truffles) and pork found a place in this ultra-sophisticated menu. It was presumed that the well-heeled gourmet who would come here would have grown up acquiring these tastes in private schools in Switzerland, not to be overawed by a chef or maitre de conversing in phrases culled from *Larousse Gastronomique*. Vegetarians were equally spoilt for choice between Belgium endive, avocado salad, warm asparagus *mille feuille*, and *hollandaise* baby artichoke. And, the long list continues. With not even a remote connection with Delhi's culinary heritage or palate. When Nandita Jain took me there for a meal after a hectic day winning over schools to the Newspaper in Education programme that I was associated with, it was a mind-blowing experience. I had read the Agatha Christie classic where all the action takes place on the train but had never imagined that I could get a glimpse into this elegant and opulent world of European luxury. Nandita was a vegetarian and I an omnivore. Obviously the diners were expected to feast their eyes and nibble at the dainties. Eating to satiate hunger was vulgarly out of question.

Hyatt Regency emerged as the proverbial 'dark horse' to sprint ahead for a very short while in the 1990s when the hotel decided to re-launch its ethnic Indian restaurant as Delhi ka Aangan. It simultaneously opened La Piazza, a high-end Italian eatery. The hotel was then run by three partners—Shiv Jatia, Sushil Gupta and Anil Shroff. All of them loved food and were keen that food and beverages should be a major attraction for the guest. The idea was to showcase many kinds of foods that have coexisted in the city, as also to let the guests savour the confluences of flavour created by gifted chefs.

Delhi has never been an isolated citadel, confined within its walls. There was frequent interaction between Agra and Delhi and the influences from Rohilkhand, Punjab and Kashmir have flowed in constantly. Chef Muhammad Farouk from Lucknow took it as a challenge to match the best food available in the city—Indian and foreign. Devendra Bungla, corporate pastry chef at the Hyatt Regency, Delhi, had learned the basics from old khansamahs employed by the British in Nainital, at the pastry shop. Farouk was an artiste with equal command over kebab and curries. Some of his creations represented the crown jewels of the Awadhi Dastarkhan. Among these were: *kham khatai* (a delicate kebab that crumbled on touch), *naqab posh* (a kebab covered with a thin lace-like mask of eggwhite), *surajmukhi* (the *shami*, wearing a veil of sunny-side up), *chaamp tazdar* (whole rack of lamb, served in a crown- like curve), *tohfa-e-zamin* (a delicious vegetarian *shami* created out of zimikand/yam), *dal saat salam* (a variation on a Hyderabadi lentil dish that is greeted with the equivalent of the royal gun salute that was the privilege of the Nizam, and is enriched with seven temperings administered at different stages of cooking) *salmon tikka*, and *kathhal ki biryani.*

Many of these recipes were copied and replicated, rarely with success, by chefs, hotels and restaurants, and some of these items in following decades have filtered down to non-deluxe eateries. What needs to be underlined here is the phenomenon of osmosis of taste, its dilution, mutation, and adulteration. The phrase has it, imitation is the best form of flattery, but almost everything is lost in translation by an incompetent interpreter.

It was during this decade that 'round the clock' coffee shops and lobbies with tea lounges became the rendezvous of 'wheeler dealers', power-brokers and influence-wielders, assorted fixers and their hangers-on. For some inexplicable reason, the tea lounge at the Taj hotels attracted the power-brokers more.

How much has changed in the hotels of Delhi is apparent by revisiting the very short reign and the long decline of the 'Emperor', Ashoka, the first five-star hotel to be set up in Delhi. The Ashoka was the child born in the high noon of socialist India. Nehru was basking in the glory of his adulation at the Bandung Conference. The first Five Year Plan was nearing conclusion. There was no sign of trouble with China. The UNESCO summit in 1956 was assigned to Delhi and Nehru took personal interest in creating a suitable venue to host the foreign guests. The 25-acre plot of land (currently valued at Rs 7,409 crore) was gifted by Dr Karan Singh, the crown prince of Kashmir, a protégé of Nehru. The Ashoka opened its doors in 1956, in time for the summit.

For years, the Ashoka remained the only five-star hotel run by the government. This is where state guests were put up. Among the many such distinguished state guests who have stayed here were Queen Elizabeth II, Fidel Castro, Che Guevara and Yasser Arafat. The entire team of Richard Attenborough's *Gandhi* stayed there while shooting the film in Delhi in the early 1980s.

Designed by Mumbai-based architect, E.B. Doctor, many traditional Indian motifs like *jharokhas* and *chhatris* were incorporated in the design. Author V.S. Naipaul, ever hard to please, dismissed these inclusions as reducing the ancient Indian culture to 'comic little cupolas'.

Many firsts can be claimed by the Ashoka, which now remain forgotten. It brought Burgundy to Delhi—the city's first French specialty restaurant. Its French chef, Roger Moncourt, was a legend for introducing French cuisine to the city at large. Tokyo, the first Japanese specialty restaurant, and Kumgang, a specialty Korean restaurant, were opened at the Ashoka as well. The Taverna Cyprus used to be the only place in town for Cypriot food, long before Mediterranean fare became the preferred cuisine of the health-conscious diners. The Samavar, the spacious coffee shop, with large, pool-facing windows blended laid-back elegance and homely comfort.

As early as 1959, the Ashoka introduced buffet lunches in Delhi at its Peacock Room restaurant, which had a stage for live musical performances. The hotel's Rouge et Noir restaurant was known for the cabaret, while the Supper Club, one of the city's first nightclubs, was famous for its haute cuisine. Some of the performers at the Supper Club went on to become famous singers, such as Usha Uthup, Sharon Prabhakar and Vijay Benedict.

The excitement and the enthusiasm of the launch, alas, didn't last long. The decline of Ashoka set in as soon as the government took over its management. The ITDC was a lethargic nominally autonomous body under the Tourism Ministry and, like many other public sector enterprises, relied totally on government patronage. It became a parking slot for hangers-on who had to be awarded a sinecure.

As state banquets moved to Hyderabad House, the chefs and the service staff were demoralized. The Ashoka had become an ageing white elephant by the mid-1960s. The emphasis continued to remain on restaurants specializing in foreign cuisine—French or Chinese. For a short while, the pastry shop enjoyed an excellent reputation. The clientele was confined to diplomats.

The old flame flickered brightly for one last time when Rajiv Gandhi wed Sonia in 1968 and Indira Gandhi hosted a banquet for 1,000 guests. The feast comprised Parsi, Kashmiri and Italian cuisines.

The Ashoka was no longer associated with great food nor remembered for refreshing beverages it once served, but had acquired the reputation of a place preferred for a rendezvous by lovers pursuing clandestine affairs.

The protagonist in Khushwant Singh's novel *The Company of Women*, extolled the conveniences of this Delhi landmark, which aided a discreet rendezvous:

> The Ashoka had some advantages which other Delhi hotels did not. It was owned by the government and was the largest hotel in the city. Most important of all, it had a third floor with a lift of its own, beside the patisserie along the parking lot. Visitors staying on the third floor did not have to go through the large entrance hall with the reception desk, enquiries and cashier's counters. Restaurants, health spa and other facilities were slowly leased out to private operators.[38]

Worse was in store for the ageing beauty. Chaudhary Devi Lal, former Deputy Prime Minister of India, even when out of power, packed enough clout to bully the India Tourism Development Corporation (ITDC) into opening Chaupal, an open-air restaurant with a village ambience, at the Ashoka. The idea was to make the joy of urban fine-dining accessible to rustic village folk. A reluctant ITDC put together the rural eatery in haste. The doors of Chaupal were thrown open and a 50 per cent discount offered to villagers. Against all expectations, the restaurant did well in its short life, thanks to footfalls of foreign tourists, who flocked to have a privileged peep into 'Asli Bharat'. The villagers didn't choose to 'own' it.

The Ashoka run by the bureaucratic ITDC was in no position to compete with others when the winds of change swept in. Unfortunately, the management totally lacked imagination and were much too smug, enjoying the monopoly.

For years, all the state guests were housed in the government-run Ashoka. International conventions and seminars provided a steady stream of business and the ITDC continued to live in a fool's paradise that things would never change. Ashoka was given a makeover for the Asian Games but the Old Lady had little energy or inclination to step out confidently in an unfamiliar world. The Ashoka was rudely woken up from its slumber by the shock administered by the economic reforms in the 1990s. New wisdom had dawned on the mandarins who were now forcefully arguing that it was not the business of government to run hotels. Disinvestment and privatization were the buzz words.

Other hotels launched by the ITDC fared no better and hardly left any lingering taste on Delhi's palate. None of them made a mark on the culinary scene in the capital. Only the Hotel Akbar, for a very short while, advertised a buffet where for twenty-one pieces of silver (Rs 21), one could partake of the spread, fit for an emperor. On a day when I had received generous remuneration for a journalistic piece and felt like splurging, I took Girijesh for lunch there. Girijesh, a vegetarian and an economist, kept eyeing what he couldn't touch and commenting how the monthly bill at the Gomati Hostel mess where he lived never exceeded Rs 80! Soon, most of these hotels were renting out office space, or for security reasons, like in the case of Samrat, several floors were leased out to the government.

Finally, after disinvestment, Kanishka made way for Shangri La, run by the Eros group, and Ashok Yatri Niwas, too, was sold to a private operator. They replicated multi-cuisine coffee shops or Chinese restaurants, which attracted a loyal clientele that was drawn primarily by its locational advantage. The owners of Shangri La hotel also built and ran the World Trade Tower, next to the hotel. The ground floor of this building is leased out to restaurants catering mainly to corporate clients. Among these, the one to become extremely popular was Oh! Calcutta, specializing in the flavours of Bengal.

It was the Great Kebab Factory at Hotel Radisson Blu in Mahipalpur that popularised the concept of eat as much as you can at a fixed price. The meal was composed of a large selection of kebab, skewers and patties but wasn't restricted to them. A pot of biryani, a bowl of dal, assorted Indian breads supplemented the unending stream of starters that left the guests almost satiated. The idea was originally Jiggs Kalra's who helped the partners in Unitech to develop it commercially. The original team that executed it comprised Jiggs' band of regulars from Bawarchi Tolla—Vakil Ahmed, Miraj-ul-Haq and Ilyas Muhammad, all bawarchis from Lucknow. Their years of apprenticeship under heritage kebabchis and Jiggs' quality control ensured that the product performed as promised and exceeded expectations. However, it lost some lustre when Kebab Factory was replicated at all Radisson hotels as the chain expanded. There wasn't enough skilled manpower to deliver exquisite Awadhi kebabs or aromatic moist biryanis.

In subsequent years, there were many imitators who flattered the concept of Kebab Factory—unlimited barbecue items served hot at the table with bread, rice and dal along with a sweet dish to give a satisfying dining experience at a fixed price.

By around 2005, Indian foodies were familiar with the concept of a 'buffet'. However, many creative chefs and restaurant managers were grappling with the challenge of serving the diners barbecue items that had not turned cold in their journey from the kitchen to the table. The founders of Barbeque Nation were the first on the block. They worked in Sayaji Hotels in Indore and the first outlet was opened in Mumbai, but it was not long before the sensation reached Delhi. Barbeque Nation may be seen as a budget version of the Kebab Factory.

The sleepy dusty Hauz Khas Village was rejuvenated in the mid-1980s in the slipstream created by the Asian Games. Bina Ramani, the socialite-fashion designer, should be given credit for initiating the facelift by starting design studios and boutiques here. The creative artsy types were followed by travel and advertising agencies and bespoke tailors. Suresh Kalmadi, the politician, was among the first to see the potential of the place. Bistro, though on the first floor, created a buzz as a multi-cuisine fun place. For the politically well-connected, it wasn't difficult to get approvals and licenses for eateries in congested lanes in buildings that seldom conformed to safety regulations in force regarding restaurants.

By the mid-1990s, Hauz Khas Village was the most happening place in town. It resembled a gastronomic Milky Way with many stellar constellations. Some blazed a trail like a comet, only to fade away, such as Gunpowder, once the go-to place for Malayali food, others seemed to enter from other galaxies. Entrepreneurs from Mumbai introduced concepts that had proved to be a runaway success in other metros: Social, Town Hall, SodaBottleOpenerWala, Naivedyam, Yeti and a number of small bakeries that started selling artisanal food and products.

Multiple cuisines became available on one main street and by-lanes branching out of it: KFC, Dominoes, Thai, Italian, Greek, Arab, Korean, Mediterranean and many other Indian and foreign flavours were available. Some were BnB facilities, popular with better-off backpacking foreign tourists. The Bella Mia, owned by a former test cricketer, offered a fusion menu, well-stocked bar and a fabulous view of the Hauz Shamsi built by Alauddin Khilji—the surrounding greenery creating the illusion of a woodland in the heart of the city.

Dilli Haat, established in 1994 by the Delhi Tourism, was first envisioned by Jaya Jaitley. It sought to bring craftspersons from all over India and provided space for eateries from different regions, to showcase the diversity of Indian cuisine. Bijoli Grill from Bengal had on its menu *kosha mangsho*, *prawn cutlet*, *fish orly*, *aloo dom*, *Radhaballabhi*; Awadhi Dastar Khwan offered *galouti* and *kakori kebabs*, *shami* and *pulav*; Kashmiri Wazwaan tempted walk-in guests with *rishta*, *gushtaba*, *martswangan qorma*, *tsuk vangun*, *aloo bukhara qorma*, and *rogan josh*. Rajasthan served *pyaaz kachori*, *mirchi vada*, *ghewar*, *dal bati choorma*. The Naga Kitchen had no qualms about mentioning pork and palate-scorching *raja mirchi* aka *bhut jholakiya*. A taste of Assam and Manipur introduced Delhi to other flavours from the North East. Peninsular India was represented by Tamil Nadu, and Anantam, that showcased delicacies from Kerala.

Prices were (and continue to be) extremely reasonable and tastes strive to be 'authentic'. Entry fee to the Haat was low and entertainment free. One could pick up good quality handicrafts at bargain prices.

Connected very well even before the Metro reached INA, and adjacent to Kidwai Nagar West, Dilli Haat was the most preferred hang-out for youngsters and families on a small budget.

The arrival of the Golden Arches—the McDonald hamburgers—created quite a sensation in the Capital. The first outlet in India was opened in the Priya PVR complex in Vasant Vihar.

For some reason this plaza, in an upmarket residential colony, never really took off. The location on paper was ideal. There was a multiplex showing the latest movies and drawing youngsters like a magnet—couples who didn't mind spending a lot more for their imported ice creams from Häagen Dazs. JNU was a short pleasant walk away—a readymade catchment area of customers always willing to try out something new.

PVR complex was one of the earliest food promenades. What let it down was poor maintenance. The fountains ran dry and became oversized dustbins. Khomchas selling momos and paranthas to menials, who manned the overcrowded parking lot and taxi stand, pulled down the stylish pretenders. It never could compete with the Vasant Vihar markets in A, C or D blocks.

Sugar & Spice started in 1989 as a bakery offering high quality cakes, pastries, puffs and patties. Its outlet at the Priya Complex in Vasant Vihar attracted a steady stream of discerning customers and created quite a buzz. Encouraged by its success, it opened shops in Khan Market, incorporating the establishment as a private limited company. This inspired other entrepreneurs to venture into the hitherto uncharted space of specialized food marts. Le Marche and Nature's Basket, originally a Godrej company now owned by Spencer's Retail, appeared when the younger generation of upwardly mobile Delhites had acquired the taste for imported cheeses, sauces, imported (frozen) sea food, assorted tinned delicacies and chocolates, artisanal breads and more. The butchers at the meat counter claimed to 'sculpt and carve' the choicest cuts. Marinated tikkas and heat and eat kebab were introduced. Not that the imported stuff wasn't available in the city before this but it was certainly not as easily accessible. Sprouting of stores selling 'everything nice' met the rising tide of expectations after the economic liberalization.

Nirula's made way for McDonald's in the Priya Complex. Earlier the trend-setting departmental store, the Modern Bazaar, was relocated here after it was gutted in the original site nearby. There were fancy bookstores like Fact and Fiction, and branches of Citibank. Other all-American fast-food joints like Pizza King soon entered the space. Across the courtyard stood 'Thank God It's Friday', positioning itself somewhere between fast-food outlets and fine dining—elegantly informal. It wasn't all American fast food. Arabian Nights did brisk business most evenings serving delicious shawarma and doner kebab. There were a few wine shops and small Chinese/Japanese restaurants dotted the scene.

Hindi-Chinee Khai-Khai

For almost seven decades, the city has always had Chinese eateries at the top end and also stand-alone restaurants catering to middle-class diners who do not wish to step out of their comfort zone. Since the mid-1970s, there has been a proliferation of more affordable, smaller, almost no-frill tiny outlets, with limited menus, doing thriving takeaway business.

Nehruvian India's honeymoon with China lasted almost a decade but had started showing strains by the mid-1950s. Slogans like '*Hindi-Chini Bhai Bhai*' were popular when the Panchsheel Agreement was signed during Chou En-Lai's visit to India in 1955, but it was becoming increasingly difficult to paper over the cracks in the relationship. The border war that exploded in 1962 ended in stunning defeat for India and there was a nationwide sense of betrayal and humiliation. The anger against the treacherous neighbour erupted in demonstrations against Chinese shops: emporia selling curios and eateries that had the image of a dragon on the signage. Laguna restaurant on Janpath, that stood where the jewellers Tribhovandas Bhimaji Zaveri now have a glittering flagship store, suffered vandalism. However, it wasn't long before those fond of Chinese food got over the trauma.

By the mid-1960s Delhi had realized that hating China and loving Chinese food were two different things. York, Nirula's China Room, Ginza all did good business, dishing out Indian interpretations of Chinese classics: 'Sweet and Sour', pork and seafood, shredded lamb, fried rice, assorted noodles and soups.

The deluxe hotels claimed to serve 'authentic' Chinese flavours though they also had to pamper the local palate preference for spicy Schezwan. Only a small selection from the Cantonese repertoire was added for variety. Recipes using black bean, garlic or oyster sauce reinforced this suggestion.

House of Ming, opened in the Taj Mahal Hotel on Mansingh Road in 1984, and soon became the elite dining destination for Chinese food. For over two decades, Tea House of The August Moon at the Taj Palace Hotel in Chanakyapuri was ranked amongst the finest Chinese restaurants in the capital. When it was inaugurated, it claimed to take discerning diners along the less travelled road. Its accent was on relatively simple ingredients. (It was inexplicably shut down in 2009, leaving a large number of patrons mourning it.)

Surya Sofitel, later Surya Crown Plaza, in Friends Colony, started with a Chinese restaurant, the Sampan, on the top floor. The panoramic view it afforded at dinner-time was stunning. It had some unusual seafood dishes like lobster that were not on offer elsewhere.

Golden Dragon started as an unabashedly Chindian restaurant in the 1980s in Vasant Kunj, and soon expanded into a popular chain. A decade later, Drums of Heaven opened in Green Park. Chopsticks provided the Chinese experience in the Asian Games Village complex. Yo! China started in 2003, and Yum! Yum! Cha! set up in 2014, cater to the lower end of the market and happily play the takeaway game.

Another prominent food cluster that has prospered developed in Greater Kailash II, M-Block Market. Most popular restaurants here have been Chinese. Hong Kong was the one that started the trend and was once frequented by former prime minister Atal Bihari Vajpayee. It was followed by Imperial Garden, then Mainland China started in 1992, and later China Garden set up by the legendary Chinese Master Chef, Nelson Wang, in 2010. China Garden, first started in Mumbai, has received accolades from far and wide for its menu, hygiene and vibe.

Nanking in Vasant Kunj is run by Baba Ling, whose family once owned the restaurant bearing the same name in Mumbai. They managed a small fleet of trawlers and assured their patrons the catch of the day was the freshest available in the city. The guests in Delhi were assured that sea food was flown in every day from Mumbai. In the intervening years, residents of Delhi had unprecedented access to seafood. The apprehensions about allergies and toxicity dissipated.

The Gujarat Fisheries Corporation outlet in Green Park as well as the fish market in Chittaranjan Park displayed prawns, shrimps, squid and lobster. Crayfish was no longer an exclusive preserve of the five-star hotels. Improvements in cold chain and refrigeration introduced Delhites to frozen seafood, pre-cleaned and packaged attractively. This contributed significantly to enrichment of the restaurants specializing in Chinese cuisine.

Hyatt Regency, on the Ring Road, started with TK's Grill (a Korean-Japanese barbeque) along with the Pearls, a Chinese restaurant. More recently, it has opened China Kitchen at the hotel as well as in the DLF Cyber Hub, Gurgaon. Hyatt Andaz, at Aerocity, has the Hong Kong Club. Then there is Shang's Place at Eros-Shangri La on Janpath.

The 'Chinese' experience periodically enjoys a revival at the top-tier hotels. In 2016, the Taj Group decided to launch Spicy Duck, a pan-Asian restaurant, at the Taj Palace, in place of The Teahouse of the August Moon. The kitchen was in the hands of the expatriate chefs Cheang Chee Leong and Chee Kuai Oon. Taipan at The Oberoi, in its latest incarnation, is Baoshuan with mentor Andrew Wong—a chef, who has been helmsman at Michelin-starred restaurants in London. Old recipes are being tweaked and renamed: Pickled bok choy, corn cakes with hot garlic sauce, steamed sliced fish in ginger sauce, chicken chilli mountain, king prawns with ginger and spring onions, and stir-fried exotic veggies in chilli garlic coriander wine sauce.

To borrow Sourish Bhattacharyya's words, the Chinese chow in the city has 'come a long way from Sino-Ludhianvi. And (fingers crossed) perhaps the influence of these restaurants will finally edge out the thick red sauces of Punjabi-Chinese cooking.'

Connaught Place, N-Block, which used to have just a sleepy Amber and Blues and Taste of China, is home today to over fifteen restaurants, the latest being MTV's Flyp, the music channel's first foray into the food and beverage business in the world.

Ichiban isn't a new restaurant but it's definitely a trend-setter for Delhi for a variety of dishes. Phuntstok from Sikkim, a veteran of Trinca's Ming Room in Calcutta, worked in New Delhi's Taj Mahal Hotel and then ran Chinatown in Ashoka Hotel. Of course, Ichiban has all the usual favourites, from hakka noodles (something that most mainland Chinese would not recognize as their own, rather like our reaction to Britain's *chicken tikka masala*) to drums of heaven, chicken wings, chop suey, sweet and sour chicken, sliced lamb in hot garlic sauce and pork spare ribs. And, of course, my favourite hot-pot soup called Ichiban Special Soup, which has a sprinkling of every meat and vegetable along with a generous helping of flat noodles.

Berco's in Connaught Place has been around since 1954. It was started by the present owner's grandfather, D.P. Advani, as a music store. The eatery started in 1982. Back then, it was a snack bar and later on, was converted into a full-fledged restaurant. From that one outlet, Berco's later expanded to different parts of Delhi and the NCR.

Momos

No one remembers exactly when the humble momo arrived in town. Some have vague memories of trying it out in Majnu ka Tila in the late 1960s but it was the *thupka* and chow mein noodles there that were really popular then. It took the rustic dumplings almost three decades to traverse the distance from North to South Delhi. To conquer the local palate, it followed the 'strategy of indirect approach'—it bypassed the Shahar (Old Delhi and Connaught Place) where the kebab was well entrenched.

As the city continued to expand wildly, new residential colonies came up. The menials—cooks, domestic servants, and drivers also immigrated to the city with their masters. They, too, required affordable food with a familiar taste.

The number of immigrants, particularly from the North East, swelled during this time. The momo for them, like for the Nepalese, was their own. Momo/chow mein stalls mushroomed near Chanakya Cinema and popularized the dish in the neighbourhood of Sarojini Nagar—until the mid-1960s the quintessential 'Babu Colony'.

Yashwant Place, Chanakyapuri, where Russian and East European tourists thronged, and the Chanakya cinema hall, popular with trendy youngsters, provided a captive clientele. The lane leading from the Satya Marg to Chanakya became a bustling hub for momo and street-style Chindian food.

The steamed stuff is considered healthier than any fried or roasted meaty snack. It needs little capital to enter the momo-making business—nor does it entail the burden of keeping glued to a place. Most of the preparatory work can be done off-site, at home.

The momo has today dethroned the *murgh tikka* and *tali macchi*. It has donned new avatars like baked and tandoori. Innovations like momo filled with chowmein noodles have a small but loyal niche following. Atta momos offer a healthier option, and the cottage industry is flourishing in markets of posh colonies like Vasant Vihar, Friends Colony, and Gurgaon. In Khan Market, malls and food courts there are outlets selling just momos.

Today, poised on the threshold of an exciting future as the first quarter of the twenty-first century draws to a close, Delhi doesn't need any official celebration to indulge in 'fun and games'. Celebrations are ongoing with food at their core. What was till a decade back accessible only to the affluent is now accessible to anyone who wishes to taste an unfamiliar dish. This isn't true just of foreign cuisines but also of diverse regional cuisines that have been a part of the identity of different communities. Young and old alike are embarking on a voyage, almost on a daily basis, on a Discovery of India in the Age of Globalisation.

Nineteen

The World on Delhi's Plate

Select Citywalk Mall, Saket, Delhi
Courtesy: Indrajit Pant

The 'Food Scene' has changed significantly, if slowly and almost imperceptibly, in the Delhi-NCR region over the past twenty-five years. Food courts in air-conditioned shopping malls and specially laid-out destination food hubs have left behind the iconic restaurants of yore—the legendary restaurants in five-star hotels that had a magnetic pull for lovers of food in the 1980s and 1990s. Accessibility to various options in the market has been furthered by the cluster of eateries in metro stations.

Economic liberalization propelled by spreading globalization opened the Indian market for imported foodstuffs—meats, poultry, seafoods and what were considered exotic fruits. A great variety of wines, cheeses and chocolates also appeared on the shelves of specialty food stores. Not that this expensive stuff was unavailable to the elite in the city earlier, there were stores who sourced this for their 'expatriate' foreign clients—Scotch whisky, wines and cheeses were delivered to their regular clients discreetly and regularly, bootlegged from smaller diplomatic missions.

The world at long last is becoming an oyster on the Delhi diner's plate. The transformation is most visible in Gurgaon, the satellite city which has played a significant role in this process.

My first memories of Gurgaon are not of a sleepy village, but long expanses of fields, with a few liquor shops, just past the border, that catered to tipplers from Delhi on a dry day in the capital. Munnu, also known as Atul Rai, drove me along with my son Indrajit, one sunny afternoon in 1977, just after the Emergency had been lifted, to guzzle some beer in Gurgaon. We downed more than a couple of bottles each, seven-year-old Indrajit had a few swigs as well, and we were tempted to smuggle in some bottles, but good sense prevailed.

The next time I visited Gurgaon was after almost two decades.

Indrajit was persuaded by some of his friends to look at a plot to build a house in the city that was coming up. Land prices were much cheaper than in Delhi. Going for the place was the clean air and the wide open spaces, besides relative proximity to the Jawaharlal Nehru University, where I had many more years of service left before retirement. We could see how much development had taken place beyond the jumbo point near the Palam Airport. The real-estate agent took us to what looked like a forsaken poultry farm, not too pretty to look at. This was close to the market of Sector 23. We did end up buying a plot but never built a house there and, finally, sold it, when buying a larger plot of land more than a decade later. At this time, the road leading from Old Jaipur Road to Palam Vihar, developed by the Ansals, was lined with shacks of property dealers who were weaving dreams of a glittering city before potential buyers. The road was dotted with tea shops and, if memory serves me right, a solitary sweet shop was there at the crossing that also sold samosa and kachori. Palam Vihar itself had no eating places worth mentioning. We were taken out for lunch at the Chancellor's Club by Professor Devendra Kaushik, a senior colleague from Jawaharlal Nehru University, who had by then, moved into his home in the sparsely populated Palam Vihar. If one wanted to try out something different than the club fare, one had to mount an excursion to Old Gurgaon to pick up things from Om Sweets or Hira Sweets. In short, the food scene in Gurgaon was rather bleak until the mid-1990s.

By the time Trident Hotel opened in Gurgaon, we were visiting Gurgaon more frequently to supervise the construction of our house where we would move after my retirement from JNU. There were times that, after hours in the sun with the contractor and architect, one felt it was okay to splurge on oneself. The Trident had a soothing water body and a 24/7 coffee shop that was like an oasis in the midst of a desert. The place was expensive, thanks to the exorbitant taxes imposed by the government on five-star hotels, but the quality of the food and service was outstanding. There were other culinary temptations. Many chef friends did pop-ups in the Trident and the Oberoi next door.

Osama Jalali was invited by the Oberoi group to reinvigorate their Indian kitchen. He and his mother brought in the flavours of Rampur and Old Delhi. Prima Kurien treated the guests with her selection of Kerala classics, refined even the rustic recipes and sublimated them for the gourmet's palate. Dr Izzat Hussain, the heritage chef-cum-Unani physician, unveiled Awadhi dishes appropriate for each season, which were not confined to the royal kitchens of nawabs. It was difficult to resist these temptations and one almost mindlessly strayed into these hotels for a leisurely brunch.

Today's locals consider Gurgaon and its culture as being divided in the middle by the highway. West of the highway is Old Gurgaon and to the east is the swiftly developing New Gurgaon. As the name suggests, until the early 2000s, the families which dwelt in Old Gurgaon had been living there for at least a generation. Their ancestors were some of the refugees redirected from Delhi, who set up large camps in small towns like Bhima Nagar, Arjun Nagar, Madanpuri and other parts of the city close to Sadar Bazaar, like Sectors 14 and 15. Since then, the most gravitating force in Gurgaon's growth story has been the presence of Punjabis, much like in Delhi. Though Gurgaon saw slow growth initially, there was a significant boost in 1966 when the state of Haryana was formed, and Gurgaon became a district. The judicial courts at Gurgaon were shifted in 1975 to nearby Rajiv Chowk (the main junction which connected the Old Gurgaon colonies to the highway), which became a bustling hub.

Restaurants and food outlets opened by entrepreneurs of this generation in Sectors 7, 14 and 15 have attained the status of local legends. The food they offered was a clear reflection of similar legends of New Delhi, resonating with same culinary sentiment. Papu Fish Corner, Civil Lines Wala for Chole-Bhature, Mangle Di Kulfi, Kishu di Hatti (KDH) for Doda, Monu Kachori Wala, Harish Bakery were local legends. As the town expanded northwards, Ansals established Palam Vihar and another set of residential colonies and markets came about.

The demographic of Gurgaon changed from the 1990s onwards

with the opening of corporate offices, which employed about half a million people in various sectors, who pulled day and night shifts. These offices were located east of the highway, in New Gurgaon, or right on the highway's edge to the west. As Gurgaon became India's second largest IT hub, largely developed by DLF, the demand for restaurants and malls opened up to cater to the new heterogeneous white-collar population.

This was when DLF's Cyber City corporate park in Gurgaon opened. Malls like Sahara, Ambience, MGF Metropolitan, DLF Mega Mall and Central Mall mushroomed in a span of a few years. All of these malls had provisions for a food court and some had earmarked spaces for specialty restaurants. This gave an unprecedented boost to the sluggish food and beverage business.

In a matter of a couple of years, Gurgaon was transformed. Buildings with glass facades, replicating the cityscapes of Singapore and Shanghai, came up seemingly overnight, along with a cluster of high-rise condominiums. Restaurants came up to cater to the needs of those who lived or worked in Gurgaon. The Cyber Hub and the 32nd Milestone soon pulled in diners even from Delhi.

The crown jewel of DLF's Cyber City, the Cyber Hub, was established in 2013. It was conceived as an enclosed food court, spread across 40,000 square yards. Designed by renowned architects, the American M. Paul Friedberg and the Indian Hafeez Contractor, it had beautifully laid-out walkways, lined by eateries offering myriad cuisines, Indian and foreign, and thus stood apart from the food courts in other malls.

On the ground level are Starbucks, Big Chill, Wine Country, Beer Factory, on the right, the purely vegetarian Panchvati, and on the left-hand side Viet Nom, Pan Asian Tapas, and Copper Chimney. As one walks, one crosses Circus, Peri Peri, Nando's, Made in Punjab, Farzi Cafe, and SodaBottleOpenerWala. Further down the footpath, turning to the left, are the Mad Botanist, Social, and China Kitchen. One can take the escalators to the first floor, to enter the conventional food court with all the popular fast-food outlets under one roof—

McDonald, KFC, Pizzas. Further down, restaurants greet you with a selection of paranthas at Parathas and More and the revamped United Coffee House, 2.0.

32nd Milestone was earlier known for the luxurious hotel built in the 1990s. But what you see today is a renovated entertainment centre. The focus is on a fine dining experience with a pleasant ambience. This spot, although renamed 32nd Avenue, is still popular as 32nd Milestone. 32nd Village, as the entire 24-acre development is called, has offices, retail space and a convention centre. Food joints here too are a healthy mix of fine-dining cuisine-specific restaurants, resto-bars and fast-food eateries.

Bhawan at 31st Milestone is a brainchild of Kainaz Contractor and Rahul Dua, the couple known for the Parsi restaurant Rustom's. Between them, they have consulted for the likes of Café Dori and Café Lota at Pragati Maidan.

Both these outlets offer classics like *tamatar chaat* and *palak pata chaat* from Banaras, *Marathi sev puri*, *bhel puri* from Chupati in Bombay, *bhutte ki khees* from Indore, *jhaalmuri* from Bengal. But, the USPs are 'new-age' versions of the chaat, snacks, and mithai like *dahi batata puri, chorizo pao bread pakora*; there's the *mutton dahi vada*—a contrast of hot and cold in each bite, and *kuliye ki chaat gulab jamun*, *jalebi*, *rabri*, *puran poli*, and many more including variations like coconut *barfi* infused with passion fruit, *Nutella peda*, *shrikhand choux* Bun, *mango motichoor ladoo.*

A number of food outlets came up in Delhi after their owners had tasted success elsewhere, in Mumbai or Bangalore, and wanted to expand their business. There is a fair sprinkling of desi 'chains' spawned by owners of profitable banquets and caterers. In many cases, those who had prospered in the real estate business branched off into the food business in search of respectability and a higher status. Listing all these eateries would serve no purpose as they open and close with almost monotonous regularity. The owners are constantly scouting for celebrity chefs who could come out with a catchy concept. Owners with deep pockets keep trying for a progressive Indian or pan-Asian winning formula. The signage changes and the churning continues without making any impact on the taste buds.

Each outlet has an interesting story to tell. Some were started by enthusiastic amateurs who took a leap of faith mid-career, others are brainchildren of professional hoteliers, restaurateurs, and chefs who were driven by the desire to try something new. There were sundry celebrities who thought that their investment and association with emerging trends in food and flavours would yield attractive dividends. Used to regular appearance on 'page 3' (when newspapers were still at least glanced at every morning), they hoped that this strategy held the promise of prolonging the fickle limelight.

BPOs and call centres triggered a boom in the fast-food business. Youngsters barely out of school, now had some disposable income for the first time. They were handed out food coupons, besides duty meals. Those who were till then considered unemployable were suddenly bread-winners. They hung out together, trying to impress their friends how sophisticated they were. Peer group pressure contributed to them taking to trendy fast-food burgers, pizzas and the occasional pitcher of beer. McDonald's was referred to as 'McDee' and self-confident kids began to differentiate between pan- and thin-crust pizzas, additional toppings and sides. Chili flakes and seasoning became familiar. French fries filled the belly. The health food era was yet to dawn, and no one was worried that this was junk food. The fare had long been aspirational and now was within reach. Chilling out with friends in these joints was affordable. Nor was the ambience intimidating, like in an elegant restaurant. This was the first wave of democratization of Western fast food.

The McDees and the Kentucky Fried Chicken (KFC) have had to make adjustments to Delhi's palate. There was no question of dishing out 'buff' [beef] or mutton burgers. Patties of chicken, fish fillet and *aloo tikki* were more promising options. KFC learned over the years that the Colonel's recipe couldn't beat the home-grown t*andoori zaika.* They had to come up with different combos, including pilau-like rice with gravy to go along with the usual cornflour-coated, deep-fried chicken.

Pizza toppings also underwent modifications: Corn kernels, paneer cubes, broccoli, mushrooms supplemented the mozzarella. *Pizza Hut,* owned by Pepsi, contributed to educating youngsters about thin-crust pizzas with extra toppings. What made pizzas popular was that sharing was not only possible but encouraged. Two of three diners could mix and match, sides like garlic bread or a pasta added variety.

Desserts were limited but became aspirational, as these were distinctly different from similarly named confections served elsewhere. Of these, the one which captivated the Delhiites' sweet tooth was the Chocolava cake, first popularized when it was added into Domino's menu. Slowly, the rather easy to prepare chocolate syrup-filled muffin found its way on the menu of various fast-food outlets. Their unique delivery model contributed significantly to Domino's spectacular success in Delhi. No other pizza outlet could match it. This is where Domino's dominated, while compromising on the authenticity, after it opened its first outlet in 1996.

During the 1990s, the relatively comfortable foreign exchange situation had made it possible for Indians to travel abroad and many had extended spells of duty on work visas in Europe and the United States. They had acquired a taste for New World wines produced in California, Chile, Argentina and Canada; to this list may be added Australian and South African wines. Although the African continent, particularly South Africa, had been colonized by European settlers by the end of the eighteenth century, its alcoholic produce had always been discriminated against by snobbish wine producers in France, Germany, Italy and Austria.

This was also the decade when vineyards were set up near Bangalore in Karnataka and Nasik in Maharashtra. Master vintners were invited to take charge of operations by the Grovers, also the vineyards owned by Sula. The Indian wines, some of them remarkably good, were looked down upon by wine snobs but they played a significant role in promoting the wine culture in the metros and Delhi was not untouched. The government that remained on paper committed to prohibition was keen to cut down the consumption of hard liquor, without losing the revenue it earned from excise. It encouraged wine and beer drinking and the licenses for these 'milder' alcoholic beverages were easily given. Draft beer, microbreweries, artisanal and craft beers made their appearance. It took Delhi sometime to surf the wave due to the confusing complexities of excise policies in different states. The net result, in any case, was the mushrooming of and increasing profitability of pubs and resto-bars.

To cater to the young millennials coming of age, New Age resto-bars proliferated across the city, in developed and developing areas alike, throughout the twenty tens.

What pushed these businesses more than anything else was the millennial's fascination and affinity for colourful cocktails like mojito, Sex on the Beach, Long Island iced tea and jáger bombs. Such drinks could not be prepared without purchasing special products and often required handy skill.

To understand the phenomenon better, a look at menus of some pubs and bars is needed. Based on an economic model, largely centred on the sale of alcohol, the food menu usually revolved around easy-to-cook and easy-to-please-with dishes like chicken-wings, fried fish, pizzas, burgers, pastas and nachos. Bringing together this set-piece menu of dishes that young Indian millennial customers were used to eating and the local cooks used to cooking, the New Age resto-bars in the capital introduced a similar pub-food menu with a north Indian (read Punjabi-tandoori) accent.

Alongside the usual Western finger food, a plethora of familiar items from the tandoors, tawas and woks were added to ensure that the items were not too alien for the modern, yet Indianized palate.

Establishments like *Social,* Hard Rock Café, Café Delhi Heights, *Imperfecto, Beer Café,* Out of the Box Café *et al* all serve similar menus with slight variations to avoid apparent monotony. What differs across these resto-bars in NCR is their ambience and aesthetics rather than the food being served.

Out of the Box Café and Café Delhi Heights became the distilled version of the Big Chill/Imperfecto formula, which seemingly could not fail as long as minimum quality standards were maintained. At times a dish or two was added, like Koliwada fish fingers at Café Delhi Heights or 'Keralian Curry (sic)' at the Hard Rock, to create, or at least to claim, a USP for its menu. Though Hard Rock never really took off, it deserves a mention for its penchant for improvisation.

Different malls and clusters attract footfalls of different generations. The first of the promenades and malls date back to the two thousands, when Indians born in the post-liberalization era were entering their teens. Dreams of a free market never really blossomed or were fully realized, but a sense of freedom from fetters in that blissful dawn set the mood for many.

By the time more malls commissioned by other builders joined the game, these youngsters were entering middle age. Double Income, No Kids (DINK) professionals were looking for different seductions and different satisfactions. The eateries in the malls changed accordingly. The teenagers and young adults who frequent malls today are many steps ahead of their parents at that age.

While the new-age bars were favourites for the college and office-goers looking for places to de-stress, the slightly older and not quite middle-aged grown-ups provided a sizeable market for another species of restaurants, more or equally focused on foods as on drinks. These included restaurants like Farzi Café, United Coffee House, Made in Punjab and SodaBottleOpenerWala.

Both of these species came together to spawn a brand which would not only change the pre-existing eatery complexes like Hauz Khas, Khan Market, Greater Kailash II, M-Block, Connaught Place and so on but also act as crowd-pullers to new malls across the NCR and complexes/clusters like Cyber Hub, World Mark, Galleria, and the Ambawatta near Mehrauli. Each new cluster had some features that made them stand out from the rest.

The Ambawatta Complex was developed by the socialite Bina Ramani who had spearheaded the transformation of the sleepy Hauz Khas Village into a fashionable happening place, crowded with design studios and informal eateries. The backdrop of the Complex was breathtaking; the Qutub Minar dominates the skyline and the incomplete Alai Minar casts a shadow on the terrace. However, Tamarind Court, the bar operated by Bina Ramani, became notorious in 1999 due to the murder of the vivacious bartender, Jessica Lal, on the premises. She was shot dead in cold blood by the son of a high-profile politician and the impression it created in public was that the watering holes in this locality were dens of vice, catering to the rich and the powerful. It took a very long time for the scandal to die down and for other restaurateurs to make a foray into this territory. With the passage of time the blood-stained memories faded.

The specialty Japanese restaurant, En, had a short, but a spectacularly successful run at Tamarind Court in Mehrauli. The Sikh gentlemen who ran it imported all the ingredients from Japan and the place did not compromise to cater to the local palate. The Japanese clientele was enough to keep the place buzzing. Next door, the space was rented out to chef-entrepreneur Sabyasachi Gorai, or Chef Saby, who opened an Indo-Armenian restaurant there.

Few Indians remember today that India and Armenia have a connection that goes back almost half a millennium. Armenians first came as refugees to Calcutta, to escape ethnic cleansing in the land of their birth. They settled down in Calcutta and preserved with great care their cultural tradition and culinary identity. Many of their recipes underwent a transformation in the land of their domicile and the city that became home to them also acquired a taste for many of their traditional recipes. Chef Saby belongs to Calcutta and brought to Delhi many of the Indo-Armenian dishes that Delhities had not tasted. This restaurant flourished until the Covid pandemic. I remember some very satisfying meals, lunches and dinners, dished out at Lavash. I was accompanied by Ishani and Parth Sharma, foodie youngsters who have travelled widely and sampled foods on different continents. All of us ordered whatever caught our fancy—*dolama*, *mantis*, Armenian soup, Lavash bread, hand tossed pizzas and wines to wash the food down with. Another magical evening was spent on the terrace of Lavash in the company of Rocky Mohan and his wife Rekha. The Qutub and Alai Minars were beautifully lit up and as darkness descended, provided a perfect backdrop for food that suddenly ceased to be exotic. (Saby's understudy, Megha Kohli, later, after recovering from a severe bout of Covid herself, opened a Mediterranean café, Café Meze, at the Wine Country in CyberHub). Vaibhav Bhargav, who had opened Viet nom at Cyber Hub, shifted base to this location and opened Cho, a pan-Asian with predominantly Vietnamese flavours. Rooh, a contemporary Indian venture, has replaced the En. None of these restaurants are going out on a limb and trying something new. Regrettably, from the diners' point of view, they seem to be comfortable serving the same 'fusion' fare, with the creativity confined to nomenclature.

Dr TSR Murali, who at that time was the head of Research and Development at Pepsi Co, was fond of exchanging notes on changing trends in food and flavours with whoever was around and available when he had the time. We often met at the Cyber Hub and if it was not at a quiet table at Starbucks, the two of us would share a vegetarian working lunch at the Parathas and More.

Parathas and More is inspired by the Paranthe Wali Gali in Old Delhi. This is a major pull for the vegetarians who can sample more than a dozen varieties of paranthas with myriad accompaniments. For those who do not like paranthas, stuffed or plain, there is a selection of tandoor baked breads and the classic *kali dal*.

Glitzy showrooms of Apple and Samsung punctuate the food outlets and the amphi-theatre beckons visitors wishing to take selfies. Many multinational companies like Citibank, Penguin, HarperCollins, American Express and Pepsi have their offices in the Cyber City and the hub provides a very convenient place to take a break or conduct a business meeting in an informal setting.

Galleria in Sushant Lok on the other hand was a little different from the rest. It was opened in 2004 in an up-and-coming area, the

DLF Phase IV. While there were other market complexes which were developed at the same time, Galleria, for the first ten years after its establishment, remained highly gentrified. Most food joints had a boutique aura which made one comfortable even in a cramped shop. As restaurants were too expensive, teenagers would be seen walking around with small bottles of DePaul's cold coffee. However, as the neighbourhood became more crowded, market forces took over and 'democratized' the complex, and more accessible food joints came up.

Beer Cafes

My first gulp of beer was from a bottle of Golden Eagle, bought by my father in Almora from the L.R. Shah Stores. The crown was removed with great ceremony and a fountain of the frothy stuff shot out as if it were champagne. The taste was bitter but not unappealing, even though the beer was lukewarm. That bottle was shared between me and my brother. It was the beginning of a long hunt chasing the perfect beer. Years later, one encountered beers other than the ubiquitous Golden Eagle, Kalyani Black Label, Sandpiper and Rosy Pelican. Some came in pint-sized bottles, cans of Tuborg, Carlsburg and San Miguel from the Philippines were more difficult to get. For those who liked their stuff stronger Thunderbolt and Guru made their appearance. Those addicted to stronger stuff used the beers as *tadka* in rum or whiskey.

In the bordering district of Pithoragarh, where River Kali marks the divide between India and Nepal, imported beers along with Nepalese brew, Gorkha, Ice and Everest, were available at a premium and irresistibly tempting. The vagaries of the then excise policy had denied residents of Delhi the joys of draft beer—available on tap in Bangalore—or variations of the Kingfisher. The drought ended when the Beer Cafe entered the scene. A haven for those who loved the bubbly hops.

Pradeep Gidwani, who represented Moet Chandon and some other top-notch wine and liquor brands in Pernod Ricard India, had spent years as a blender-taster in Scotland and gained experience in wine-making in French vineyards before returning to India.

It was only natural that when he decided to take a mid-career break, he would draw from an experience of almost a lifetime. He thought the business would boom if more Indians were persuaded to drink less hard liquor and consume beverages that had a small percentage of alcohol. He was convinced that it was beer that would register a breakthrough. Economic liberalization had paved the way for import of beers and wines from across the world. Pradeep thought that if he could provide a beer-tasting experience in a café-like ambience, many young Indians as well as old would flock to it. This was an idea whose time had come.

Beer Cafe was opened first in the Ambience Mall, Gurgaon, in 2010, the next one followed in the Pacific Mall, in West Delhi, and another welcomed guests in the Vasant Kunj Promenade. The outlet that made the greatest waves was arguably the Beer Cafe at the Cyber Hub. Pradeep remembers, with a sense of pride and a touch of sadness, that this was the place where, at one time, he served almost a hundred brands of imported beer. The establishment went beyond the usual menu of Kingfisher, Carlsberg, Budweiser and Corona and curated a long list of beers and ales from across Europe and the Americas. They clubbed them with a typical pub menu of fried foods, pastas and pizzas. My young friend, Tanmay, still gets excited when he recalls first sipping Oranjeboom, a Dutch beer, and the oddly named Bishop's Finger, that his friend was bold enough to make risqué jokes about, relating to the instances of paedophilia among the Catholic clergy. The beer bliss did not last long as stringent and unpredictable excise policies fettered the operations. It was the killjoy government that dictated what could be served at the Beer Cafe.

The restaurant Social, which started in Hauz Khas Village and now has multiple locations including Cyber Hub, varied its menus to suit the local palate. It made it fashionable to eat out of brass plates and drink out of glass jars. Certain outlets serve 'all day breakfast', English as well desi-puri-sabzi, Irani and Parsi breakfasts. Some mash up dishes like the pancakes with bacon bits were truly for the hearty eater. For quick meals, the menu offers *keema spaghetti*, *anda-mutton parantha* besides khichdi and kadhi. For lighter snacks one can choose between *vada pav* and rolls. I remember, on two different occasions, I was served iced tea in a miniature bath-tub and a Long Island iced tea in a long beaker. It was such quirks that made the Social experience the most 'instagramable' of all.

The Italian Trend

Italian cuisine has always lured the Delhi diners because it has many affinities with Indian cuisine. Tomatoes, eggplants, chilis, bell peppers remain familiar as well as exotic. This is partly due to the fact that Italian flavours are close to north Indian flavours, but also to the influx of American fast-food pizza chains which became the gateway for the Delhi diner into the larger, 'more authentic' Italian repertoire.

The full range of Italian flavours was first introduced with great fanfare in the 1990s by La Piazza at Hyatt. It had the traditional wood-fired oven, but the Italian chef in-charge was equally proud of his *antipasti* and the main course dishes, far more elaborate and substantial than the pasta and pizza. Even earlier, the Taj Hotel had experimented with Casa Medici on the top floor of the Taj Mansingh. It was elegant and formal but failed to meet the expected response. La Piazza had a far more informal ambience, and though it was expensive, it offered a very different dining experience.

Tonino Ristorante was started by Parmeet Sawhney, whose business interests took him on frequent trips to Italy. His family had bought the Plaza cinema in Connaught Place from Sorab Modi and the children were keen to try their hand in the food business. Their first Italian venture called Pyramid had opened in Old Delhi. It really took off when the location was shifted to South Delhi in the vicinity of farm houses in Andheria Mor and Chattarpur. It is an expensive place but has retained the authenticity of flavours. It soon became the go-to place for Italian expatriates in the capital. Under the charge of Chef Suman

Sharma, who has been with Tonino for over two decades, Sawhney expanded their business by opening Caffe Tonino, a restaurant in New Gurgaon, and Dolce Tonino, a scaled-down bakery and cake shop.

Olive Bar and Restaurant is one of the greatest success stories in the restaurant business in Delhi. A.D. Singh, a food lover and restaurateur, came up with the idea of serving elegant Italian meals in informal alfresco setting. The first restaurant was opened in Mehrauli and popularized the idea of laid-back Sunday brunches, savouring wine and food in the lap of nature, for the well- heeled. Uncompromising about quality, the entrepreneur put as much emphasis on the quality of food as on service. Many of the celebrity chefs working today independently started their career at the Olive. A branch was opened in Hotel Diplomat in Chanakyapuri, and a clone appeared at the Cyber Hub.

Ritu Dalmia opened Diva, the Italian eatery in Greater Kailash II, a chef-owned and led, upper-crust restaurant. It has from the beginning been a runaway success with the cognoscenti. She also introduced affordable authentic Indian recipes at the cafeteria of the Italian embassy accessible to the staff and guests. She has written *Italian Khana*,[39] a book of Italian recipes adapted for the Indian palate. Her experience provides interesting insights into foreign foods evolving to suit local tastes.

Other cuisines that have had to go through the same process are the Chinese, Thai and Mexican. The Japanese and Koreans have resisted the local pushback but have had to make compromises for commercial reasons. The popularity of the pan-Asian cuisine or pub foods, drawing upon multiple cuisines and on fusion delicacies, has greatly blurred the borders between pure Chinese, Italian, Mediterranean and other cuisines.

Warm Glow of the Big Chill

The Big Chill started as a small eatery in 2000 in East of Kailash. It catered to a niche customer base who were fond of well-made pastas and cheesecakes. The enterprise was spawned by an interesting couple. The husband, Aseem Grover, had served for years with the 3rd Gorkha Rifles regiment and the wife, of Pakistani descent, worked with an NGO in England after her parents settled there. The two met by chance in Rwanda in the course of duty, fell in love, and decided to get married. They also decided to quit their jobs and start up something in Delhi. Neither of them had any professional training in culinary arts or restaurant management, but loved food passionately. Fawzia, the wife, had done a ten-day ice-cream making course as a student in America. The Big Chill began with a healthy flavourful and light Mediterranean menu—stuff like the baked penne with pepperoni and Gouda, fusilli with sun-dried tomato and cheese and baked potato with ham and cheese. Essentially, comfort food that can attract diners across generations. For dessert, there was a slice of chocolate truffle cake. Encouraged by friends, the couple decided to expand. When the first floor of Khan Market was commercialized, they moved into a friend's flat to set up shop there. By the time the Big Chill opened in Khan Market in 2003, the operation had become more professional. Hands-on management ensured the heart and soul remained unchanged.

Imperfecto was conceived and developed by the Spanish Chef Nuria Rodriguez, who came to India in 2011, because of her husband's work. She started teaching Spanish gastronomy at the Cervantes Institute; and in the afternoons at Olive Bar and kitchen. She joined Imperfecto, owned by Sharad and Naresh Madan, and transformed it. Imperfecto, like the Big Chill, offered risottos, blue cheese pasta and raviolis but retained some time-tested staples—chili chicken/paneer, noodles, spring rolls and burgers. The 'pure' desi side of the menu included tandoori *tikke*, kebabs, dals and assorted naan and roti.

East-Asian, beyond Thai and China

As the Delhiites' fascination with Japanese cuisine peaked and then started to diminish, the *'Hallyu'* wave, popularized by the internet, swept across the world with K-pop music, K-dramas, K-movies and

Korean TV shows taking the main stage in global culture throughout the twenty tens. 2010s. The wave swept into Delhi, further enriching the city's culinary repertoire.

Till then niche Asian restaurants were usually ensconced within five-star hotels, making them accessible to only the cream of society. The new wave of Asian restaurants which served Korean dishes, including Kori's, Gung the Palace, Dalgrak, Dongne the Town, in South Delhi, opened independently around the same time in Green Park and Humayunpur in Safdarjung Enclave. Sensing good business prospects, Kori's and Gung the Palace expanded and opened more outlets in the NCR. The prices matched other fine-dining restaurants in the city. These provided the middle- and upper middle-class diners a new way of consuming Korean culture, usually limited to the audio-visual media. Diners enthusiastically flocked to check out first-hand the spongy rice cakes, succulent pork appetizers and myriad seafood preparations paired with Soju (Korean wine). As Sushi became a commonplace food item, readily available in all parts of the city, Korean cuisine flourished as a niche and is on the cusp of capturing the zeitgeist and exploding into the mainstream.

The combination of an increasing number of people with high purchasing power, cultural awareness charged by TV and internet, alongside a fascination for food, backed by the impact of being the capital for over a century has deeply impacted the palate of Delhiites and their food.

Today, while cities like Lucknow, Amritsar, Hyderabad, Kolkata and Bengal, all take proprietorial pride in their local cuisines, and promote it zealously, Delhi boasts of going beyond the local and embracing global flavours.

The most apparent indicator is the competitive market in the high and mid-level restaurants where the old and new constantly compete. The competition has bred a wave of generations increasingly sensitive to quality over anything else. A wide repertoire of cuisine which caters to an audience which vehemently rejects those who don't live up to their standards.

Food Courts and Experiential Eating Hubs

Eatopia at India Habitat Centre (IHC) came up in the early 1990s as Delhi's first carefully and lovingly curated food court. It offered diverse cuisines through five specialty kiosks: Granma's Homemade (European bakery and confectionery), Pahalwan's All India Dhaba (South Indian and North Indian), Oriental Lee (Chinese and Thai), Wild Willy (American burgers, pizzas and Mexican food) and Golooji's Chaat Waat (street food).

This thoughtfully compiled exposition of myriad cuisines outlived Eatopia itself, as it was adopted by all food courts which opened across malls in the NCR. Paired with added attractions like a cyber café to surf the internet and a video game arcade to entertain the kids made Eatopia a wholesome destination for a family outing. Similar food courts soon surfaced in early malls like the Sahara Mall in Gurgaon and Select City Walk in Saket.

The role of serving different cuisines was fulfilled by a mix of legacy fast-food outlets—Starbucks, Burger King, Subway, KFC, Dunkin' Donuts, Taco Bell—and local chains—Keventer's, Yo China, Wokstar, Moti Mahal Express, Karim's, Sagar Ratna, Crunch Box, House of Candy, Pizza Express, Mad About Donuts, Chicago Pizza, Dimcha, Chaayos. Permutations and combinations of these varied offerings featured across malls established between 2000 and 2015 in different parts of Delhi, like the MGF Gurgaon, Ambience in Gurgaon and Vasant Kunj, Great India Place in Noida, Pacific Mall in Janakpuri and DLF Promenade in Vasant Kunj.

It was in the DLF Promenade that some of the most talked about eateries first opened to create a mild culinary sensation. The designer Rohit Bal, who had a knack for hogging the limelight and remaining in headlines, set up Veda, that sought to replicate, the suggestively sinful atmosphere of the restaurant of the same name in Connaught Place that he was once associated with. The food was expensive and it was hoped that celebrities would be drawn to it automatically. Despite initial reviews that were encouraging, it never came alive. Myntra was owned and operated by Marut Sikka, who had once worked with Jiggs Kalra, and sought to cast himself in the mould of a food curator and impresario, like his one-time mentor. Food at Myntra was much better as it was cooked by the team that had once been headhunted and trained by Jiggs. Ilias Ahmed from Lucknow cooked his signature biryanis and subtle curries. Marut's wife, Anusuya, a fashion designer, added a touch of glamour. The service was elegant and Myntra did good business till it got into trouble with the excise department. Also, competition was catching up in the same space. It was here that Zambar first served delectable South Indian non-vegetarian delicacies, showcasing all the southern states. Although some of these dishes had earlier been put on the menu by Sagar in Defence Colony, the ambience at Zambar was of a fine-dining restaurant, with flavours that were subtler and service more elegant. Zest was more eclectic in its offerings. It had a range of pan-Asian, fusion and contemporary Indian items on its menu. It sported an informal ambience and attracted the younger crowd.

Besides these, the trio of these malls also had an affordable food court on the top floor and the perennially popular with the young American chains like Chilis, McDonald's and Subway.

However, unlike its cousin malls in Saket and Gurgaon, the Vasant Kunj malls could never establish themselves as a food hub. The students from JNU and IIT could not afford the niceties, and others found the familiar options in PVR Priya and B-block market more appealing and less overwhelming.

The basic idea of serving a mix of North Indian, South Indian, Oriental, Continental and street food at budget-friendly prices has remained a constant. Even the post-security-check food court in the Delhi IGI Airport terminals replicate similar, though smaller food courts.

Metro stations and food joints

Metro stations in prime parts of metropolises across the world naturally attract food joints to open in and around them. Foreseeing high footfalls in busy stations across the various lines, the Delhi Metro Railway Corporation since its early days had adopted the idea of incorporating malls with eateries and retail shops inside the metro station to stabilize earnings.

In some primary junctions and busy stations like Rajiv Chowk, HUDA City Centre, Dwarka Sector 21, Dhaula Kuan, Tees Hazari, and Shivaji Stadium, there is dedicated space to house large food courts similar to those usually encountered in malls to cater to the commuters looking to get a quick coffee or a snack before going to the next train.

Epicuria in Nehru Place metro station stands apart from others. It takes a step beyond setting up a run-of-the-mill food court with prominent indigenous brands and instead offers a wider variety of dining experience. Conceptualized by Vivek Bahl, with the aim of creating a bouquet, colourful and flavourful, in South Delhi, it attracts customers with all kinds of palates and pockets, with over thirty different outlets operating.

Nehru Place has been a bustling commercial district in the 1990s. But, in spite of attracting a large footfall, it has always lacked mid to high-end fine-dining options, similar to those already growing in other busy areas like Hauz Khas and Khan Market.

Epicuria sought to fill this gap as a transit-cum-food destination which caters to both the metro traveller out for a quick bite and the affluent diners from the surrounding up-scale neighbourhoods—Greater Kailash, New Friends Colony and Maharani Bagh.

Elements like the greenery provide an open air park-like ambience and the growing crop of lounge-bars blending features of fine-dine restaurants are equally popular with families and youngsters. The lounge-bars have a deliberately split personality—they offer a relaxed environment in the day but as the night falls, the club aura sets in as high-spirited music of DJs and bands envelops the atmosphere.

Besides Social, these include lounge-bars like The Flying Saucer Café, The Chatter House, Lord of the Drinks, The Beer Café.

Fine-dining restaurants like Fio, an Indian-Italian fusion restaurant, which expertly combines two very varied cuisines, provide a solid avant-garde yet pop experience which offers a unique fusion experience with a 60-40 split between Italian and Indian items. The names may change but they cannot avoid the *dal makhni* and butter chicken, or Moroccan hotpot and prawn squid risotto. However, things are kept interesting by serving dishes like *murrabba paneer tikka*, crunchy *dahi aam papad*, pulled mutton phyllo cup and tamarind butter sole. The food hub space is shared harmoniously with local chains and MNC fast food outlets alike. The collective whole of the sum of these restaurants manifests itself as a gastronomical fiesta.

Almost all states in India have state guesthouses in Delhi that double up as the office of the Resident Commissioner. Many run a dining room/ canteen that showcases the cuisine of the state. However only a few have found favour with the discerning Dilliwalas or left an imprint on the city's cuisines.

Andhra Bhavan was the first to open a section of its canteen to non-resident, walk-in guests and became immensely popular on the strength of its value for money spicy thali. I recall being taken there by a friend in Doordarshan for lunch in 1985, to celebrate the completion of a commemorative programme. On other busy days, to save time, an errand boy was sent to bring back lunch packets from the United News India (UNI) canteen—*upma* and *idli-vada* wrapped in banana leaf parcels. Impressive long queues formed much before the gates were opened and sharing a table with strangers was quite common. The star of the non-vegetarian thali was a large piece of deep-fried fish—a red hot scorcher.

Sikkim House has also built a loyal following among lovers of foods, not easily available at a reasonable price, in clean comfortable surroundings. Bihar Bhavan has allotted space to Potbelly and Gujarat Bhavan has outsourced its vegetarian cafeteria to Veda.

As Delhi's palate acquired a taste for cuisines around the country and the world, food in the city has become experiential. Restaurants are conceived conceptually. Food isn't necessarily the central core of the concept. Ambience and innovation plus the celebrity quotient of the associated chef are assigned greater value. This pattern is repeated from malls to metro stations and other curated food hubs/clusters.

Dining at these exciting eateries, it is impossible to escape the sobering thought that, despite tall claims about 'creating new dishes inspired by the classics', in the end, no one is really interested in taking the slightest risk of a novel recipe being rejected by loyal patrons. The fall back is always more comfortable—*kali dal, paneer makhni, aloo dum, malai kofta*. Just for the sake of providing a choice, sundry mushroom curries made an appearance. The kebabs remained clíches—*dahi ke, bhutte ke, hara-bhara* and so on.

Epilogue:
The Past is the Future

Sunrise at the Yamuna Ghat in Delhi
Courtesy: Freepik

Majestic monuments are reduced to rubble or cannibalized to build new cities. The forest reclaims what once belonged to it. Memories fade of those who lived there—their foods and festivals. The past becomes an alien land, far away, that is of no immediate or great concern to most people. What matters is the present. Don't we owe everything to the living? The young have short attention spans; they swing to constantly changing rhythms. New trends emerge in food as in fashion. For the Indian Gen-X, Y and Z, the Midnight's Children are Jurassic.

But the present can't cut itself from the past or remain oblivious of the future. Several generations co-exist at any given point in time. The distance between generations is steadily being telescoped and the gap blurred. It would not be quite correct to talk of the 'clash of generations' in the context of Delhi's food in the past four decades or so. The generations cannot be identified clearly; they overlap, as do their tastes.

Residential colonies and settlements in Delhi-NCR at the end of the first quarter of the 2020s resemble puddles, pools and ponds of water in a concrete jungle. And, when a river changes its course, with passage of time, water dries up in some channels and some ponds are reduced to shallow pools. Others dry up completely, or are swallowed up by larger water bodies.

While travelling between Chandigarh and Delhi, one takes small breaks at Kurukshetra or Karnal, and cannot help hearing echoes from the past.

The great fratricidal war was fought between the Pandavas and Kauravas at Kurukshetra and today it is considered a place of pilgrimage. People come here to perform *shraddha* for their ancestors. Devout villagers undertake circumambulation of the place, spread over hundreds of square miles. It is a strictly vegetarian *teerth*. (Karnal is very different. Haryana Tourism owns and manages a lakeside tourist resort, where serving fish, fowl and flesh or alcohol is permitted.)

According to legends, this was the spot where the eldest son of Kunti, who was disowned by her right after his birth, practiced austerities to receive the boon of invincible weapons from his celestial father. Karna is a complex character, an anti-hero, certainly not a villain, who fought on the side of the Kauravas at Kurukshetra and remained loyal to his friend Duryodhana to the end. No purpose is served by trying to verify the historicity of each single event or the existence of individuals who played an important role in the epic narrative. More important is that, indeed, this vast tract of land has been inhabited by people for thousands of years and many foods and flavours have travelled across it for centuries, more or less unchanged. This is particularly true of the rural repast—what the villagers ate.

Before Haryana was carved out as a separate state from Punjab, the large province was known to be the bread basket of the subcontinent. Those who lived in the Land of the Five (according to some, Seven) Rivers, have always had a penchant for dairy, green leafy vegetables, grams and chickpeas. These ingredients continue to provide the core of the staple daily diet. It is reasonable to suggest that *saag*, paneer and lentils, that are an indispensable part of Delhi's food, have come via this route.

And, as one bites into a succulent seekh kebab or murgh tikka, one is reminded that these delicious morsels have travelled along the Grand Trunk Road that was originally built by Emperor Ashoka and later restored by the Afghan Shershah Suri. This historic highway was regularly used till the decline of Shahjahanabad and acted as the backbone of a mighty river system from which tributaries and distributaries branched off to serve cities and towns far removed from the its main course.

Driving further down, one reaches Panipat (Paniprastha of the Mahabharata) that was one of the five villages the Pandavas asked for from their quarrelsome cousins, in lieu of which they would hand over the rest of the territories controlled by them in the kingdom of Indraprastha. Panipat is also the site of three important battles that changed the course of history. All these military clashes must have resulted in great loss of life and property, but the town has risen like a Phoenix from the ashes repeatedly. At present, it is a bustling industrial hub. There is a large oil refinery and hundreds of handlooms that export their produce and provide livelihood to thousands. It is also known for the Panchranga pickle made here. This cottage industry was set up by a Punjabi refugee after the Partition.

Similar memories are rekindled on the road linking Delhi to Mathura. Sri Krishna was born in Mathura and grew up in nearby Brindavan, with the milkmaids there. This swathe of land is also considered hallowed. Mathura is listed among the seven holiest cities in India and is located on a historic trade route connecting the Indo-Gangetic plains with ports on the western coasts. Archaeological excavations have brought up evidence, dating to before the Christian era, that testify to the city being a flourishing centre of trade and a repository of culture in the millennia after the big battle of the Mahabharata. When it comes to food, Mathura is famous for its milk-based confections—*peda*, *rabdi*, *makhan misri* and rich creamy curds. Many of the halwais, traditional sweetmeat makers, in Delhi, come from this region. The areas of Rajasthan adjacent to Mathura and Brindavan are also included in what is termed as Braj bhumi. Braj bhasha, a dialect of Hindi, is commonly spoken here and the repast is largely vegetarian.

The experience is uncannily similar on the road leading east across the river Yamuna. Shahdara, Ghaziabad and Meerut today are connected to Delhi, almost umbilically, like they were in the ancient past. It was the mythological engineer architect Maya, who built the marvellous palace for the Pandavas at Indraprastha. The city of Meerut is named after him (the original name was Mayarath). Close by is Sardhana, the large principality, once ruled by the gutsy Begum Samru. This was the route followed by travellers heading towards Awadh and Bengal from Delhi. The riparian route flowed alongside.

Garh Mukteshwar was the point where the road branches off towards Amroha, Rampur and Lucknow. Food travelled well on this road, like it did on the Grand Trunk Road and the highway to Mathura and Agra. The best kebabchis in Delhi have always come from Meerut, Sambal and Rampur.

When Delhi was attacked by marauders, its terror-stricken people sought refuge in these sanctuaries. When peace returned, they headed back to the city, bringing back ingredients, cooking techniques and spicing from different places. The influence of Rampur and Awadh is deep and discernible in the culinary heritage of Delhi.

Emerging Trends

The first thing immediately striking any observer is that the more things change, the more they remain the same. The constant 'churn' appears to be illusory. There is large-scale cloning and homogenization. There are a dozen brands that greet us today with familiar signage and predictable fare at locations as far apart as the suburbs of East Delhi, beyond the River Yamuna, and the outermost fringes of Gurgaon.

The continuously emerging culinary trends in Delhi are confusing. Manish Malhotra, owner of Indian Accent, was the one who first came up with the idea of an elegant tasting menu, showcasing classic dishes from different gastronomic regions of the subcontinent. It started in the 1990s with him introducing a tasting menu at the Indian Accent, in a boutique hotel, the Manor, in New Friends Colony. It had small portions and a lot of mix and match (not necessarily fusion) of flavours from different regions in India. This experiment was a great hit with foreign tourists who could get acquainted with a wide range of delicacies in one sitting. Great care was taken to pair wines with different courses. Chef Manish Malhotra ensured that the base remained Indian, despite the plating and milder spicing that would not singe or scorch the foreigner's palate.

In the process, they indulged in an exercise in brilliant fusion. Indian Accent soon became a landmark dining destination. It has remained the flagship of Contemporary Indian. Indian Accent has moved to a new home in the renovated Aman, at Lodhi Hotel. Bits and pieces of the contemporary ideas (pork kulcha, blue-cheese naan and paan flavour in drinks and desserts) from Indian Accent have found their way, in some form or the other, into the menu of resto-bars and pubs who do not promote themselves as avant-garde joints.

In the years since, there have been many attempts—with varying degrees of success—to replicate and reinterpret 'Contemporary Indian'. The terminology has changed from time to time: Progressive Indian, Avant-garde Indian, Modern Indian and so on. Some chefs have tried to impress the diners with molecular jugglery, others have tweaked familiar recipes, unabashedly borrowing the tricks of the trade from successful Indian restaurants abroad from Bangkok (Gaggan) to San Francisco.

The emphasis remains on elegant plating, inspired not only by visual aesthetics but also nutritional balance. The restaurant that undertook exploration of this theme and serious improvisation on it was Masala Library. Eateries like it are at the top tier of the market and their primary target are the foreign audience; they seek to 'demystify' Indian food for them.

Contemporary Indian or Avant-garde Indian or Progressive Indian, call it by any name, it seems here to stay.

Cultural anthropologist Kurush Dalal has proposed a less abstract and more concrete method of studying the evolution of food and its effects on the process of civilization and urbanization. In his talk on Basics of Food Anthropology, he elaborates his theory about how the neolithic revolution was driven by food—how new agricultural techniques led to surplus food production, leading to promotion of craft specialization, further leading to creation of towns, which became market towns, leading, ultimately, to incipient state formation.

The food and cuisine of a city are shaped by a wide range of concrete factors such as geography, climate, cultural practices of different communities that inhabit it, the history and circumstances of their immigration, and historical events. As cities grow and change, their culinary traditions also evolve, reflecting the shifting social and economic dynamics of urban life.

Cities also often have distinct culinary identities that reflect their unique histories and cultural heritage. In Delhi, the interactions within and between communities which have made the city its home, have defined the city's food. Of these cultural factors, some deserve a closer inspection, to understand their influence on the culinary culture of the city. These include, gender biases and the divides created by class, caste and creed.

Gender bias

As we look back, one disturbing feature in the historical evolution of food in Delhi is the discrimination practiced against women. It was not only the Muslim women who were constrained to observe purdah and not allowed to step out to savour the famous street foods of the city; the veiled Hindu women were also assigned a subordinate role in respectable households. They, too, could enjoy only the sweets and savouries that the menfolk brought home from the bazaar, or partake of a small portion of the delicacies they cooked at home. Even in affluent families, they ate last, after feeding all the male members. Most interesting perhaps is the case of Kayastha women, who cooked meat for male members in the family, but only rarely tasted it themselves. It is amazing how they turned out perfect recipes even without tasting or checking the seasoning. Patriarchy prevailed in all families, Muslims and Hindus—Brahmin, Baniya or Kayastha. It is only years after Independence that we see partial liberation of women. The independence in matters of what and where to eat was restricted to a small elite. Women professionals—doctors, college professors, musicians and artists were reluctant to push the envelope. Highly Anglicised Christians and Parsis were happy to be accompanied by their spouses to clubs and parties.

The transitional phase was marked by kitty parties, in which women could mingle with other women, without the presence of a male chaperone, in public places. They were allowed to imbibe mocktails, with, occasionally, a daring lady ordering cocktails. It was only in the twenty-first century, when single women raising kids on their own, became the breadwinners and heads of the household that those in the food business had to cater to this segment. Previously, women who frequented bars were automatically stigmatized, but now social drinking was no longer a male privilege.

Caste-Creed-Class

Delhi, like any other imperial capital, has always been a highly stratified city. Class divisions were always reflected in the residential areas as also in the food consumed and the manner in which it was prepared and served. Subjects of the Mughal Emperors could not even aspire to ever taste the fabulous dishes that are listed in the royal spread. Those who lived outside the palace and did not belong to the aristocratic circles of courtiers ate very frugally. Vendors on street corners quelled the hunger pangs of those who lived in galis and kutchas. The basic fare was bread and kebabs or a plateful of biryani.

There were few men who ate both meals at home. *Qorma* and *kaliya* and different kinds of *salan* were cooked when entertaining close friends or relatives at home. On social occasions like marriages and other celebrations, catering was handed out to professional cooks.

Snacks and sweets were very seldom prepared at home in Muslim households. On the other hand, in Baniya and Khatri households, sweets and savouries were routinely prepared at home. Male children were allowed to go out and buy snacks like *dahi vada* or *aloo chole* on their own but the girls had access only to what the khomchewala brought to the doorstep.

The khomchas sold chaat and did lively business in predominantly Muslim areas. Perhaps this is explained by the caste taboos that the Hindus observed more strictly. As a number of chaat sellers and halwais belong to the Vaishya caste, food bought from their shops, but not from khomchas, was considered acceptable by even the orthodox Hindus. The deep-fried items are considered *pakki rasoi*—free from any taint of pollution. Those who lived in shanty towns outside the city walls subsisted on coarse grains, millets prepared as one-dish meals of porridge or khichdi. Inhabitants of settlements in the proximity of a village would supplement their diet, if lucky, with seasonal vegetables and occasional delicacies handed out by rich peasants during marriages and other festive feasts.

Before Independence, the new capital built by the British resembled a circular maze with the Vice Regal Lodge flanked by North and South blocks at its core. The residential areas were plotted strictly hierarchily consigning residents to quarters resembling caste-based bastis. One occupied space according to social and economic status. The old elite moved over the years following the violent upheaval of Partition from the Walled City, Daryaganj and Civil Lines to New Delhi.

The elite lived their lives in cocoons. They entertained each other, and with the departure of the British jostled to move up the social ladder. Those who could claim friendship with top echelons of political power—distinguished freedom fighters with many belonging to privileged aristocratic families like the Nehru family—put some aspirants in pole position. The newly-arrived also registered their presence by cultivating foreign diplomats and holding mini-durbars, with a lavish spread of food and drink with the added temptation of congenial company. Malvika Singh has mentioned an open house on New Year that for decades was an unbroken tradition at the home of her parents, Raj and Romesh Thapar. Hundreds of persons turned up for the event, to swill rum punch and nibble at kebabs and to have a blast dancing to the popular tunes.

Ashok Mitra, a Marxist economist from Calcutta, who lived for some years in Delhi and had many friends in the city from pre-Independence years was an acute observer of the social scene.

His comments on parties like this provides a different perspective on the Open House and exclusive dinners. He believed that the Delhi Establishment didn't bother about ideology, revolutionary or reactionary, as long as the person was considered interesting and, the guest, however outlandish, adhered to the accepted norms of etiquette.

Doors to good food and expensive drinks opened to the privileged automatically but not always or easily to those born outside the circle of entitlement.

So Who is an Asli Dilliwala and What is His Cuisine?

Until the 1980s, Delhi was never really a melting pot. It more resembled a confluence where different streams intermingled, imbibing and imparting what they carried, to create something different. Only Kayastha gastronomy was shaped by a confluence of Muslim and Hindu delicacies and cooking styles, enriched by the innovative adaptation of some elements of Anglo-Indian cooking.

Today, Delhi foods can be visualized as a giant mosaic that at the same time was a jigsaw puzzle. Different pieces had to be put together lovingly to appreciate the pattern. The grand design may also be seen as a tapestry woven together with different strands of colourful yarns.

Recipes for different delicacies cannot be separated on a sectarian or communal basis. Over centuries there has been an invisible but unceasing process of intermingling of techniques ingredients and styles.

At present, food in Delhi looks like a cross-section of sedimentary rock, where many layers are distinctly discernible. What is interesting is that one can savour any one of these or more layers at the same time, without having to drill deep to reach the lower levels. Perhaps a more apt metaphor is the glass of Parsi faluda, where with a long spoon you can scoop out whatever you wish to taste and enjoy—the frozen dessert, fresh fruit, custard or jelly (the American parfait comes close to this confection). The different layers in Delhi's culinary sediments happily coexist: The Muslim-Turko-Afghan, 'Mughaliya' and Rohilla, the Punjabi (original settlers and the post-Partition refugees), the Baniya and the Kayastha, different shades of 'South Indian', with smaller veins of Christian-Anglo-Indian, Parsi, Marwari, Rajasthani, Bengali and, more recently, North Eastern.

The interesting thing about emerging and receding food trends in Delhi seems to be their cyclical nature. When the robust Punjabi dhaba repast has jaded the palate, the diners move to other regional cuisines, Indian and foreign. One fad fades out and something else is in vogue. Tex-Mex, Mediterranean, Italian, Greek or Japanese. For a short while, it appears that this is what will endure. Suddenly, the rising wave subsides and recedes. Experimenting with fusion or molecular gastronomy to return to what conveniently is labelled 'Mughaliya' (including Awadhi and Hyderabadi). Traditional 'classics' reappear in slightly changed form, both in terms of spicing and plating. The kebabs and tikkas, lentils and paneer, the milk-based desserts, have survived recurring assaults by multinational fast-food chains to conquer the Indian palate.

Delhi's special connect with the tandoor and rich aromatic gravies is pretty strong. The gravies at times may be lightened by reducing the amount of ghee or oil used, and spicing may become milder but they along with the kebab and tikka remain indispensable. The big business of food has been trying hard to manufacture a homogenized taste that obliterates the diversity of local flavours. This strategy has only partially succeeded in Delhi. They have had to make changes to their trademark recipes to retain a foothold in the world's second largest market.

Delhi, from the time of its existence as Indraprastha to that of the NCR, has never had a common or shared identity of its own. It has received a diversity of cultural influences and residents have adapted these to their own needs. From language to food, music to poetry, pastime to architecture, it has borrowed freely, improved upon and refined recipes as well as modes of expression, giving them a Delhi imprimatur. The closest we can get to answering the question, 'who is an asli Dilliwala and what is his cuisine?' is that whoever chooses to live in Delhi, calls it home and enriches its culinary repertoire with his own, while enjoying the confluence of flavours, is a Dilliwala. Dilli hain Dilwalon ki!

Acknowledgements

My interests in Delhi's cuisines was kindled by Jiggs Kalra when we were engaged in conceptualising a new restaurant at the Hayat Regency hotel—*Delhi ka Angan*. Preliminary research was published in a series of page long article in three parts in the *Times of India* and made us realise that we had only touched the tip of the iceberg. It dawned on us that Delhi had not one but multiple streams of cuisine. While the Mughalia and the Punjabi refugee were the most visible the underlying currents of Baniya, Kayasath and Khatri foods were no less resplendent.

Research and writing about food with Jiggs was a very pleasant addiction. Having him around opened many doors. It was through Jiggs that I could get an opportunity to spend valuable time with Mr PL Lamba of Kwality and Gaylord fame. It also made it possible to have enriching conversation with younger members of the Nirula Family and a number of chefs working in different hotels.

I owe a large debt to Mayank Austen Sufi, better known as 'Dilliwalah' who's passionate love affair with the city is not matched. His blog particularly the section on the city's food is a rich mine of priceless information. He has been generous to let me use whatever I could from his writings.

There are a number of Chefs who have very generously shared their knowledge and distilled essence of their experience, not only about Delhi foods but the different streams that find a confluence here. Among them Manjit Gill, ex-corporate chef of ITC, Devender Kumar of Le Meridian Hotels, Sudhir Sibal of Ashoka hotel, are the ones who have been most generous and come to my help whenever I needed it. Of the heritage chefs, Osama Jalali, journalist turned culinary curator, along with his mother and wife, have helped me verify roots of some recipes in old Delhi.

I miss my Hyderabadi late friends Javed Alam and Prof Ali Baqar who patiently explained to me the differences that separated Delhi's cooking from that of Hyderabad.

Gunjan Goela the author of *Baniyas of Old Delhi*, is a veritable goldmine of information. I have been fortunate to discuss the food related contents of her book with her.

Sunita Narain, the renowned environmentalist, belongs to a vegetarian Baniya family near Chandni Chowk. Her invitation to curate a vegetarian meal and subsequent discussions with her colleague Dr Vibha Varshney helped me fill some gaps in the Delhi Baniya story.

Dr S.Y. Quraishi is an internationally renowned expert on elections, a public intellectual and keen foodie. I have greatly enjoyed my conversations with him about the days spent during his adolescence and early youth in the shadow of Jama Masjid.

Vinod Dua, who was snatched away by Covid, was a *yaron ka yar*, who enjoyed the city's food, exchanging notes with him provided many clues about obscure eateries and old masters whom time has passed by.

The Christian population in Delhi comprises a minuscule minority. But they have left indelible imprint on Delhi's food repertoire. My friends John Dayal, Satish Jacob, S Samraj have educated me about cooking at home and how different strands from Kerala and Tamil Nadu mingled with local Delhi and Agra flavours. They fed me at home or took me out to their favourite eateries underlining without speaking that they were not outsiders but *Delhiwalle* first.

I remember with more than a tinge of sadness many a happy meals shared with late Nandita Jain and Sabina Sehgal. All of us used to go out together to introduce the 'Newspaper in Education' program in various school in the morning and ended the hard days work with a sumptuous lunch at one place or another. Over time this became a passionate exploration of whatever old and new was taste worthy in the city.

When shooting *Raja, Rasoi aur Anya Kahaniyan,* I met Raghav Khanna who was producing the show for Rangrez. His family had lived for generations in old Delhi and he was extremely well informed about the flavours flourishing and dying out in that locality.

I can never forget long sessions spent with my dear friend Anirban Bora who was obsessed with food. He passed away during the first wave of Covid, but I will always cherish memories of working with him and comparing notes. Before his untimely demise, we were planning to work on a pictorial food atlas of Delhi. Alas that dream will remain unrealised.

My friends Vijay and Laxmi Jambolkar are a most loveable odd couple. Vijay is from Nagpur, a voracious meat eating Maharashtrian and Lakshmi Ji is strict vegetarian from Dharwad, Hubli. They fell in love and married when both were research scholars at Sapru House. For past fifty years they have been generous hosts maintaining two separate kitchens in peaceful coexistence.

This book could not have been written without the research and referencing assistance rendered by Tanmay Regal. He not only took meticulous notes, drove me around and exposed himself to hazards of overeating while sampling food all over the city. His incisive comments on generational changes reflecting on food culture, emerging trends, passing vogues and the strong pull of local taste has helped me overcome my subjective biases and generational prejudices. I can't thank him enough.

Milton has a great line in Paradise Lost—'They also serve who stand and wait'. Govind Kirola has more often than not just done this. He has had to stay back home most of the time holding fort in my absence and missed out all the food tasting sessions. Many thanks.

I have had to rely on many books, some of them not easily available. Mirza Zuber and his father Mr Afsar Beg of the Midland Bookshop were of immense help to procure for me the rarest of the books I required. The Indian International Centre Library was another repository which never let me down. Special thanks are due to Hema Yadav & Mishra in the reference section.

Indrajit, my son, took great pains to look for material that would provide reliable substantial information about what Mughals ate, which went beyond anecdotage and paraphrasing of *Ain-e-Akbari, Akbarnama* and accounts of foreign travellers. I do not know how many hours he spent surfing the net to discover doctoral dissertations and monographs on Mughal Food meticulously researched, exhaustive in scope and combining urban history with food lore. As always, his support and love have been my greatest strength. He shares my love for Delhi and its cuisines and through the hours spent with him discussing the drafts of this book, I have been able to refresh fading memories of many a shared memorable meal in the city over half a century.

Recipes

MAKHANA-MATAR SABZI

Preparation time: 20 minutes
Cooking Time: 30 minutes
Serves: 4

Ingredients

Makhana ¾ cup
Green peas 1 cup shelled preferably fresh
Khoa ¼ cup crumbled (optional)
Tomato puree ½ cup (optional)
Cumin seeds ½ tsp
Turmeric powder ½ tsp
Coriander powder 1-½ tsp
Cumin powder 1 tsp
Red chilli powder 1 tsp
Ginger paste 1 tsp
Hing large pinch
Ghee ¼ cup
Green chillies 2 (slit lengthwise, deseeded)
Fresh coriander leaves 2 tbsp (chopped fine)
Salt to taste

Method

Dry roast the makhana for a minute till they acquire light brown colour. Heat ghee in a pan and put in the hing and as it dissolves the cumin seeds. When these begin to crackle add the ginger paste stir briskly for twenty seconds then put in the powdered spices along with salt dissolved in ¼ cup water to avoid burning. Stir fry for 3-4 minutes. Pour in the tomato puree, if using, and stir well before adding the peas. Stir fry till fat separates. Add khoa, if using. Mix to blend well. Stir fry for a minute before adding 2-3 cups of water. (This depends on the consistency of gravy you prefer.) When the water comes to boil add the roasted makhana saving some for garnish. Cover and cook on simmer for about 10 minutes. Uncover, garnish with green chillies slit and deseeded and coriander leaves.

NIHARI

Preparation time: 1 hour
Cooking Time: 2-4 hours
Serves: 4

Ingredients

For the curry
Mutton or lamb 1 kg (shank meat cut into large chunks)
Marrow bones 1 kg
Ghee or refined oil 500 gm/500 ml
Onions 2 large, finely diced
Garlic paste 1½ tbsp
Ginger paste 1 tbsp
Red chilli powder 1 tbsp (or as per taste)
Deghi mirch 1 tbsp
Coriander powder 2 tbsp
Turmeric powder 1 tsp
Garam masala 1 tsp
Salt to taste
For thickening
Whole wheat flour ½ cup
Garam masala ½ tsp
For special nihari masala
Fennel seeds 1½ tbsp

Cumin seeds ½ tbsp
Black pepper 1 tbsp
Cloves 7-8
Coriander seeds 1 tbsp (optional)
Dried ginger (saunth) powder ½ tbsp or 1 inch piece of saunth
Nutmeg ¼
Cinnamon piece 2 inch
Mace 2 pieces
Star anisel
Black cardamons 4
Bay leaves 6-7 (small)
Peepli or kabab chini 5-6

For the garnish
Green chillies, chopped 7-8
Ginger 2 inch piece (julienned)
Coriander leaves, chopped 2 bunches
Lemons 2 (cut into wedges)

Method

Heat the oil in a large pressure cooker (5 litres or more) or a *deghchi*. Fry the diced onions till golden. Strain and take out the onions and put them on a large plate. When they cool, reserve half for garnish and dry grind or crush the rest and set aside. In the heated ghee, add the rest of the curry masalas and bones. Sauté on a medium flame, and keep adding splashes of water to prevent the curry from burning. When the oil separates from the masala, add the nihari masala powder, about l to 1½ litres of water and bring to a boil. Lower the heat and pressure-cook for 45-50 minutes. If slow-cooking, it will take about 5 hours. You have to add 2 to 3 litres water if you are slow-cooking. Add the meat pieces after the bones are done and cook for about 20 minutes in the pressure cooker. It will take an hour in an open pan. The meat should be well done and the gelatine in the bones should be soft. Remove and take out the marrow. Put it into the bones curry. Add half crushed onions. Dry roast the flour till it slightly changes colour but does not become brown. Mix it into a cup of water and stir making sure that lumps do not form. Tilt the pan and remove the oil on top. Add the wheat flour mixture to the curry to thicken it. Stir and boil for 5 minutes on low heat. You can put a tava under the pan so that the curry doesn't burn. When serving the nihari, add the ghee removed earlier. Garnish with coriander, green chillies, ginger and the rest of the fried onions and serve hot. Put extra garnish in small bowls along with lemon wedges before serving. Nihari tastes best with khameeri roti.

PASANDE

Preparation time: 20 minutes plus marination overnight
Cooking Time: 30 minutes
Serves: 4-6

Ingredients

Pasanda 1 kg (boneless fillets, culled from the shoulder or hind leg, flattened with the back of a heavy butcher's knife and scored with deep criss-cross cuts to tenderize the meat.)
Ghee or oil ¾ cup
Milk ½ cup
Green papaya paste ½ tbsp
Onions 4 medium sized (peeled and finely sliced)
Onion paste 2½ tbsp
Garlic paste 1 tsp
Ginger paste 2 tsp
Red chilli powder 1-2 tsp
Yellow chilli powder 1 tsp
Coriander powder 4 tsp
Turmeric powder ½ tsp
Green cardamoms 8-10
Cardamoms 2 (black)

Black peppercorns 2 tsp (fresh ground coarsely)
Cloves 6-8
Bay leaves 2 (large)
Curd 400 ml (hung and drained of all water)

Method

Trim wash and pat dry the *pasande*. Apply raw papaya paste or 2 tbsp dahi to tenderize. Keep aside for at least 1 hour. Heat ghee/oil in a pan and stir fry the onions till golden brown. Remove with slotted spoon and place on kitchen towels to remove excess fat. When cool grind them with cardamom and cloves to a paste. Keep aside. Heat oil in the pan and fry the *pasande* on medium flame till they are browned. Gently flip once to ensure even cooking. About 2 minutes on each side. Then put in the garlic, ginger and fried onion pastes along with turmeric, chilli and coriander spices. Add bay leaves and salt at this stage. Continue to stir fry, sprinkling a little water to avoid scorching the spices till the oil separates. Add a cup of water mixed with milk and cook uncovered on low flame for about 45 minutes till the meat is done to taste.

DAHI BHALLE/DAHI BADE

Preparation time: 30 minutes + soaking time overnight
Cooking time: 30 minutes (including soaking in water after frying) + chilling for 30 minutes
Serves: 4

Ingredients

Urad Lentil 1 cup (soaked overnight)
Moong Lentil 1 cup (soaked overnight)
Ginger 1 tbsp (grated)
Raisins 2 tbsp

Curd 2 cup (sieved and whisked)
Hing large pinch
Green chilies 2 (chopped finely)
Cumin seeds 2 tsp
Red Chilies 2-3
Ajwain seeds 1 tsp
Black rock salt 1 tsp
Chaat powder 1 tsp
Sugar 2 tsp
Salt to taste
Oil to deep fry
Garnish Pomegranate seeds/Bundi (optional)

Method

Grind cumin and ajwain seeds along with whole dried red chilies after frying them on low heat in a pan for about a minute. Grind to a coarse powder. Add 1 tsp of chaat powder and miw well. Rinse the soaked lentils and grind separately adding minimal water to a smooth paste. Add salt and black rock salt to taste. Sprinkle raisins, grated ginger and green chilies. Whisk for 10-15 minutes with light touch to incorporate air to make the bhalle fluffy. Heat oil in a deep pan and fry bhalle in batches on medium flame. Add the hing in a large bowl of hot water and keep it aside. Remove bhalle with slotted spoon and place them immediately in hing tinged water to get rid of excess fat and swell up in size. After 10 minutes remove them one by one. Press gently between palms to squeeze out water then place on a platter. Add sugar, salt, black rock salt to the curds, mix to blend and pour generously on top pf the bhalle. Drizzle with powdered spices. Enjoy with sweet and sour sonth and green chutney.

Murgh Biryani

All images except where specified courtesy Neeraj Pant

Butter Chicken

Chicken Steak

Malai Jhinga

Fish Tikka

Fish in Mustard

Roast Ran

Pasande

Ishtoo

Roast Chicken

Aloo Methi

Image courtesy: AnnaMaya Food Hall at Andaz Delhi.

Kathal Biryani

Dahi ke Kabab

Dahi Bada

Idli Sambhar

Makhana Matar

Dum Aloo

Matar Paneer

Lauke ke Kofte

Khatta Meetha Kaddu

Kheer

Phirnee

Steamed Apple and Figs

Kulfi Falooda

Zarda

MUTTON TAWA TIKKA MASALA/BOTI KEBAB

Preparation Time: 20 minutes
Cooking Time: 40 minutes
Serves: 4

Ingredients

Mutton boneless 500 gm cut into 2" chunks
Curd 2 tbsp
Ginger paste 1 tbsp
Salt ½ tsp
Butter/oil ⅓ cup

Masala mix
Roasted besan (gram flour) 1 tbsp
Turmeric powder ⅓ tsp
Cumin powder ½ tsp
Garam masala 1 tsp
Red Chili powder 1 tsp
Black peppercorn ½ tsp (freshly pounded coarsely)
Lemon juice 1 tbsp

Method

Wash the mutton and put in a pressure cooker along with curds, ginger paste and salt. Cook under pressure 10 minutes after the first whistle on medium low flame. Let the pressure come down on its own. Uncover and boil away excess water on high flame. Heat oil/ butter in a pan and sprinkle cumin seeds. As these begin to crackle add roasted besan then the powdered spices except the peppercorn dissolved in little water to avoid burning. Stir fry for a minute then put in the boiled mutton chunks. Stir fry on medium flame for 8-10 minutes. Sprinkle peppercorn and lemon juice. Check seasoning and serve with lime wedges and green chilies.

ISHTOO

Preparation time: 20 minutes
Cooking Time: 1 hour 30 minutes
Serves: 4

Ingredients

Mutton 500 gm
Onions 500 gm diced
Mustard oil 1 cup
Garlic 8-9 cloves chopped
Ginger 1 inch, finely chopped
6-7 cloves
Black cardamoms 2 crushed
Bay leaves 2
Peppercorns 6
Cinnamon ½-inch stick
Cumin seeds
Mace 1
Nutmeg ¼ crushed
Dried red chillies 3 or 4 (or as per taste)
Curd 1 cup
Salt to taste

Method

In a pressure cooker, heat the oil till it smokes. Add half of the onions and fry them till they turn translucent. Add all the whole spices. Put the meat into the pan and stir-fry. Now add the rest of the onions, ginger, garlic, curd, salt, chillies with 2 cups of water. Cook until the meat is done to taste. Continue cooking on low flame till the excess water evaporates and oil rises to surface.

CHICKEN STEAKS

Preparation Time: 30 minutes + marination time 4 hours
Cooking Time: 30 minutes
Serves: 2-4

Ingredients

Chicken Breast 2-4 (skin removed sliced lengthwise in halves)
Lemon juice 1 tsp
Red chilli powder 1 tsp
Peppercorns 1 tsp (coarsely pounded)
Cumin seeds 1 tsp (freshly roasted and ground)
Garam Masala powder 1 tbsp
Mustard oil 1 tbsp
Vinegar 1 tbsp
Curd 2 tbsp
Salt to taste

Method

Wash, trim and pat dry the chicken breasts. Prepare a marinade mixing all the ingredients along with salt and massage the chicken breasts well with it ensuring that it is evenly applied on both sides. Keep in a cool dry place for 4 hours. Thinly line a grill pan or pan a film of oil and place the marinated chicken steaks on it and fry on medium heat for 7-8 minutes on each side. Serve with boiled or sauteed vegetables.

SORSE MAACH

Preparation time: 30 minutes
Cooking time: 20 minutes
Serves: 4

Ingredients

Fish of choice (preferably bhetki or sole) 750 gm (cut into darns or steaks)

Mustard (rai) seeds ½ cup
Poppy seeds 1 tsp (optional)
Green chillies 4-6
Lemon juice 1 tbsp
Turmeric powder 2 tsp
Red chilli powder 1 tsp
Panch phoren 1 tsp (mix of kalonji, saunf, ajewain, jeera and methi seeds in equal measure)
Mustard oil 1 cup
Salt to taste

Method

Wash, trim and pat dry the fish. Sprinkle over with salt , turmeric and 1 tsp mustard oil. A pinch of red chilli is optional. Ensure that the fish pieces are well coated. Keep Aside for 30 minutes. Grind the mustard (rai) seeds with slit green chillies and poppy seeds if using to a smooth paste mixing a little water. Heat mustard oil in a pan to smoking point reduce flame to medium and fry the fish in batches for about 4-5 minutes till golden brown evenly. Remove with slotted spoon and place on paper towels. Take half a cup of mustard oil from the pan in which fish was fried and heat it again. Temper with paanch phoren. Now pour in the mustard (rai) paste and cook for about two minutes. Stir and add about four cups of water. Add salt. Cook uncovered till desired consistency of gravy is obtained. Adjust seasoning. Garnish with fresh finely chopped coriander leaves.

KHATTA MEETHA KADDU
(Sweet and Tangy Pumpkin)

Preparation time: 20 minutes
Cooking Time: 45 minutes
Serves: 6

Ingredients

Red pumpkin 1 kg
Tamarind 50 gm
Mustard oil 4 tbsp
Cumin seeds ½ tbsp
Coriander seeds ½ tbsp
Fenugreek seeds ½ tbsp
Nigella seeds ½ tbsp
Bay leaf 1
Aniseed powder ½ tsp
Asafoetida powderlarge pinch
Ginger ½ tbsp chopped
Turmeric powder ½ tbsp
Red chillies 2 dried, whole
Saltto taste
Coriander powder 1 tsp
Jaggery 1 tbsp grated
Garam masala powder ½ tbsp
Green chillies 2 sliced
Fresh coriander leaves ½ cup chopped

Method

Peel the pumpkin and cut it into 2" cubes. Extract tamarind paste using 1 cup of water. Heat the oil in a pan. Add the whole spices, bay leaf, aniseedpowder and asafoetida powder and sauté over moderate heat for a minute. Mix in the ginger and pumpkin. Stir-fry for about 2 minutes. Add the turmeric powder, red chillies and salt. Stir and add the coriander powder. Cover and simmer over low heat for about

15 minutes, till the pumpkin is half cooked. Sprinkle some water, if required. Mix in the tamarind paste, jaggery, garam masala and green chillies. Cover and cook over low heat, till the pumpkin is tender. Garnish with coriander leaves and serve hot.

ALU DUM KASHMIRI

Preparation Time: 30 minutes
Cooking Time: 30 minutes
Serves: 4

Ingredients

Potatoes ½ kilo (medium sized, round)
Saunf powder 2 tsp
Saunth powder 1 tsp
Kashmiri red chilli powder 2 tbsb
Red chilli powder 1 tsp
Bay leaves 2
Brown cardamon 2
Green cardamon 4
Cinnamon 1x2-inch stick
Cloves 4
Hing ½ tsp
Salt to taste
Mustard oil to deep fry

Method

Wash and parboil with salt. Peel and prick with tooth pick or fork all over. Put mustard oil to smoking point in a karahi, allow to cool a little add potatoes and fry on medium flame till they are golden brown and are crisp on the outside. Let cool. Coarsely powder the whole spices. Take about 1 cup of oil from the pan in which potatoes were fried. Reheat it and put in the hing and as it dissolves the powdered whole spices. Stir fry briskly for half a minute before adding the salt and other spices dissolved in quarter cup of water to prevent burning. Fry on medium flame for a minute and add the potatoes. Mix well and cover with a tight lid. Reduce the flame to low and cook on dum for about 20 minutes. Uncover and stir with a light hand once turning the potatoes gently. Remove from stove. Check seasoning. Serve hot.

SAAG GOSHT

Preparation time: 1 hour
Cooking Time: 1 hour
Serves: 4

Ingredients

Mutton 1 kg whole spices
Onions 2 chopped
Ginger Paste 2 tsp
Garlic Paste 2 tsp
Red chilli powder ½ tsp
Coriander powder ½ tsp
Turmeric powder ½ tsp
Tomatoes 6
Curd ½ cup
Spinach (Palak) 200 gm
Ginger 1x1-cm/2-inch piece fresh cut into juliennes
Black cardamom 2
Garam masala ½ tsp
Lemon juice 1 tbsp
Salt to taste

Method

Heat the oil in a flat-based pan over medium heat and add the whole spices. Add the onions and cook for about 5-7 minutes, or until golden brown. Add the mutton and cook until well seared. Add the ginger and garlic pastes and stir-fry for a minute then add the chilli powder, ground coriander and turmeric cook for about 20 minutes. Put the tomatoes into a blender and process to make a smooth purée. Add them to the pan along with the curd and cook until the oil separates. Pour in enough water to cover the meat and gently simmer until done to taste. Add the spinach and ginger to the pan and cook for 2 more minutes. Finish with the ground black cardamom, garam masala and lemon juice.

LAUKI KE KOFTE

Preparation time: 30 minutes
Cooking Time: 30 minutes
Serves: 4-6

Ingredients

For the koftas
Bottle gourd 1 kg (tender), peeled, grated, lightly squeezed to drain some of
Gram flour (besan) 50 gm lightly roasted
Green chillies 4 gm chopped
Ginger (adrak) 1x2 inch piece (scraped, finely chopped)
Dried mango powderl tsp
Green coriander (hara dhaniya) 2 tbsp chopped
Salt to taste
Oil for frying

For the gravy
Ghee ⅔ cup
Onions 2 medium-sized, peeled and sliced
Cumin (jeera) seeds ½ tsp
Cinnamon stick 1x2 inch

Cloves 4
Ginger paste 1½ tbsp
Garlic (lasan) paste 1 tbsp
Cashew nuts (kaju) 20
(15 ground to a paste and the rest saved for garnish)
5 fried for garnishing
Poppy seeds (khus khus)
1½ tbsp soaked in water, ground to a paste
Coconut grated 2 tbsp
Red chilli powder 1 tsp
Coriander powder 1 tsp
Tomatoes 2 large-sized blanched and puréed

Method

For the koftas, mix all the ingredients listed under this head except the oil and shape into small balls. Heat the oil in a kadhai; deep-fry the koftas till golden brown. Keep aside. Prepare the gravy by heating oil in a pan and adding onions to it. Stir-fry the onions till rich brown. Remove and crush. In the same ghee, put in cumin seeds, cinnamon and cloves. Stir in the ginger-garlic pastes along with poppy seeds and cashew nut pastes. Sprinkle over the fried crushed onions. Add the cashew nut coconut, red chilli, and coriander powders mix well. Add 1 cup of warm water, bring the mixture to boil reduce flame and pour the tomato puree. Cook on low flame till the ghee separates and floats to the on the top of the gravy. Gently lower the fried koftas and simmer for a minute. Garnished with green coriander and fried cashew nuts.

KATHAL BIRYANI

Preparation time: 45 minutes
Cooking Time: 1 hour
Serves: 4-6

Ingredients

Kathal (Jackfruit) 500 gm (skinned and cut in 2 inch chunks.
Basmati rice 300 gm
Curd ½ cup (hung to drain all water then whisked)
Onions 2 (medium sized, finely sliced and deep-fried)
Ginger and garlic paste 1 tbsp
Bay leaf 1 (medium sized)
Cloves 2-3
Cinnamon 2 inch stick
Brown cardamoms 2
Black peppercorns ½ tsp
Kashmiri red chilli powder 1 tsp
Coriander powder 2 tsp
Cumin powder 1 tsp
Turmeric powder 1 tsp
Ghee/refined oil 1 cup
Salt to taste

Method

Pick, clean, wash and soak the rice in water for 15 minutes. Drain and spread on a flat tray. Boil with plenty of water in an uncovered pan till almost nine-tenths done. Heat ghee in a pressure cooker and add the bay leaf along with other whole spices. When these change colour, add kathal and fry till rich brown. Now add garlic-ginger paste along with powdered spices and curd. Pour in a quarter cup of boiling water and cook in a pressure cooker till one whistle. Remove pressure and uncover. Now start layering the biryani in a thick bottomed pan, first a layer of rice, then the cooked kathal with some gravy, topped with another layer of rice till both rice and cooked kathal are used up. Sprinkle few drops of . Cover, sealing the pan tight and finish on 'dum', placing on pre-heated griddle and cooking on low heat for about 15 minutes.

DAHI KE KEBAB

Preparation time: 20 minutes + Hanging time 4 hours
Cooking Time: 25 minutes
Serves: 4

Ingredients

Hung Curd/ Natural Yogurt 500 ml (Ensure than all moisture is drained)
Paneer 100 gm (grated)
Cashew nuts ¼ cup (ground to paste)
Raisins 2 tbsp (chopped)
Green chilies 2 (wiped clean and chopped fine, deseed after slitting lengthwise to avoid pungency)
Ginger 1 inch piece scraped and diced finely
Coriander leaves 1 small sprig (chopped fine after washing well with tender stems, discarding roots)
Bread crumbs/Suji ½ cup
Salt to taste
Oil to deep fry

Method

Place the hung curd, grated paneer, cashew nut paste chopped raisins, green chilies, ginger, coriander leaves along with salt in a bowl. Mix well and knead gently to obtain soft dough. Divide into equal portions and shape into round patties. Flatten just a little. Spread bread crumbs/ suji on a platter and carefully coat the kebab with it. Keep aside. Heat oil in a pan and fry the kebabs in batches over medium flame for about 3 minutes—turning once or twice gently to ensure even cooking. Remove with slotted spoon and place on kitchen towels to drain excess oil. You may pan grill the kebabs if you wish to avoid deep fried stuff. Serve with green mint, coriander, green chilli chutney or sweet an sour sauce.

BUTTER CHICKEN

Preparation time: 90 minutes, plus marinating time
Cooking time: 30 minutes
Serves: 4

Ingredients

Chicken 1 kg (cut into pieces)
Vegetable oil 2 tbsp
salt

For the marinade
Garlic Paste 1 tsp
Ginger Paste 1 tsp
Kashmiri red chilli powder 2 tbsp
Coriander powder 2 tsp
Cumin powder 1 tsp
Turmeric powder ½ tsp
Garam Masala 1½ tsp
Lime juice 2 tbsp
Curd 500 ml

For makhni gravy
Unsalted butter 125 gm
Tomatoes 750 gm (blanched and pureed)
Red chili powder 1 tsp
Fenugreek leaves, dried 2 tsp (crushed)
Garam masala 2 tsp
Cream 3 tbsp

Method

To prepare the marinade, mix all the ingredients listed under this head in a bowl and season with salt, then add the yoghurt and mix together. Put the chicken in a large shallow dish, pour over the marinade, then cover and put in the for 2-3 hours, preferably overnight. Heat oil in a large, heavy-based pan over low heat add the chicken and marinade, cover and cook, stirring occasionally, for 25 minutes, or until done to taste. For the sauce, melt it tablespoon butter in a frying pan (skillet), add the tomato, and cook for 5 minutes until the moisture has evaporated. Add the rest of the butter, allow it to melt, then add the chilli powder and cook for 1 minute. Sprinkle over the crushed fenugreek leaves and garam masala, then season with salt. Stir in the cream just before serving.

ALU METHI

Preparation Time: 25 minutes
Cooking Time: 20 minutes
Serves: 4

Ingredients

Fenugreek leaves 2 cups (net chopped after cleaning and washing)
Potatoes 2 medium sized (parboiled peeled-cut in halves or quartered. You may retain skin)
Hing large pinch
Whole dried red chilies 2
Turmeric powder ¼ tsp
Cumin powder ½ tsp
Coriander powder ½ tsp
Amchur powder ½ tsp
Salt to taste
Kasoori methi (dried) 1 tbsp

Green Chilies 1 chopped
Salt to taste
Mustard oil 2 tbsp

Method

Blanch the methi leaves in boiling water to wilt. Remove plunge in ice cold water. Remove and place on paper towels to dry out completely. Heat oil in a pan to smoking point. Reduce flame to very low and after the oil cools down put in the hing and cumin seeds. Stir briskly. As the seeds crackle, add the powdered spices dissolved in ¼ cup of water to avoid burning. At this stage add the fenugreek leaves and cook for 3-4 minutes. As the methi releases water put in the potatoes. Crumble kasoori methi and sprinkle all over the dish. Break chilies into small pieces distribute evenly on top. Stir to mix and cook covered for about five minutes on low medium flame. Uncover to check if potatoes are fully cooked. If not sprinkle 1 tbsp water and cook for 2 more minutes. Check seasoning before serving.

IDLI SAMBAR

Preparation time: 20 minutes + soaking overnight
Cooking Time: 30 minutes
Serves: 2-4

Urad lentils (husked) ¾ cup
Mung lentils (husked) ¼ cup
Rice Rava (or plain rice) ½ cup

Wash well the lentils and rice and soak separately. Grind separately then mix the batters adding salt. Blend and keep aside to ferment overnight. Line a idli maker or steamer with a thin film of oil and pour fermented idli batter into moulds. Steam for about 7-8 minutes. Remove carefully and put on a platter.

Ingredients

For Sambar

Toor/Arhar dal ½ cup

Mung dal ¼ cup

Shallots 2 (peeled and halved)

Carrot 1 (medium sized. Scraped washed and cut in chunks)

Beans handful (strung and cut in 3" pieces)

Tamarind extract 1 tsp

Sugar/jaggery to taste

Curry leaves 10-12

Samabar Masala

Urad dal 1 tsp

Chana dal 1/ tsp

Methi dana ½ tsp

Dhania seeds 1 tsp

Whole dried red chillies 3-4

Turmeric powder ½ tsp

Hing ¼ tsp

Method

Soak the lentils for 30 minutes. Rinse well and cook under pressure till one whistle. Let the pressure come down on its own. Uncover and mash a little with back of a ladle. Heat ghee in a pan temper with cumin seeds, fenugreek seeds, red chillies and add the vegetables. Sprinkle the powdered sambar masala. Stir fry for about 3-4 minutes. Then add the cooked vegetables in the mashed lentils. Add 2 cups of water , bring to boil and mix well. When desired consistency is obtained remove from stove. Prepare a tempering in hot ghee with ½ tsp pf urad lentils, ¼ tsp of mustard and fenugreek seeds, one whole dried red chilli and the curry leaves. Pour over the sambar . Serve hot with idlis.

PHIRNI

Preparation time: 45 minutes
Cooking Time: 1 hour
Serves: 4-6

Ingredients

Milk full cream 4 cups/1 lt
Rice 3 tsp soaked in water for 1 hour, drained, ground to a paste
Sugar 250 gm (powdered)
Green cardamoms 4 pods coarsely ponded
Raisins 10
Rose water 1 tbsp
Saffron large pinch
Almonds 20 (blanched, skinned, slivered)
Pistachios 10 (blanched, skinned, slivered)

Method

Boil the milk in a heavy-bottomed pot; add the rice paste. Stir constantly, so that there are no lumps. When the mixture is thick and creamy, add the sugar and cardamom powder. Add the raisins, rose water, and saffron mixture mix well. Pour into earthen bowls. Serve sprinkled with slivered almonds and pistachios.

MEETHE CHAWAL

Preparation time: 45 minutes
Cooking Time: 1 hour
Serves: 4-6

Ingredients

Sugar ½ kg
Rice 3 cups Basmati rice

Cloves 8-10
Cinnamon 1" stick broken into 2 pieces
Green cardamoms 8-10
Khoa (whole milk fudge) 250 gm (crumbled)
Dried fruits 50 gm (almond, pistachios, charoli), slivered
Ghee 1 cup
Saffron (kesar) a big pinch dissolved in 7-8 drops of gulab jal or kewara jal

Method

Bring to boil 2 litres of water in. Large pan along with cloves, cinnamon, green cardamoms, and rice. Par-boil the rice and drain in a colander. Remove the whole spices. Prepare the syrup of one string consistency by dissolving sugar in 2 cups of water. Add the rice to the syrup put on flame low and stir gently for a minute with a fork. Cover and cook on dum till all the liquid is absorbed. Uncover and sprinkle the *khoa* dried fruits, ghee, and the strands of saffron along with the liquid they were soaked. Serve garnished with silver leaves (optional).

KULFI FALUDA

Preparation time: 20 minutes
Cooking Time: 1 hour 30 minutes + freezing time 4 hours
Serves: 4

Ingredients

Milk 1-1/2 litres
Sugar ¼ cup
Cardamom seeds 1 tsp
Saffron 4-6 strands
Kewra water 1 tsp
Mixed nuts (almonds, pistachio, cashew chopped 2 tbsp

Method

Boil the milk on high flame stirring constantly till it is reduced to almost 1/3 its original volume. Scrape the cream that stick on the side and mix it with boiling milk. Add powder cardamon seeds, saffron, chopped nuts and kewra water stir to mix. Continue on low flame for another 5 minutes to thicken to rabri consistency. Allow to cool then pour in molds and place in deep freezer for 3-4 hours. Prepare faluda by mixing corn starch with ice cold water and stirring continuously to avoid lumps for about 10 minutes to obtain fluffy batter. Then put in a press to make sev and pour out the noodles in to a bowl of ice-cold water. Refrigerate for 3-4 hours until required.

Appendices

Appendix 1: Sherbet

Khari Baoli, in Old Delhi, is the largest spice market in Asia. The congested road that runs through it is lined by sellers of pickles and preserves. The shop Harnarain Gokalchand occupies the pride of place, as it has carried the signage 'By Appointment to Their Majesties', since 1944. The shelves are lined with colourful bottles of syrups—traditional *sherbets*—rose, *khus*, *bael*, and sandalwood. The products, once made at home following family recipes, are now manufactured in a factory but the formulations have not changed.

Harnarain Gokalchand is perhaps the oldest sherbet shop in the city—more than 200 years old. The founding family claims that the business was started in 1808 by the late Lala Harnarain. Family partitions led to a split in the firm in the 1940s and the name was changed accordingly. The late Gokalchandji shared the business with his brothers and the shop was named after him.

The firm identifies itself as 'fruit preservers' and from the beginning has sold all things fruit-based—pickles, preserves, chutneys, glazed and crystallized fruits (candied used in baking) and syrups. In 1975, the manufacturing was shifted to the industrial area in Britannia Chowk and the variety of *sherbets* was increased from just rose, *kewra*, khus and sandalwood to *aam panna* and *bael* as well.

The firm takes pride in having served their *sherbets* to prime ministers like Jawaharlal Nehru, Indira Gandhi, and visiting dignitaries at banquets hosted for them.

At the time of Independence, thirst-quenching *sherbets* and cold drinks were prepared at home with seasonal fruits. Over the years, life in the city became more hectic and the practice was given up. Factory-made bottled syrups displaced home-made beverages. Many exotic flavours were lost. Commercially produced, a greater variety of syrups was on offer—*banafshah*, *nilofer*, *brahmi*, *khus*, *kewra*, besides *bael* and *amla*—few cared that these were artificially coloured and flavoured, with preservatives being added. Many found the convenience of bottled *aam panna* and *thandai* irresistible. It was not long before the exotic *shahtoot* (mulberry) and non-fruit-based cold drinks like *raat ki raani* and *saunf ka arq* became extinct. Even *imli ka panna* is rarely encountered these days.

This specialized shop used to make *false ka sherbet* till some time back, but has stopped it, as *falsa*, a seasonal fruit, is not easy to procure nowadays.

Hakim Ajmal Khan, born in 1864, is remembered as a distinguished physician and prominent freedom fighter and advocate of communal harmony, who once served as the president of the Indian National Congress. Few are, however, aware that a *sherbet* created by him was considered a panacea for all ills at the turn of the twentieth century. Khan Sahib's ancestors had come to India with the troops of Babur and served as royal physicians. He established the Hindustani Dawakhana and played a most significant role in keeping alive the traditional systems of medicine. Tibbia College, with a large herbarium attached to it, was set up by him in Karol Bagh, and inaugurated by Mahatma Gandhi. *Sherbet Sadar Ajmali* was trusted as a '100 per cent safe herbal remedy for cough, cold, flu and bronchitis.' It was dispensed free to the poor as an expectorant and decongestant for the treatment of dry prickly cough.

The signature *sherbet* of Delhi, Rooh Afza, traces its roots to the tradition of *sherbet* making introduced by the Mughals. In 1908, Hakim Hafiz Abdul Majeed, a traditional physician practising Unani medicine in the by-lanes of Jama Masjid, prepared a herbal mix that would help the people in Delhi cope with scorching summer. He started with blending herbs and other ingredients believed to have inherent cooling properties and prepared a sweet syrup base to make it palatable. The hakim compounded a formula that would help counter heat strokes, reduce palpitation and prevent water loss. He called it Rooh Afza, literally something that revives the soul. The original idea was to provide oral rehydration therapy to reinvigorate the exhausted body and flagging spirits.

A few years later, he decided to reposition the medicinal *sherbet* as a cold drink. The fragrance and flavour were enticing, and it was claimed that the *sherbet* was full of the natural goodness of fruits and vegetables. According to folklore, when the first batch was being prepared, the wafting fragrance drew a large, curious crowd to the shop. The first batch of it was sold out in an hour. There has been no looking back. Mirza Noor Ahmad, an artist, prepared the labels of Rooh Afza in several colours, in 1910. Such colourful labels could not be printed in Delhi then. It was, therefore, done, under special arrangement, by the Bolton Press, a Parsi outfit of Bombay. Rooh Afza soon found its way into *lassi*, *kulfi faluda*, milk shakes, and a few drops even tinted and enlivened the staid *shikanji*. In 1947, most of the family migrated to Pakistan, but Hakeem Abdul Hameed, son of Hakim Hafiz Abdul Majeed, and his two sons chose to stay back. Historian and author, Rakhshanda Jalil, remembers Hakeem Abdul Hameed's visits to her childhood home in Nizamuddin, when the old man would drive up in his Fiat and present her father, his friend, a bottle of Rooh Afza.

In Chandni Chowk, Ved Prakash Lemon Wale is a small shop near the Town Hall, where the co-owner Chand Behari runs a self-contained bottling and refilling operation. The family claims that they have been selling lemon-based thirst quenchers at this site since the 1870s. Codd-neck bottles, imported from England, were introduced in the early 1900s. (A Codd-neck bottle or *goli/banta* soda bottle is used for carbonated drinks. Its closing design is based on a glass marble which is held against a rubber seal.) Legend has it that these bottles were considered 'dangerous' and were banned by British authorities in the mid-1940s as rioting protestors used them as improvised explosive devices—deadly as canons!

In the pre-refrigeration era, the desi lemonade bottles were stored in large matkas—earthen pitchers. Particularly on Fridays, there would be a long queue of customers addicted to his banta-carbonated soda, embellished with a generous pinch of black rock salt.

The inexpensive, refreshing drink has for years held its own against the fancier cola and orange flavoured drinks marketed by multinational companies. It continues to do brisk business, selling around 100 crates of *banta* every day. Rim jhim, a jeera drink, was introduced by Parle's. However, a vendor of cold drinks in Old Delhi remains hopeful of the resurrection of traditional *sherbets*. 'In the past few decades or so, people had given up on desi drinks and were completely sold over colas. However, I see that people are realizing the benefits of traditional coolers and coming back to nature,' he says.

In the early part of Akbar's reign, water used to be cooled with saltpetre, by a process described in detail by Abul Fazl. Later ice was commonly used. Abul Fazl records in *Ain e Akbari*:

> Since the thirteenth year of the Divine Era, when the imperial standards were erected in the Punjab, snow and ice have come into use. Ice is brought by land and water, by post carriages or bearers, from the district of Panhan, in the northern mountain, about forty-five kos (145 kms) from Lahore. The dealers derive a considerable profit, two to three seers of ice being sold per rupee. All ranks use ice in summer; the nobles use it throughout the whole year.

The last solace of the English in the hot weather was ice. Down country none was available until 1833, when it was imported by ships from America as ballast. The captain of the first ship received a letter of gratitude from the Governor General. In Delhi, the old Mughal custom of bringing ice from Srinagar in Teri Garhwal by relays of runners was too expensive for revival. It continued in Lahore for the supply of Ranjit Singh's court. But the method of making ice in the cold weather by running water into shallow pans in the season of the cold winds and storing the ice in pits against the hot weather, was continued. Companies were formed, whose members received ice regularly during the hot weather in proportion to the number of shares they held. The cutting off of the supply of ice from the ice-pits was one of the hardships suffered by the garrison during the siege of 1857.

The ice-bed was divided into six-foot squares, each about eighteen inches deep. In these were strewn straw of various kinds. Water-pots were provided for each square, and should the weather promise a cold clear night, water was poured into cloth-bottomed pans, which were then fitted into the earthen squares or hollows. On a good night, ice would form to the depth of one and a half inches on the pans. The frozen harvest was cropped by miserable coolies who toiled in winter chill. The ice thus gathered was stored in ice-pits. The pits were covered with a low mud house, thickly thatched, drained by a well, and further protected from the air by layers of straw. Within the pit, the ice was beaten into a solid mass by relays of blanketed coolies. The highest temperature at which ice could be made was about forty-three degrees Fahrenheit; the pits were opened at the beginning of the hot weather and the supply lasted as late as August. Each night in December and January, the old *abdar* would keep his watch. If the winds were fresh and likely to increase, he wrapped his blanket around him and retired to his bed, but if the air was clear and frosty, a drum was beaten, and from the nearest bazaar came lines of muffled figures to fill the pans and fix them in the beds. The ice-beds of Delhi were between the Delhi and Turkman Gates of the city and the ice-makers lived in the village of Banskauli.

Appendix 2: Kebab and Biryani

Delhi's fascination with kebab and biryani has remained undiminished through the rise and fall of empires, ravages of wars and the painful process of rebuilding lives. Delhi remains partial to the seekh and the *barra,* with a bite very unlike Lucknow, where melt in the mouth *galouti* and *kakori* reign supreme, and prefers biryani to pulav.

It must be emphasized here that biryani wasn't something overly common in Delhi until recent times. While *pulav* was a fairly common dish, served across generations, biryani is only mentioned once in established historic records, by Munshi Faizuddin.

It is interesting how biryani has come to dominate the culinary imagination of Delhi. We hardly find a mention of this elaborate and exotic, extravagantly rich, rice dish in the descriptions of what the Mughal princes and their predecessors partook. *Pulavs* of many kinds were cooked and appreciated. Munshi Faizuddin in *Bazm-i Aakhir*, which describes the banquet of the Mughal badshah, mentions in passing a *birinj pulav* among a long list of many other *pulavs*.

In less than a hundred years, the biryani has completely ousted the *pulav* from its pedestal. Shirir, the chronicler of the last phase of Nawabi culture in Lucknow, in his *Guzishta Lucknow* makes derogatory comments on Delhi's biryani as it was cooked at the turn of the twentieth century. He considered it a far inferior product than the delicate yakhni *pulav* of Lucknow and compared it to a *malgoba* (a crude blending of mismatched ingredients). It is difficult to understand how and when the rage for biryani started.

The memoirs and travellers accounts do not mention biryani among the signature dishes of the city. Nor is biryani a recipe that the refugees brought to the city. It is only in the last half century or so that biryani of different kinds has become immensely popular.

The only landmark associated with biryani is the *Matka Pir ki Dargah,* nestling under the shadow of Purana Qila, almost across the road from Pragati Maidan, as you drive from Shahjahanabad and Firozabad to even older cities of Delhi. The Sufi saint here is associated with *matka* (earthen pot) that was offered to him by devotees and favour seekers. By the 1960s, a small eatery had come up here that served flavourful Delhi biryani. Babu Khan, the cook who presided over the kitchen, claimed to have been descended from *Shahi bawarchis* in Shahjahanabad. One could pre-order biryani and take away the *degh,* to surprise guests with the exotica.

The Delhi biryani was upstaged in the 1980s by the biryani on the menu of the Dum Pukht at ITC's Maurya Hotel. Actually, this was a biryani carefully assembled from parboiled rice in *yakhni* and premium cuts of meat marinated expertly to melt in the mouth. The best quality, long-grained Basmati was used, and the aromatic spices were top grade. After the 'assembly' the saffron tinged biryani was put in a *matka* and the lid was sealed with dough paste. It was finished on *dum,* and when the biryani was unveiled before the guest, an overpowering aroma spread around, and the taste lingered on much after the meal was over.

The city famous for its *dum ki biryani,* Hyderabad, was the first to claim primacy. Originally prepared with mutton and cooked on *dum,* it was valued for its creamy texture, aromatic spicing, long-grained rice and fragrance that lingered. It was a time-consuming, one-dish meal, not easy to replicate in commercial kitchens. The biryani in Delhi, when it made its debut, was cooked by specialist *bawarchis* on celebratory occasions or festive feasts.

With the passage of time, other biryanis with regional flavours made their appearance. The Kolkata biryani, with reduced quantities of meat and addition of potatoes and boiled eggs, was popularized by the Bengali diaspora. The Sindhi biryani, which has no inhibitions about including assorted vegetables and pickling spices, did not find favour with the discerning Delhi diners. It was not long before that peninsular India introduced biryanis from Kerala and Andhra. The Kerala biryani, also known as Moplah biryani is cooked with mutton but has a very different spicing. Andhra biryani is not even distantly related to the Hyderabadi *dum ki biryani* and is far more piquant. *Tellicherry and Mattancherry biryanis* are prepared with mutton as well as beef. In Tamil Nadu, the *Chettinad* biryani has distinctly different spicing that relies on black peppercorns, cardamoms and star anise. Kerala biryanis are also prepared with fish and prawn. Today, one can taste any of these biryanis in the capital.

There are a number of biryani vendors who all have a loyal clientele. Some of them have built a following over forty years. One of the earliest was Deez, who started serving a local version of *dum ki biryani* in an earthen pot, with different portion sizes. These could be pre-ordered and picked up. Then there was the small shop, Rama Pulav, adjacent to a mosque, in K-Block, Connaught Place. In the 1960s it was derided as a place pervaded by frying-pan biryani, suggesting that meat curry and pre-cooked rice were blended in a frying pan and overlaid with ingredients to masquerade as a biryani. In Connaught Place, near Rivoli Cinema, stands a multi-storied building called Mohan Singh Place. The ground floor has a small restaurant, more a shop, Tee Pee O, which became famous for a short while as a place where a passable biryani could be enjoyed at a reasonable price. Mohan Singh Place had shops tailoring jeans, shirts, t-shirts and so on and the top floor housed the India Coffee House after it had been uprooted from the Theatre Communication building during the Emergency. The footfalls here were good.

None of these old-timers have been able to keep up with the new kids on the block. Biryani Blues had a considerable first-mover advantage. It was also attractive due to its low prices. Besides the mutton and chicken biryanis, cooked Hyderabadi style on dum and served with *mirchi ka salan* (gravy), it had on its menu, paneer and vegetarian biryanis. Others were quick to spot the opportunity. Biggane, Behroz and Biryani-by-Kilo replicated and extended the range of vegetarian and non-vegetarian biryanis. Some list the Punjabi Soya Chaap biryani and Tofu biryani as their specialties. Behroz caters to the upper end of the market. It has a large selection and generous portions. It again claims to be inspired by the home recipes in Hyderabad.

The latest craze is the Muradabadi biryani. No one had heard of this biryani even in the city allegedly of its birth, less than a decade back. This biryani has more robust flavours, with no pretensions at subtlety. The spicing is strong, and to reduce the confusion in most outlets, only the chicken biryani and vegetarian biryani are dished out. The 'shahi' Muradabadi biryani is spruced up by some dried fruits and nuts to claim a premium price.

By now, the biryani in the city has become a receptacle in which one can put whatever you like and think that would find favour with the customer willing to pay for novelty. There is no compulsion for the perennial favourite to retain its old garb.

Even before the Covid-19 pandemic, 'heat-and-eat' foods had become popular in Delhi. It was not only the big brands like ITC, Godrej and McCain who had launched kebabs, skewers as well as patties (frozen products) but also the neighbourhood butcher who had started selling pre-marinated fish and chicken that needed minimal cooking at home. Each vendor has slightly different spicing and quality of meats used from one outlet to another. The consumer also has the option to add spices and preferred garnishes. These products are not strictly 'heat and eat' but they do reduce kitchen chores to a large extent.

Appendix 3: Swadeshi Burger

After the fall from grace of Nirula's in the late 2000s, McDonalds reigned supreme in the budget burger market. Its sustained presence was grounded on the childhood nostalgia of the millennials and Gen X-ers and further fuelled by children of the day. Other reputed burger chains from the United States have tried time and again to disturb the market but none have been able to dethrone the golden arches. In 2012, Dunkin Donuts beat its rivals in both the cafe and burger market. They served a wide variety of vegetarian and non-vegetarian burgers. Burger King opened various outlets with much pomp and show at the end of 2014, showing off the Whopper, a burger slightly larger than most of those available on McDonald's repertoire. The next year, Wendy's decided to test the waters by launching its first outlet in Sector 29 in Gurgaon. Taking a bold approach, it served chicken burgers along with optional bacon strips. Due to the sensitivities of Muslims in the country, pork products had been abandoned by most large burger chains while trying to adjust their brand to the Indian palate. Johnny Rockets tried to stand out by creating its own version of the American Diner aesthetic. They served burgers with ingredients of higher quality than their peers, of course at a premium. But the customers' mood was kept up with the thick shake, and music from an old-fashioned juke-box. In most of these chains, however, the menu shrunk over time and many outlets had to close down. Johnny Rockets simply perished in Delhi. The golden arches retained their throne. However, one indigenous brand grew and flourished.

While most of the branded burgers that vowed the Delhi diners were marketed by Western chains there is one burger story that is Delhi's own. *Burger Singh* was started by a Gurgaon boy, Kabir Jeet Singh. When studying for his MBA in Birmingham, in 2007, he worked at a burger joint. Kabir missed home spicing in the insipid burger patty and the sauces and pickles failed to make it tempting. He decided to spike his burger by mixing some masalas produced by the Shan company, in the patty. The humble burger was dramatically transformed and became delicious. The owner of the shop where he worked was impressed and included his recipe in the menu. The new product was well received by the South Asian community in the city.

Kabir returned to India in 2011 and joined the *Beer Cafe* as a member of the founding team. After acquiring experience of a quick-service restaurant, he decided to branch out on his own. Towards the end of 2014, the first Burger Singh outlet was opened in a tiny, 98 square feet shop, on Golf Course Road in Gurgaon. The Indo-British burger proved to be a runaway hit and in a matter of five to six years, Burger Singh has twenty stores in Delhi/NCR, another five in other states, and two outlets in London.

Appendix 4: Zomato Saga

Deepinder Goyal and Pankaj Chaddah, graduates from IIT, Delhi, were working at Bain & Company, in New Delhi, when they came up with the idea of Foodie Bay. They came across many people having to wait for a long time, just to get a flash of the menu card. Foodie Bay scanned the menus of restaurants and posted them on Bain's private website. Soon the employees of Bain started using the website and thus saving their time. This, in turn, increased the traffic to their website. Eventually, they decided to expand their website to make it accessible for everyone. In a matter of nine months, Foodie Bay became the largest restaurant directory in Delhi/NCR. (Soon, its services were extended to Mumbai and Kolkata.) The popularity encouraged the duo to scale up the project, and in 2010, Foodie Bay was officially changed to 'Zomato'. The rest as they say is history.

Some enterprising chefs took the leap of faith by experimenting with doorstep deliveries of delicacies that extended the choice of what to eat beyond the run-of-the-mill tikka and kebab.

Aggregators like Zomato and Swiggy could deliver these orders across NCR in reasonable time, offering hefty discounts. The growing specialty food joints offering niche cuisines from India and abroad also found easier access to curious customers. The boom in the cloud-kitchen based business model—food prepared in the service provider's kitchen and delivered to the customer's home—catalysed by the shuttering of restaurants during lockdowns, has seemingly revolutionized the market. While consumers have gotten used to munching on professionally prepared delicacies, sitting in their cozy homes, the format has also been beneficial to the restaurant owners, who do not need to spend money on customer service and additional rent for the seating area. Even as the government restrictions after Covid were lifted, the delivery model has worked very well in the NCR and it is highly unlikely that it will go away any time soon.

Appendix 5a: Enterprising Refugees Spicing Up the City's Food

There were some refugees who did not open up dhabas to strike new roots but contributed to the changing flavours of food by processing and supplying ready to use spices to those who cooked meals commercially or set up small bakeries to provide 'Indianized' biscuits that were popular in undivided Punjab.

'Mahashay' Dharampal Gulati, the founder of MDH Spices, hailed from Sialkot, Pakistan, and had moved to Delhi in 1947. In the beginning, he ferried passengers on a horse-drawn carriage for a living. Sometime in the early 1950s, he was allotted shop number 37 in Karol Bagh. Gulati also rented another shop in Chandni Chowk, and as business grew, he bought a plot in Kirti Nagar in 1959, to start a factory for producing ground spices. One of the most innovative things the company did was introducing packaged masala. The founder showed exceptional flair for advertising and succeeded in registering the presence of his product quite dramatically.

Once during a TV commercial shoot for his company, the hired actor failed to turn up in time. Mahashay ji, who hated wasting time, decided to play the role himself. The target audience loved the cameo and from that day onward the pearl necklaced old man became the face of the brand. The punchline, 'assi masala di duniya de shahenshah', delivered against a fantastically changing backdrop became the USP.

Before the advent of MDH on the scene, the wholesale spice market was at Khari Baoli. Traditionally, spices were blended and pounded at home or at the shop floor. Partition changed all this. Joint families were splintered and few had the time to do chores at home. There was a need for ingredients that were cost-effective and reduced the chores. Others followed the footsteps of the founder of MDH to market pre-processed and packed spices.

Appendix 5b: Bakeries

Munshi Ram Sethi was just seventeen when he left Hoti Mardan, in West Pakistan, for Delhi, and crossed the border as a refugee. As an adolescent, he served a long and hard apprenticeship with his father, Mangal Sain, who had set up a small biscuit-bakery in Old Delhi to continue the business he had established in Pakistan in 1921. When the shop initially opened, it was operated by two to three workers who knew just four or five recipes. Customers brought the ingredients—flour, butter and sugar—and paid a small sum to bake fresh atta biscuits, namkeen-zeera biscuits and rusks. The labour charges were a mere 50 paisa per kg. The shop did not even have a signboard.

In 1947, when opening a shop in Sadar Bazaar, Munshi Ram took the initiative to rebrand the shop as *Frontier Bakery* and expanded their repertoire to include kaju-pista biscuits, wholewheat biscuits, rusks and chocolate-chip biscuits. Their 'homemade' biscuits were very popular in the 1950s and 1960s, especially among the refugees. Factory-made branded biscuits were more expensive and considered not very healthy as they were made with maida and were artificially flavoured. In the mid-1960s, shortages of ingredients and rationing created unforeseen problems for the bakery. Munshi had to travel from Rajouri Garden or Sadar Bazaar to Modi Flour Mills in Okhla to procure the raw materials and load them in a truck. The state government also ordered that such bakeries should move out of residential areas, as their ovens, fired by charcoal, were polluting the environment.

Like many other refugees, the family acquired a plot in Lawrence

Road Industrial Estate, but profits plunged. Popular taste also changed and consumers switched to biscuits and cookies with different flavours, packaged more attractively.

Defence Bakery started off as a hole-in-the-wall outlet that supplied bakery items on a wholesale basis to other retailers. It was founded by Jagdish Mitra Dhingra, a refugee from Multan, who shifted from Bombay to Delhi in 1961. Later, it expanded its business with door-to-door delivery via trunk riders. The real turnaround came over the next decade, when his son, Dalip Kumar Dhingra, a graduate of the Institute of Hotel Management, Pusa, introduced new products like butter cookies. The bakery was also one of the first to introduce pre-made pizza bases into the local market.

Appendix 6: Bihari Cuisine

Bihari cuisine is not just about litti chokha. The rich, ancient heritage of the place is infused in their cuisine, courtesy its authentic flavours, aromas of the spices and condiments all put together to serve the most sumptuous fare that a food aficionado can ever dream of.

And Potbelly Rooftop Cafe, tucked away in the heart of South Delhi, imbibes the culture of Bihar, and promises to offer the most authentic Bihari cuisine to savour.

The restaurant is one-of-its kind, since it is Delhi's first ever Bihari restaurant. And introducing the Delhites to the Bihari cuisine wouldn't have been possible without Puja Sahu and Vivita Relan, who despite knowing the Bihari stereotypes, decided to bring the richness of Bihari food to Delhi.

Potbelly was started on the first floor of a small flat in Shahpur Jat by Puja Sahu, who was inspired after her stay in the United States to showcase her home cuisine from Bihar in the capital. Shahpur Jat by then was growing into a creative workspace, as the low rentals there and central location attracted potters, painters, designers and other arty-crafty types. Visitors from outside Delhi carried tales of this new cauldron, bubbling with ideas, to other metropolitan cities. It was Babso Konwar who persuaded me to accompany her to Potbelly, negotiating that rickety wrought iron staircase that wound up to the Potbelly terrace. Puja herself was present and curated a wonderful meal comprising *madua* puris filled with *hilsa chokha*, Bihari mutton curry and *sattu makhuni*. The food was basic but served with flare, without compromising on original tastes. Later, she acquired a toe-hold in the Bihar Bhavan, eventually to take a long leap to the 32nd Milestone in Gurgaon. Much before the Champaran meat craze had enthralled the city, Potbelly's mutton, slow-cooked in a clay pot had cast a spell on the guests who visited it. *Aloo ka chokha* and *arhar ki dal* were no less enticing. The food has remained consistent at different venues. No mean achievement.

Notes

1. *Delhi Between Two Empire: 1803-1931—Society, Government and Urban Growth* by Naryani Gupta, published by Oxford University Press, 1981.
2. *City of Djinns: A Year in Delhi* by William Dalrymple, paperback edition published by Penguin Books, 2003.
3. *White Mughals: Love and Betrayal in the Eighteenth Century India* by William Dalrymple, paperback edition published by Penguin Books, 2004.
4. *Where Stones Speak: Historical Trails in Mehrauli, the First City of Delhi*, published by Element, 2016.
5. *Perpetual City: A Short Biography of Delhi* by Malavika Singh, published by Aleph Book Company, 2013.
6. *The Last Spring Part I: The Saga of the Great Mughals* by Abraham Eraly, published by Penguin India, 2014.
7. *The Last Spring Part I: The Saga of the Great Mughals* by Abraham Eraly, published by Penguin India, 2014.
8. *The Last Spring Part I: The Saga of the Great Mughals* by Abraham Eraly, published by Penguin India, 2014.
9. *Delhi Through the Ages: Essays in Urban History, Culture and Society* by R.E. Frykenberg (ed.), from The Delhi Omnibus edition, published by Oxford University Press, 1994.
10. Ibid.
11. *Delhi in Historical Perspectives* by K.A. Nizami, published by OUP, 2020.
12. From *A Short History of Aurangzeb* by Sr. Jadunath Sarkar, published by Orient BlackSwan, 2009.
13. *The Emperor's Table: The Art of Mughal Cuisine* by Salma Husain, published by Lustre Press, 2008.

14. *Twilight in Delhi–A Novel* by Ahmed Ali, published by Rupa, 2007.
15. *The Sword of Persia: Nader Shah, from Tribal Warrior to Conquering Tyrant* by Michael Axworthy, published by I.B. Tauris, 2006.
16. *Twilight of the Mughals: Studies in Late Mughal Delhi* by Percival Spear, published by OUP Pakistan, 1981.
17. *Kai Chaand The Saare Aasman* by Shamsur Rahman Faruqi, Hindi edition published by Penguin India, 2010.
18. *Zikr-e-Mir* by Mir Taqi Mir, Hindi edition published by Rekhta Foundation, 2023.
19. *City Improbable: Writings on Delhi* by Khushwant Singh (Ed.), published by Penguin India, 2001.
20. *The Mirror of Beauty–A Novel* by Shamsur Rahman Faruqi, published by Penguin Random House, 2014.
21. *Three Mughal Poets: Mirsauda, Mir, Hasan* by Islam Khurshidul and Russell Ralph, published by OUP, 1998.
22. *Murder at the Mushaira: A Novel* by Raza Mir, published by Aleph Book Company, 2021.
23. *Dastan-e-Ghadar: The Tale of the Mutiny* by Zahir Dehlvi, English edition published by Penguin India, 2017.
24. *Bazm-i Aakhir* by Munshi Faizuddin, English edition published by Roli Books, 2021.
25. *The Baniya Legacy of Old Delhi: Culture and Cuisine* by Gunjan Goela published by Empty Canvas Publishers, Delhi, 2023.
26. *Climbing the Mango Trees: A Memoir of a Childhood in India* by Madhur Jaffrey, published by Alfred Knopf, US, 2006.
27. *Raga'n Josh: Stories from a Musical Life* by Shiela Dhar, published by Permanent Black, 2005.
28. *The Courtly Cuisine: Kayastha Kitchens Through India* by Preeta Mathur, published by Lustre Press, 2013.
29. *Smoke Without Fire: Portraits of Pre-Partition Delhi* by Abdul Rahman Siddiqi, published by Aakar Books, 2011.
30. *Dil-o-Danish* by Krishna Sobti, published by Rajkamal Prakashan, 2018.
31. *Qabze Zaman* by Shamshar Rahman Faruqi, published by Rajkamal Prakashan, 2021.
32. From *Raj on the Move* by Ritika Bhandari, published by Lotus/Roli Books, 2019.

33. Ibid.
34. *Delhi: Light, Shades and Shadows* by D.N. Chaudhuri, published by Niyogi Books, 2005.
35. *Delhi Durbar 1911: the Complete Story* by Sunil Raman and Rohit Aggarwal, published by Lotus, an imprint of Roli Books, 2016.
36. *Climbing the Mango Trees: A Memoir of a Childhood in India* by Madhur Jaffrey, paperback edition published Ebury Press, UK, 2006.
37. *V.P. Menon: The Unsung Architect of Modern India* by Narayani Basu, published by Simon and Schuster, 2020.
38. *The Company of Women* by Khushwant Singh, first published by Viking Press, an imprint of Penguin Random House, 1999.
39. *Italian Khana* by Ritu Dalmia, published by Penguin India, 2009.

Bibliography

Ahmad, Qeyamuddin, *India by Al-Biruni*, New Delhi: National Book Trust, India, 2005.

Alam, Muzaffar, *The Crisis of Empire in Mughal North India: Awadh and the Punjab, 1707-48*, Delhi: Oxford University Press (Oxford India Paperbacks), 1986.

Ali, Ahmed, *Twilight in Delhi: A Novel*, 2nd edn., Bombay: Oxford University Press, 1967.

Babur, *Baburnama: Memoirs of Babur*, ed. A.S. Beveridge, Chennai: Atlantic Publishers and Distributors, 1989.

Basham, A. L., *The Wonder that Was India*, London: Sidgwick and Jackson, 1956, p. 300.

Battutah, Ibn *The Travels of Ibn Battutah.*, ed. Tim Mackintosh-Smith, New Delhi: Picador, Pan Macmillan (Macmillan Collector's Library), 2003.

Bernier, Francois, *Travels in the Mogul Empire*, tr. Irving Brock, London: W. Pickering, 1826.

Bhandari, Rajika, *The Raj on the Move: Story of the Dak Bungalow*, New Delhi: Lotus Collection, Roli Books, 2012.

Blake, Stephen P., *Shahjahanabad: The Sovereign City in Mughal India 1639-1739*, Cambridge: Cambridge University Press, 2002.

Brennan, Jennifer, *Curries and Bugles: A Memoir and a Cookbook of the British Raj,* New Delhi: HarperCollins, 1990.

Chishti, Seema, *Sumitra and Anees: An Indian Marriage--Tales and Recipes from a Khichdi Family*, New Delhi: HarperCollins, 2022.

Dalrymple, William, *City of Djinns: A Year in Delhi*, New York: Penguin Books, 2003.

———. *White Mughals: Love and Betrayal in Eighteenth-Century India*, New Delhi: Penguin Books, 2004.

_______. *The Last Mughal: The Fall of a Dynasty, Delhi, 1857*, United Kingdom: Bloomsbury Publishing, 2009.

_______. *The Anarchy*. United Kingdom: Bloomsbury Publishing, 2020.

Dayal, Maheshwar, *Dilli meri Dilli*, Delhi: Santosh Nath Parkashan, 1978.

Debroy, Bibek, *The Mahabharata*, New Delhi: Penguin Books India, 2015.

Dehlvi, Sadia, *Jasmine and Jinns: Memories and Recipes of My Delhi*, New Delhi: HarperCollins, 2017.

Dehlvi, Zahir, *Dastan-e-Ghadar: The Tale of the Mutiny*, Gurgaon: Penguin Random House, 2017.

Dhar, Shiela, *Raga'n Josh: Stories from Musical Life*, Ranikhet: Permanent Black, 2015.

Douglas-Home, Jessica, *A Glimpse of Empire*, New Delhi: Rupa Publications, 2012.

Elliot, H. M. and J. Dowson, *The History of India, as Told by Its Own Historians: The Muhammadan Period*, London: Trübner and Company, 1867.

Elliot, H. M., *Memoirs of Jahangir*, Delhi and Noida: Islamic Book Service, 1975.

Eraly, Abraham, *The Last Spring: The Lives and Times of Great Mughals*, New Delhi: Penguin Books India, 2000.

Faizuddin Munshi, *Bazm-i Aakhir*, tr. *The Last Gathering* by Ather Farouqui, Lotus Collection, New Delhi: Roli Books, 2021.

Frishta, Muhammad Qasim, *Tarikh-i-Firishta*, or History of the Rise of the Mahomedan Power in India, till the year AD 1612, vol. I, tr. John Brigg, Bombay: Government College Press, 1st edn., 1829.

Goela, Gunjan, *Baniya Legacy of Old Delhi (Culture and Cuisine)*, ed and tr. Indrani Ganguly, New Delhi: Empty Canvas Publishers, 2022.

Gupta, Narayani, *Delhi Between Two Empires, 1803-1931: Society, Government and Urban Growth*, New Delhi: Oxford University Press, 1981.

Habib, Irfan, *Akbar and His India*, New Delhi: Oxford University Press (Oxford India Paperbacks), 1997.

Hameed, Syeda Saiyidain, *Maulana Azad, Islam and the Indian National Movement*, New Delhi: Oxford University Press, 2014.

Husain, Salma, *The Mughal Feast: Recipes from the Kitchen of Emperor Shah Jahan*, New Delhi: Lustre Press, Roli Books, 2021.

_______. *The Emperor's Table: The Art of Mughal Cuisine*, New Delhi: Lustre Press, Roli Books, 2008.

_______.*Nuskha-e-Shahjahani: Pulaos from the Royal Kitchen of Shah Jahan*, New Delhi: Rupa & Company, 2004.

Jaffrey, Madhur, *Climbing the Mango Trees: A Memoir of a Childhood in India*, United Kingdom: Knopf Doubleday Publishing Group, 2006.

Jahangir, E. o. H., *The Jahangirnama: Memoirs of Jahangir, Emperor of India*, Washington D.C: Freer Gallery of Art, Arthur M. Sackler Gallery, 1999.

Jha, D. N., *The Myth of the Holy Cow*, London: Verso, 2004.

Kabir, Nasreen Muni and Zakir Hussain, *Zakir Hussain: A Life in Music*, New Delhi: HarperCollins, 2018.

Khan, Dargah Quli, *Muraqqa'-e-Delhi: The Mughal Capital in Muhammad Shah's Time*, Delhi: Deputy Publication, 1989.

Khan, Mir Yar Ali., *The Incomparable Festival*, ed. Razak Khan, tr. Shad Naved, Gurgaon: Penguin Random House India, 2021.

Khan, Syed Ahmed, *Asar-us-Sanadid*, The Remnants of Ancient Heroes), tr. and ed. Rana Safvi, New Delhi: Tulika Books, 2018, 2024.

Khurshid, Salman, *At Home in India: The Muslim Saga*, New Delhi: Hay House, 2014.Liddle, Swapna, *Chandni Chowk: The Mughal City of Old Delhi*, New Delhi: Speaking Tiger Books, 2017.

_______.*Connaught Place and the Making of New Delhi*, New Delhi: Speaking Tiger Books, 2018.

Losty, Jeremiah P. and Pramod Kapoor, *Delhi: Red Fort to Raisina*, New Delhi: Lustre Press, Roli Books, 2012.

Mahmood, Saif, *Beloved Delhi: A Mughal City and Her Greatest Poets*, New Delhi: Speaking Tiger Books, 2018.

Malhotra, Inder, *Indira Gandhi*, New Delhi: Directorate of Advertising and Visual Publicity, Government of India, 1975.

Malhotra, Anchal, *Remnants of a Separation: A History of the Partition Through Material Memory*, New Delhi: HarperCollins India, 2017.

_______.*Remnants of Partition: 21 Objects from a Continent Divided*, London: Hurst, 2019.

Manekshaw, Bhicoo J., *Parsi Food and Drinks and Customs*, New Delhi: Penguin Books India, 2000.

Manekshaw, Bhicoo J. and V. Thukral, *Secrets from the Kitchen: Fifty Years of Culinary Experience at the India International Centre*, New Delhi: Niyogi Books, 2013.

Mathur, Preeta, *The Courtly Cuisine: Kayastha Kitchens Through India*, New Delhi: Lustre Press, Roli Books, 2013.

Moosvi, Shireen, *Episodes in the Life of Akbar: Contemporary Records and Reminiscences,* New Delhi: National Book Trust, India, 1994.

Mir, Mir Taqi, *Zikr-i Mir: the autobiography of the eighteenth century Mughal poet, Mir Muhammad Taqi 'Mir', 1723-1810*, tr. annot. and intro. C.M. Naim, New Delhi: Oxford University Press, 1999.

Mukhlis, Abdul Rozak, *Encyclopaedic Dictionary of Medieval India*, New Delhi: Sundeep Prakashan, 1993.

Narang, Gopi Chand, Ameer Khusro: Hindavi Lok Kavya Sankalan, New Delhi: Vani Prakashan, 2021.

Narayanan, Divya, Cultures Food and Gastronomy in Mughal and post-Mughal India, unpublished doctoral dissertation Heidelberg, 2015.

Nizami, Khwaja Hasan, *Tears of the Begums: Stories of Survivors of the Uprising of 1857*, tr. Rana Safvi, New Delhi: Hachette India, 2022.

Panigrahi, D. N., *Charles Metcalfe in India: Ideas & Administration, 1806-1835*, New Delhi: Munshiram Manoharlal, 1968.

Panjabi, Camellia, *50 Great Curries of India*, United Kingdom: Kyle Cathie, 2004.

Patil, Vishwas, *Panipat*, tr. Moreshwar Tapaswi, Bharatiya Sahitya Sadan, 1991.

Prakash, Om, *Food and Drinks in Ancient India (from Earliest Times to c. 1200 A.D.)*, foreword B. Ch. Chhabra, New Delhi: Munshiram Manoharlal, 1961.

Raman, Sunil and Rohit Agarwal, *Delhi Durbar 1911: the Complete Story*, New Delhi, Lotus Collection, Roli Books, 2012.Rehman, Habib, *Borders to Boardroom: A Memoir*, New Delhi: Roli Books, 2014.

Reshii, Marryam H., *The Flavour of Spice*, New Delhi: Hachette India, 2017.

Rizvi, S. A. A., *The Wonder that Was India*, vol. II, New Delhi: Picador, Pan Macmillan India, 2005.

Roe, Thomas and William Foster *The Embassy of Sir Thomas Roe to India, 1615-19: As Narrated in His Journal and Correspondence*, rpt. new and rev. edn., New Delhi: Munshiram Manoharlal, 1990.

Safvi, Rana, *Where Stones Speak: Historical Trails in Mehrauli, the First City of Delhi*, New Delhi: Element, 2015 Sahni, Bhisham, *Tamas*, tr. Jai Ratan, New Delhi: Penguin Books, 2001.

Sarkar, Jadunath, *A Short History of Aurangzib*, Hyderabad: Orient Black Swan, 2009.

Shankar, Sondeep and Pavan K. Varma, *Mansions at Dusk: The Havelis of Old Delhi*, New Delhi: Spantech Publishers, 1992.

Singh, Khushwant, *Delhi*, New Delhi: Penguin Books, 1990.

_______.*City Improbable: An Anthology of Writings on Delhi*, New Delhi: Viking, Penguin Books, 2001.

_______.*A History of the Sikhs: 1469-1838*, New Delhi: Oxford University Press, 2004.

Singh, K. P., *Whatever the Odds: The Incredible Story Behind DLF*, New Delhi: HarperCollins, 2015.

Singh, Malvika, *Perpetual City: A Short Biography of Delhi*, New Delhi: Aleph Book Company, 2013.

Sihota, Kikky, *The Ultimate Army Cookbook: A Memsahib Cooks*, New Delhi: Lustre Press, Roli Books, 2013.

Smith, R. V., *From the Bylanes of Delhi, Agra & Jaipur*, New Delhi: Vitasta, 2019

_______.*Delhi: Unknown Tales of a City*, New Delhi: Lotus Collection, Roli Books, 2015.

_______.*Delhi's Curly Tales*, Gurgaon: Shubhi Publications, 2020.

Sobti, Krishna, *Dilo-Danish*, New Delhi: Rajkamal Prakashan Pvt. Limited, 2021.

Soofi, Mayank Austen, *The Delhi Walla–Hangouts*, New Delhi: HarperCollins, 2010.

Subramanian, Lakshmi, *History of India, 1707-1857*, Hyderabad: Orient Black Swan, 2010.

Tandon, Prakash, *Punjabi Saga (1857-2000)*, New Delhi: Rupa & Company, 2000.

Thapar, Raj, *All These Years: A Memoir*, New Delhi: Seminar Publications, 1991.

Timms, Pamela, *Korma, Kheer and Kismet: Five Seasons in Old Delhi*, New Delhi: Aleph Book Company, 2014.

Tribe, Caste, and Religion in India, ed. Romesh Thapar, Delhi: Macmillan Company of India, 1977, 2002.

Truschke, Audrey, *Aurangzeb: The Man and the Myth*, Gurgaon: Penguin Random House India, 2018.

Vishal, Anoothi, *Mrs LC's Table: Stories about Kayasth Food and Culture*, New Delhi: Hachette India, 2016.

Index

G

M

N

ALSO IN THIS SERIES IN SPEAKING TIGER

A TASTE OF TIME

A Food History of Calcutta

Mohona Kanjilal

Calcutta, once the nucleus of the Raj, was at the heart of a thriving economy and unparalleled administration. Over the centuries, this teeming, cosmopolitan metropolis has become home to people from various communities who have lent its food and culture their distinctive tastes and culinary rituals. The heady romance of palates and flavours in the 'Royal Capital' has fostered diversity in food and culture all the while adhering to the city's Bengali roots.

A Taste of Time is an insightful journey through the ever-changing landscape of Calcutta's food and cultural milieu, from its decades-old cutlet, jhal muri, and puchka stalls to its iconic continental restaurants like Firpo's and Flurys; from its oldest tea shop, Favourite Cabin, set up in 1924, to the 21st-century fine-dining restaurant threesixtythree°. Mohona Kanjilal, through her immaculate research, deftly captures the stories behind the city's endearing culture of 'bikel chaar-ter cha' (tea at 4 p.m.); its renowned bakeries like Nahoum's; and the invention of rasogollas and samosas (or shingara). Diving into Calcutta's dazzling history, she explores how the food habits of early European settlers, Jewish, Armenian, Chinese, Parsi and other expats, and the city's next-door neighbours like Darjeeling and Odisha, have made the culinary fabric of Calcutta immensely rich and layered.

This delightful and comprehensive history of food in Calcutta, peppered with mouthwatering nuggets, recipes and intriguing accounts of some revolutionary personalities of Bengal will appeal to the mind and tastebuds alike.